THE
NEW
WORSHIP

Straight Talk on Music and the Church

Barry Liesch

Foreword by Donald P. Hustad

BAKER
A DIVISION OF
Baker Book House Co

©1996 by Barry Liesch

Published by Baker Books
a division of Baker Book House Company
P.O. Box 6287, Grand Rapids, MI 49516-6287

Printed in the United States of America

Library of Congress Cataloging-in-Publication Data

Liesch, Barry Wayne, 1943–
      The new worship : straight talk on music and the
church / Barry Liesch ; foreword by Donald P. Hustad.
      p. cm.
      Includes bibliographical references and index.
    ISBN 0-8010-9001-6
    1. Music—Religious aspects—Christianity. 2. Public worship.
3. Church music. 4. Evangelicalism. I. Title.
    BV290.L54 1995
    264'.2—dc20   95-2576

Unless otherwise noted, Scripture is taken from the HOLY BIBLE, NEW INTERNATIONAL VERSION®. NIV®. Copyright © 1973, 1978, 1984 by International Bible Society. Used by permission of Zondervan Publishing House. All rights reserved.

Scripture marked NASB is taken from the New American Standard Bible, © the Lockman Foundation 1960, 1962, 1963, 1968, 1971, 1972, 1973, 1975, 1977.

Scripture marked KJV is taken from the King James Version of the Bible.

Scripture marked NKJV is taken from The New King James Version. Copyright © 1979, 1980, 1982, Thomas Nelson, Inc., Publishers.

Scripture marked ICB is taken from the *International Children's Bible, New Century Version,* copyright © 1983, 1986, 1988 by Word Publishing, Dallas, Texas 75039. Used by permission.

Contents

Foreword

During the last twenty years we have seen a spate of books on corporate Christian worship, by such well-known evangelicals as Robert G. Rayburn, Anne Ortlund, Ronald Allen and Gordon Borror, Ralph Martin, Robert Webber, Warren Wiersbe, C. Welton Gaddy, and Barry Liesch. Seven years after Liesch's first volume, *People in the Presence of God,* he is back with a second, *The New Worship: Straight Talk on Music and the Church.* The timing says something significant about Barry Liesch: He is caught up in the importance of what's happening in the modern church, and is constantly studying and reevaluating the changing situation, in order to answer the barrage of questions that is being asked by ministers, worship artists, and laypersons.

"Straight talk" is a desirable thing, and I believe Liesch has given his best, quoting extensively from a number of evangelical experts, and "fleshing out" the argument with his own unique scripture-plus-common-sense approach. That is not to say that every reader will find the material easy to understand at first glance. But that is an acknowledgement of the complexity of the issues, rather than the failure of the writer.

Barry Liesch's approach is not "linear" or "progressive." Rather, in what seems to be a "mini-library," he has chosen seven issues that he feels are central in the divisive debates going on in the church, and has dealt with each issue honestly and quite thoroughly in a pair of chapters. On pages 14 and 15 (in his introduction) Liesch gives excellent advice about different ways to read the book. To these suggestions, I would add: Go back and read each section you think is important, a second and a third time. There is so much significant material included that it needs to be considered again and again!

In preparing to write the foreword to Liesch's earlier book, I differed with him at so many points, that, on first reading, I didn't think I could produce the required piece. Yet the manuscript contained so much good material that I pressed on and encouraged the reader to do so, as well. In this volume, I have only one disagreement, but it is so important that I must mention it.

In chapters 3 and 4, Liesch presents Praise and Worship music in the context of "Free-Flowing Praise" (the prolonged service of chorus-song in the first part of contemporary services) and "Journey into the Holy of Holies." P & W music itself originated with the Charismatic Renewal Movement; all of the approaches identified in these chapters (as described by Wimber, Cornwall, and Wohlgemuth) are carefully devised according to charismatic theology and Scripture interpretation, and are expected to lead to characteristic pentecostal experiences. However, this origin, association, and expectation are not clearly stated in these pages. I believe that much of today's confusion in noncharismatic churches arises from a failure to make these distinctions. Charismatic believers have a right to develop their own worship to match their own theology and exegesis, and they have done this well. Noncharismatics should not thoughtlessly copy or imitate their worship formulae, unless they expect to enter the same "Holy of Holies" in the same way. Instead, they should develop their worship rationale based on their scriptural understanding, and then sing up to their own theology! (See my *Jubilate II*, 273–4, 282–97.)

Donald P. Hustad
Emeritus Senior Professor of Church Music
Southern Baptist Theological Seminary
Louisville, Kentucky

Acknowledgments

Rising on the shoulders of many authors, this book has particularly benefited from the following writers: Harold Best, Judson Cornwall, Donald Hustad, Calvin Johansson, Graham Kendrick, David Pass, Bob Sorge, and Paul Westermeyer.

Friends, pastors, worship leaders, and musicians also graciously took their time to critique the text and contribute ideas: Paul Anderson, Dan Bauman, Laurey Berteig, Mel and Dianne Bowker, Vickie Fisher, Doris Friessen, Paul Stelian Goldheart, Ismael Gurrola, Edna Grenz, John Harris, Tom Keene, Mike Kent, Jay Martin, Dave Morgan, Ken Pendergrass, and Leonard Peyton. My sincere thanks to each one of you!

In addition, members of the Biola University academic community offered advice, read various chapters, and improved them: Clint Arnold, Harold Dollar, Bob Krauss, Lloyd Kwast, Bill Lock, Inez McGahey, Gary McIntosh, Wally Norling, and Jack Schwarz.

I must acknowledge two individuals who have profoundly impacted my life. Richard Johnson, a church elder and trusted confidant and faithful friend, has nurtured me as a father for over twelve years. I thank God for you, Richard! I also want to express my appreciation to my grade-school piano teacher, Rowlie Hill, who taught me as a boy to place a high value on ministry. I can't forget the many times he picked me up at my home Sunday nights and involved me as pianist in his youth choir. Thanks, Rowlie, for the stimulating environment, the YFC piano competitions, and for bringing into my life inspiring guys like Tom Keene and Franklyn Lacey in those crucial, formative years.

To Dave Russell (director of Media Center at Biola University) my extra special thanks for his great work on the "concept icons" and figures, which have added "dimension" to this book, and for his suggestions that improved the title and table of contents. David put about fifty hours of his spare time into the graphics, an incredible effort I won't forget.

To Paul Engle, Mary Suggs, Jack Johnson, and Wendy Peterson at Baker Book House, I appreciate your friendly manner, attention to detail, and for going the extra mile on the design and layout.

And, Mom, I love you! I'm thankful for telephones that carry your wonderful, eighty-year-old voice.

To everyone, my deepest gratitude.

Introduction

Nothing short of a revolution in worship styles is sweeping across North America. Worship leaders, pastors, and trained musicians face new and powerful forces of change—forces that bring renewal to some churches and fear to others. No denomination or group can sidestep the hot debate between the benefits of hymns versus choruses, seeker services versus worship services, choirs versus worship teams, organs versus synthesizers, and flowing praise versus singing one song at a time. Even traditional Southern Baptist churches, strongly committed to graded choir programs, are transitioning to free-flowing praise and worship teams.

The New Worship is a practical resource for everyone involved in music and worship planning: pastors, worship leaders, teachers and students in seminaries and colleges, and professional musicians. If you need practical material you can use every Sunday, *The New Worship* is for you. It will aid you not only with the entire scope and direction of your worship program but also with your philosophy of worship. Though I particularly focus on worship that employs a blend of traditional and nontraditional music in the free-flowing praise format, I don't limit my attention to that. The free-flowing style is not without its flaws—in fact, I think the concept needs some refining. So I'll be tackling head-on some tough questions and controversial issues that don't always get answered, offering both practical application and analysis. This book aims to accomplish the following:

- provide biblical perspective
- inform readers of contemporary culture, trends, and technology
- teach concepts and illustrate techniques
- present strategies for implementation
- build up the pastor/musician relationship

Ways to Read This Book

I've designed the chapters to be interactive, not rigidly compartmentalized. Issues raised initially, for example, are revisited in subsequent chapters. So you may enjoy reading this book in different ways than simply straight through. Here are a few options:

1. Begin with part 2
2. Read pairs of chapters
3. Read appendix 1, "The Book in Brief," first

I'm attempting to do a difficult thing in this book—keep two very different types of readers, pastors and musicians, engaged throughout. The opening chapter, for instance, may address musicians somewhat more than pastors. Hang in there pastors! Your issues are also central to this book, but the material here unfolds in the reverse of most books. Solutions are sometimes presented before the problem is discussed in detail: For example, I dive into application in the first seven chapters. Why? Because musicians are application hungry. Nevertheless, you'll find at least some theory and application in every chapter. But if you want the complete rationale before the application, then read chapters 8 through 16 first and return later to chapters 1 through 7.

Or you can select a pair of chapters to read. Let your area of interest guide your choice:

The argument for hymns, choruses, and variety (1, 2)
Understanding free-flowing praise (3, 4)
Service design (5, 6)
The issue of performance (8, 9)
Theology of church music (10, 11)
Reducing divisiveness over music style (12, 13)
Staff relations (14, 15)

Before beginning a chapter you may want to read its summary to get a quick overview of the major points. Summaries usually come at the end of chapters. Appendix 1 ("The Book in Brief") provides a handy, point-by-point summation of the principles in each chapter.

Field-tested in worship seminars, Sunday school classes, and the college classroom, this book has been greatly shaped by the concerns many individuals have raised. I hope the "Questions for Reflection and Discussion" at the end of each chapter will spark lively and constructive discussion between pastors and musicians, students and teachers.

This logo is your signal that follow-up material is available on the supplemental disk dealing with keyboard modulation and improvisation.

Chapters That Are "Must Reading"

Musicians who have critiqued this text have offered the following recommendation: Chapters 7, 14, and 15 are "must reading" for pastors. Pastors, too, have underscored the value of certain chapters—chapter 5 on service design and 8 and 9 on performance were recommended repeatedly. I regard chapter 3 as the book's major contribution.

This volume is not a rehashing of my previous book, *People in the Presence of God*, but it does develop ideas I alluded to there. Nor is it a repetition of materials written elsewhere. When I draw on other works, it's integrative to add new perspectives.

I do not expect 100 percent agreement from readers. Donald Hustad's foreword suggests that aspects of this book will be controversial. The mature Christian approach should allow us to disagree in an honest and respectful manner and get issues into the open. I'm honored that Hustad has expressed himself so strongly, and I urge you to hear him out and read the pages he cites in his book, *Jubilate II*, which I heartily recommend. Concerning this book, my advice is, absorb what you find useful. A decade of personal experimentation and observation convinces me that free-flowing praise does not lead to "characteristic Pentecostal experiences." I firmly believe that if we are to move ahead in worship, pastors, musicians, and seminaries need to work through these issues and forge a strong partnership.

Charts May Be Photocopied

The charts convey a lot of information succinctly and are frequently requested at seminars. You are at liberty to print or make overheads of them for your sermons or Sunday school classes, college or seminary teaching, seminars you may conduct, or any other noncommercial activity. I want them to be readily accessible for your use.

Finally, I want to declare myself as being passionately *for* the church! I want to be numbered among those building it up. For three years I've been thinking about this book—crafting, refining, eating, and sleeping it. I believe it has the potential to do some good, and with joy I present it to you.

If you have questions regarding this book or the disk, you may contact the author in the following ways:

Biola University
Music Department
13800 Biola Avenue
La Mirada, CA 90639
FAX: 310-903-4748
EMAIL: barry_liesch@peter.biola.edu

PART ONE

CONTEMPORARY WORSHIP SERVICES

Hymns or Choruses?

They function like the "top forty," a kind of musical fireworks. Each new one shoots into the air, bursting into a kaleidoscope of color, only to fall all too quickly, burned out through overuse like songs on the hit parade.

"Worship choruses!—are they here to stay?" pastors ask. Definitely! "Should their use be supported?" Absolutely! Their spectacular rise in importance is simply uncontestable. Choruses communicate a freshness to our faith. They powerfully relate Christianity to contemporary culture. And they effectively express intimacy—our personal relationship with God. Their contribution is enormous, and I love them and play them continually. *But we need balance.*

It's a fact: Some churches have not sung one hymn in five years! Others sing at most one hymn a month. Their worship is devoid of hymnbooks, choirs, solos, and corporate Scripture readings. Even corporate prayers have dwindled greatly.

For these churches, music forms the heart of their service. Their worship, led by a "worship team," may consist of two guitarists (bass and lead), two vocalists, a percussionist, a synthesist, and perhaps someone doubling at the flute or sax, as the congregation sings. The words to the music are projected on slides, overheads, or are printed in the worship folder.[1]

19

Walk into these churches and—putting aside hymns for the moment—you may not hear even one *chorus* that is familiar! Newness is the rage, and each church has its unique repertoire. Though the congregations are always learning new songs, singles, young families, and even senior citizens find these churches very attractive. And some are growing—fast! The effort they put into their "worship sets" deserves high commendation.

But here's my point. We have to recognize the danger of becoming too "market driven" by the immediate. Despite the many benefits of worship choruses, we must acknowledge that they tend to reflect values of popular culture that should not be "bought into" unquestioningly—values that include "instant gratification, intellectual impatience, ahistorical immediacy, and incessant novelty."[2] Used exclusively, choruses have real limitations. In general, choruses lack intellectual rigor and fail to offer a mature exposition of biblical doctrines. Choruses bracket the cross and resurrection together in their lyrics but shortchange the full reality of sin and human weakness and fail to capture adequately the agony and suffering of Christ on the cross. They put the weight on sin defeated and therefore gloss over persistent sin in our lives. There's very little emphasis on corporate confession or repentance. And the cost of discipleship and need for endurance and perseverance in the Christian life get scant attention.[3] Hymns address these shortcomings. Yet many consider the flowing praise of choruses, despite their deficiencies, to be the form of preference.

How should we look at different forms of music and worship? The issues of form and content will rise to the forefront throughout this book and they command our attention.

Forms—Confused with Spirituality

We often confuse form with spirituality. Worshiping a certain way or in a certain style doesn't make us spiritually superior. True, the content in forms can encourage us to pursue maturity in Christ, but the forms themselves don't make us spiritual. Rather, *behavior and holy living reflect spirituality.*[4]

Free-flowing praise, for example, does not have a monopoly on the Holy Spirit. Similarly, the form of Baptist worship is not more spiritual than Reformed; nor is the form of Presbyterian or Methodist worship less spiritual than Calvary Chapel or Assembly of God.

It is unfair (and dangerous!) to equate spirituality with any form. I mention this even though I'm an avid supporter of flowing praise. In fact, in chapters 3 and 4 I attempt to enrich it, make it more viable for everyone, and elevate it to a new level of sophistication conceptually. Ultimately, the Spirit of God must animate *any* form with his presence and power if we are to experience authentic worship. We are dependent on God, not forms.

Is something of value being neglected, though, in some nontraditional worship? I think so and this is what I want to convey to nontraditional worship leaders: "I love your band and I wholeheartedly support your use of choruses. But couldn't you include at least *one* hymn?" I don't think this is unreasonable or unbiblical, as I will try to explain later. Put as much energy into it as you do choruses. Perform it to the very best of your ability *within your style*.[5]

I teach at a fine Christian university, and I've observed a disturbing trend. Increasingly, our incoming students—which I take to be representative of the evangelical population—are ignorant of even the most well-known, historic hymns. Our young people are committed Christians and many are exemplary students, but when it comes to their knowledge of hymnody—they're ignorant! Their local churches have let them down.

Jeremy Begsby rightly challenges us: "*Roots down! Walls down!*" We need to learn our musical heritage first, then explore widely. Once we know our tradition, then we can expand. Everyone needs a center.[6]

Given this unhealthy state of affairs, I'm focusing on two basic questions in this chapter:

1. What different yet valuable functions can both hymns and choruses perform?
2. What can we do to make hymns interesting?

Stars or Fireworks?

Hymns may not explode or dazzle like fireworks, but like stars, their light shines. Stars, ablaze so many millions of miles away, pierce our distant atmosphere and reach us with their light. Similarly, hymns bring deep theological truth within our reach in portions we can grasp and with melodies we can remember. So why not seek a *blend* of hymns and choruses that reflects the composition of your church? Or look at it another way: What will our sons and daughters have after thirty years of *exclusive* chorus singing? A few choruses of enduring quality and the memory of hundreds of worn-out ones?[7] To dismiss hymns and what they offer as culturally irrelevant is a mistake—that's what passages in Ephesians, Colossians, and the Psalms teach us. I'll expand that thought in the next chapter.

The Hymn Society of America defines a hymn as follows:

> A Christian hymn is a lyric poem, reverently conceived, designed to be sung, which expresses the worshiper's attitude to God or God's purposes in human life. It should be simple and metrical in form, genuinely emotional, poetic and literary in style, spiritual in quality, and its ideas so direct and so immediately apparent as to unify a congregation while singing it.

One could argue that hymns are ultimately more rewarding than choruses. Hymns have stood the test of time. They underscore denominational distinctives, communicate the profundities of faith, and offer a thoughtful exposition of church doctrines. Take, for example, this weighty stanza of "It Is Well with My Soul":

> My sin—O the bliss of this glorious thought—
> My sin, not in part, but the whole,
> Is nailed to the cross, and I bear it no more:
> Praise the Lord, praise the Lord, O my soul!

Great lines! Or consider Wesley's encapsulation of his conversion experience, which echoes Romans 8 in "And Can It Be":

> No condemnation now I dread:
> Jesus, and all in Him, is mine!

Hymns provide texts for a wider variety of subjects and themes than most worship choruses. There are hymns for virtually any sermon topic or occasion, including Christmas, Easter, weddings, and funerals. And time-tested hymns such as "How Firm a Foundation" and "O God, Our Help in Ages Past"[8] paraphrase whole Scripture passages. When we sing "How Firm a Foundation," we are singing a text rich in substance.

"How Firm a Foundation" Paraphrases Isaiah[9]

Scripture	Hymn Paraphrase
Fear thou not; for I am with thee. Be not dismayed; for I am thy God.	Fear not, I am with thee, O be not dismayed; For I am thy God, and will still give thee aid;
I will strengthen thee; yea, I will help thee; yea, I will uphold thee with the right hand of my righteousness. (Isa. 41:10 KJV)	I'll strengthen thee, help thee, and cause thee to stand, Upheld by my righteous, omnipotent hand.
When thou passest through the waters, I will be with thee; and through the rivers, they shall not overflow thee. (Isa. 43:2 KJV)	When through the deep waters I call thee to go, The rivers of woe shall not thee overflow; For I will be with thee thy troubles to bless, And sanctify to thee thy deepest distress.

Consider Martin Luther. He called his people "theological barbarians" and taught them basic theology by devoting Thursday evenings to congregational hymn singing.[10] Two centuries later, the Lutheran composer J. S. Bach tells of his congregation singing up to forty stanzas of one hymn. An unrelenting *perseverance* pervaded their culture! Some services lasted four hours. The Hebrews in the Old Testament, too, under the leadership of Ezra, read the Scriptures for three hours and praised God for another three hours (Neh. 9:1–6). Think about that! But we press the edge when we ask people to sing four stanzas. Question: Is our "sound bite" culture serving our long-term interests?[11]

Incredible Stories behind Incredible Texts

Hymns have been written under incredible circumstances. The hymn "It Is Well with My Soul" was composed by Horatio Spafford, a lawyer born in 1828 who had a close relationship with the evangelist D. L. Moody. Tragedy profoundly struck Spafford. His only son died. The Chicago Fire of 1871 wiped out his real estate

23

holdings. Desiring a vacation for his wife and four remaining daughters, he sent them by ship to Great Britain to join Moody, last-minute business detaining him from going along. He was making preparations to join them when he received a cable from his wife that read, "Saved alone." For on November 22, 1873, the English vessel his wife and daughters were on, the *Lochearn,* was struck and sank in twelve minutes. Anguished and heartbroken, he immediately left by ship to join her. It is believed that near the place where his four daughters drowned, he penned the words so familiar to us and yet so graphic in their disclosure of overwhelming grief: *"When sorrows like sea billows roll."* Prevailing faith was granted Spafford, however, for he was able to write: "Whatever my lot Thou hast taught me to say, *It is well, it is well with my soul.*"[12]

Or consider the story behind the Thanksgiving hymn "Now Thank We All Our God" composed by Martin Rinkart, the son of a poor, German coppersmith. During the Thirty Years' War, pestilence and famine ravaged the city of Eilenberg where he was pastor, leaving in its wake widespread death and destruction. Pastor Rinkart opened his home to the afflicted, providing them with food and clothing—though he barely had sustenance for his own family. It is reported that he conducted almost 4500 burial services. At the height of the plague of 1637, Rinkart, the only surviving minister, conducted as many as forty funerals a day, often digging the graves himself. These were not easy days for thanksgiving! It was Rinkart's caring pastor's heart that wrote what almost sounds like a benediction: "And keep us in His grace, And guide us when perplexed, And free us from all ills, In this world and the next."

We must share these stories! They are our heritage. Knowing the circumstances behind hymns helps us love and appreciate them all the more. So encourage young people to take a second look. If we unthinkingly allow our young people to be severed from their magnificent past—their cloud of witnesses—are we serving them well?

Overcoming Polarization

Besides visiting contemporary churches, I also visit older, traditional churches. My heart goes out to them. In some cases, the youngest person may be fifty years old. They have not adjusted to today's cultural patterns. Some members would like to draw in younger blood if they could, but to achieve this they, too, must be willing to undergo transformation and be open to the newer choruses and associated technology. Let's not underestimate the problem. This is an extremely difficult proposition, especially for the elderly, who are usually established in their ways.[13]

Intergenerational congregations in our culture often experience tension between the young who want choruses performed in contemporary styles and the old who want hymns performed in traditional ways. Polarization is not uncommon. Both sides often insist on their own rights and experience untold hurt and rejection.

Is there an answer? Some churches have separate traditional and contemporary services on the same Sunday morning (see chapters 5 and 11). Or they have a traditional service Sunday morning but a contemporary service Saturday or Sunday evening. In some contemporary services, the pastor and the people don't wear ties. They meet in the church gym, where they can set up their guitars, synthesizers, and percussion instruments; whereas the traditional service (occurring the same morning) meets in the sanctuary with a choir and the organ, and dress is formal. Pastors report that separate services target the divergent cultures represented in individual congregations.

One church reported that their baby busters (eighteen- to thirty-year-olds) found interactive software and interactive worship services appealing. More interested in singing than in being sung to, they felt "empty" unless they had participated in the music in some way. Background tapes were unacceptable, but a "tight" band or a perfectly played guitar or piano solo was appreciated. Live performance with a few flaws was preferred to "canned" music.[14]

Churches subscribing to separate services, however, should resist a class mentality where each group stands in judgment of the other.

Another solution, if you have several services or only one worship service, is to seek a blend of the old and the new.

But "blend" does not necessarily mean a 50/50 balance. Blend could mean a 25/75 or 60/40 weighting of hymns and choruses, for example, depending on the composition of the people and the church's history and traditions.[15] These factors must be taken into consideration, because church music programs are not interchangeable.

25

How can this blend be achieved? One way is to share life experiences during a "what this hymn/chorus means to me" time during the service.[16] Seek out progressive individuals who will agree to contribute. Elderly persons telling how a hymn has impacted their faith in times of crisis help young people understand where the older generation is coming from. Moreover, if a young person *sings* the same hymn as a solo and that sharing is followed after the service by expressions of appreciation and affirmation, improved relations between the young and old are given a real chance to develop.

Again, it's important that leaders on either side not undertake this task with a begrudging attitude that smacks of tokenism. The effort must be a real and costly one—it should summon your very best. This kind of give-and-take pleases God because it promotes and advances spiritual maturity and is a powerful demonstration of Christian respect on the congregational level.

Some Values of Worship Choruses

It is also helpful for the older generation to learn precisely how the texts of contemporary choruses relate to the younger generation. Take the text of "Sweet Perfume," a unique chorus that could only have been written during our time. When people struggle with low self-esteem and the consequences of divorce or abortion, words like these speak acceptance and healing:

> Consider how He loves you,
> His arms of love enfold you,
> Like a sweet, sweet perfume . . .
> Don't ever think that you're worthless,
> You have His life within.
> You are a sweet, wholesome fragrance,
> So valuable, to Him . . .
> He'll light up all your darkness,
> And fill you with His Spirit
> Like a sweet, sweet perfume. . . . [17]

The text speaks to their experience of brokenness. And the music uniquely reflects current styles.

A pastor friend of mine was at a halfway house encouraging the women there to attend his church. Some confessed their apprehensions to him: "We don't think we would belong. We're afraid. If we were to come, the walls might fall on us!" Those were their feelings—that's exactly how they expressed it.

Another young man shared with me that though he found our worship service immensely helpful, it was also the most painful time of the week for him. As he looked around and saw healthy couples and families interacting, it brought to mind his own dysfunctional family. The newer choruses can speak words of renewal and intimacy with God to those who experience pain. That's a valuable function.

Personal Ownership of Hymns

On the other hand, hymns can renew and console also. But we must acknowledge that some hymns may require the passage of time or special circumstances before they come alive and take hold.

I personally observed this when a university student, a comparatively new Christian, got up and gave his testimony at a church where I had just accepted the music position—in fact it was my first Sunday evening there. He said he had found hymns boring and in a style he couldn't get into or identify with until his experience of the previous night: "I was worshiping with a large group of believers who began to sing 'Amazing Grace.' Something came over me," he said. "I began to cry . . . it was such an awesome experience."

I don't know what triggered this young man's response, but I listened and decided to do everything I could to make old hymns come alive. I identified with him and appreciated his honesty. He helped me and all of us remember how we were once impacted by hymns.

When I was a youth I didn't care for the lyrics of great, historic hymns. My attention those days was focused totally on music—the latest rhythms, the hottest chords. But as I matured, the words gradually became meaningful, and a whole universe of hymns opened up to me. I became amazed at the insight packed into their lyrics. Today I am grateful my home church taught me so many of them. I also discovered that the words I was ignoring (at the time) were being memorized and internalized without my conscious knowledge. Like Augustine, I became captivated:

27

How I did weep, in Thy Hymns and Canticles, touched to the quick by the voices of Thy sweet-attuned Church! The voices flowed into mine ears, and the truth distilled into my heart, whence the affections of devotion overflowed and tears ran down, and happy was I therein.[18]

Broader Options for Using Hymns and Choruses

What can we do to keep hymn singing exciting? *First,* sound a call for new hymns. Young congregations should employ contemporary hymns and innovate their own new hymns.[19] Charles Wesley, brother of John Wesley, wrote more than six thousand of them for his generation. Today, writers like Brian Jeffery Leech ("We Are God's People" and "Kind and Merciful God") are making contributions. Let's be a part of this. A new genre of hymns is badly needed.

Second, compose new tunes and rhythms to old texts. Or the reverse. Compose new texts to old tunes. You could even make this a family project.

Noted missiologist Alan R. Tippett related to me a revealing missionary story from the Fiji Islands along these lines. In the 1840s, missionaries who had real insight into the Fiji language paraphrased Wesley's lyrics into Fijian and invited the native people to chant them in their own scales and idioms. The project was a spectacular success. Forty years later, a new group of missionaries arrived and insisted that the old rhythms and tunes be sung exactly as notated in their English hymnbooks. This new constriction, he told me, was never well received; the tunes and rhythms felt strange to the people. This is highly insightful for our situation. The practice of composing new tunes and rhythms to old lyrics is as valid for us as it was for the people of Fiji.

In fact did you know that many classic hymns we use today have undergone revision melodically, rhythmically, and textually over the centuries? For example, today we do not sing "A Mighty Fortress Is Our God" the way it was sung in Martin Luther's time. The rhythm has been changed. Current settings have a sturdy, military feeling to them, whereas the original setting around 1550 had a lighter, dancy, Renaissance feeling to it.

Third, encourage new musical arrangements of historic hymns that are in the public domain.[20] Public domain hymns (those without a copyright sign)[21] may be altered, arranged, displayed, reproduced, and distributed by any means without fear of copyright infringement. Hymns need not be performed precisely the way they are written in hymnbooks in terms of their notes, rhythms, and wording.[22] You can *alter* their tunes and rhythms and *reorchestrate* the harmonies. That's a tremendous advantage. For example, "Blessed Assurance," "Come Ye Disconsolate," and "My Tribute" (refrain) can be sung in a black gospel swing style (see endnote for music notation in 12/8 time and pointers on how to obtain a "black" style).[23]

What about changes in the lyrics? A friend sent me a photocopy of the original lyric of Charles Wesley's "O for a Thousand Tongues to Sing" obtained from a library in England.[24] The original contained about sixteen stanzas, some breathing hell, fire, and brimstone. One stanza had something like this:

That stanza has been omitted from our hymnbooks! The wording of other stanzas has also been "toned down" by editors so as to not offend the sensitivities of today's worshipers. Understand, I'm not suggesting you have to change *all* hymn lyrics or melodies, rather that adjustments have been and will continue to be made.

Altering the harmonies and rhythms of hymns is a tricky business requiring skillful crafting, but that process may have to be undertaken if the current generation is to find hymnic material attractive.

With these thoughts in mind, I invited students in my electronic music class to innovate synthesizer arrangements on the public domain hymn "Come, Christians, Join to Sing." They loved the tune and found they could do a lot with it. One student conceived an exciting fiesta version with Latin percussion—interesting, because it is a Spanish hymn. Another's version captured all the sparkle of "Disneyland on Parade." The students were impressed, and the piece was no longer perceived by them as "dead."

Encourage such efforts! These students were performing a real service. By shaping the hymn material to their culture, they were not only keeping it alive but extending the vast tradition behind it. Some may object that hymnbook settings should not be tampered with. Agreed, there *is* a place for historical purism, and we need to retain the sense of reverence that many hymn settings project. But *we need to see tradition as an ongoing, ever-renewing process.* In these days of breathtaking change and cultural pluralism, we must take calculated risks to bridge communication barriers. We too want to feed into the ever renewing river of song.

In summary, both hymns and choruses are valuable. Each can contribute edifying functions to the full scope of worship.

Hymns and Choruses Edify Differently

Hymns	*Choruses*
enduring "stars"	momentary "fireworks"
historic, classic	contemporary, popular
lengthy, developed	short, repetitious
numerous thoughts	one general thought
transcendent	intimate
more intellectual	more emotional
appealing to mature believers	appealing to mature believers, children, and the unchurched
full of content	minimal content
require attention to text	free attention to God
lyrics dated	lyrics contemporary
vocally demanding	vocally easy
rhythmically stiff	rhythmically freer
medium for specific doctrines	medium for basic character of God

Some may question individual contrasts cited above, and others may rightly argue that many choruses today have more spiritual depth than those of previous years (e.g., "Our God Reigns"). Yet all of us (I hope) can accept the central point of the chart, namely that both forms can yield different, yet positive functions.

Does Scripture offer any guidance along these lines? Yes! Paul reports that the early New Testament church was already employing a *variety* of forms of song. Let's look into that in the next chapter.

Questions for Reflection and Discussion

1. How can intergenerational polarization be overcome?
2. What blend (percentage) of hymns and choruses is appropriate for your church? Why?
3. What is your favorite hymn or chorus? Why?
4. What are the major themes of worship choruses today? Are there gaps?
5. What support systems need to be in place before implementing two contrasting worship services?
6. If we are not singing, what does that say about our lives?

Psalms, Hymns, and Spiritual Songs

> Let the word of Christ *richly* dwell within you, with all wisdom teaching and admonishing one another with psalms and hymns and spiritual songs, singing with thankfulness in your hearts to God.
>
> Colossians 3:16 NASB, emphasis added

Sometimes we come across a critical verse in the Bible that both informs and tantalizes. Our understanding is enlarged, yet the specifics of how to apply it are not completely certain. That is how I find Colossians 3:16. A scriptural argument for variety in worship is clearly stated in the verse through the use of the terms *psalms* and *hymns* and *spiritual songs*. But what exactly is meant by "psalms, hymns, and spiritual songs"?

Are you ready to be stretched? Prepare yourself for the unusual! Let's look into the scriptural basis for why a blend of hymns and choruses may be desirable. We'll begin with Colossians 3:16, which may well contain the most explicit statement for the use of music in the New Testament.

Let Christ Dwell Richly

Let Christ dwell richly—*richly!* That is Paul's major emphasis in this incredibly compact and instructive passage (see

33

also its counterpart in Ephesians 5:19). The opening clause has the central verb; the rest of the sentence is directly tied to and dependent on it.

> *Let the word of Christ richly dwell within you,* with all wisdom teaching and admonishing one another with psalms and hymns and spiritual songs, singing with thankfulness in your hearts to God (NASB, emphasis added).

Simply put, the passage says to let Christ richly dwell in our worship by

- teaching and admonishing one another through song
- singing to two audiences (God and one another) with thankfulness
- embracing a variety of forms

Paul wants Christ to dwell in us *richly*—"abundantly" or "in a constantly new way"[1]—and links that richness to *a richness of expression.* Think about that. For us this could suggest the use of both hymns and choruses, as well as other kinds of responses. Moreover, observe that *two* audiences are addressed: we minister to one another and to God (see chapter 8).

Songs can *teach.* The text reads, "teaching . . . psalms and hymns and spiritual songs." The New American Standard Bible properly brings out the teaching function as a point of immense significance. All three—psalms, hymns, and spiritual songs—can teach strongly in their own way.

Unfortunately, in the New International Version the teaching function does not come out as clearly as it does in the NASB and other versions. Notice why. Below I've bracketed the comma and the *and:* this denotes that they are not in the original Greek.

> Let the word of Christ dwell in you richly as you teach and admonish one another with all wisdom [, and] as you sing psalms, hymns and spiritual songs with gratitude in your hearts to God.

When the comma and the conjunction *and* are improperly retained, "teach . . . with all wisdom" and "sing psalms, hymns and spiritual songs" are separated, muting the teaching function of music. But when the comma and the *and* are omitted, two parallel clauses emerge:[2] "as you teach" and "as you sing" are connected, thereby relating "psalms, hymns and spiritual songs" to the words "teach and admonish."[3] It restores their teaching and admonishing function.

What Exactly Are "Psalms, Hymns, and Spiritual Songs"?

Can we determine exactly what the three terms *psalms, hymns,* and *spiritual songs* were like musically? Not with certainty. Two basic views on the terms exist: they describe and emphasize either (1) the *full range* of style employed or (2) *three different forms.*

The "full range" view de-emphasizes the distinctiveness of the three terms individually and emphasizes the cumulative effect of the terms (their plerophoric value). It's similar to using three words in Scripture (*spirit, soul,* and *body*) to describe the composition of human beings. In other words, it took Paul three terms to describe the full range of the musical activity going on.

That may be the most prudent way to view them. Etymologically it is difficult to distinguish the terms absolutely "because of the small number of passages in the New Testament for comparison."[4] Sometimes the terms *psalms* and *hymns* are used interchangeably.[5] Furthermore, no early Christian treatise on ecclesiastical music has survived. The earliest full text we have of a Christian hymn is dated around A.D. 200.[6] Not until about A.D. 560 are there substantial descriptions of Christian liturgy and its music, although Saint Ignatius of Antioch (d. 110), Tertullian (d. 220), Clement of Alexandria (d. 212), and Augustine (d. 430) talk much about music practice in their time.[7]

What sources did early Christian music draw on? Answer: popular Greek idioms. Scholars believe that Christian music developed not from *classical* Greek music, but from a freer, less strictly metered *popular* Greek idiom that developed during the fourth century B.C.[8] Apparently, the early Christians also improvised much of their chant: "The church Fathers gave a surprising amount of attention, in music and worship, to improvisation and charismatic utterance . . . [and] spontaneity in prayer."[9] Early church father Tertullian wrote: "Anyone who can, either from holy Scripture or from his own heart, is called into the middle to sing to God."

On the other hand, Egon Wellesz, an authority on music of this period, holds to the three forms argument—that the forms were *stylistically differentiated.* Based on a study of early Jewish music and later recorded Christian chant, he views the terms the following way:

35

1. Psalmody: the cantillation of the Jewish psalms and of the canticles and doxologies modeled on them.
2. Hymns: songs of praise of a syllabic type, i.e., each syllable is sung to one or two notes of the melody.
3. Spiritual songs: Alleluia and other chants of a jubilant or ecstatic character, richly ornamented.[10]

That is, Wellesz believes that the psalms probably refer to unmetered psalms and their early church derivatives that reflect the parallelism inherent in Old Testament materials. The hymns were likely syllabic (one note for each syllable)—more like our hymns. They were probably Christological expressions, similar to hymnic passages in Paul's letters that show evidence of Greek poetic patterns (see Phil. 2:6–11; 1 Tim. 3:16). The designation "psalms, hymns, and spiritual songs" may also reflect a Trinitarian emphasis: psalms were addressed to God, hymns to Christ the Son, and spiritual songs were spontaneous expressions under the inspiration of the Holy Spirit.

Arro holds a view similar to Wellesz, believing that psalms, hymns, and spiritual songs reflect the three influences that shaped early Christianity—Judaism, Hellenism, and the Asiatic Near East region—and bases his judgment on the "subsequent course of history, not on a strict literary interpretation of St. Paul's terms."[11] This view, too, seems sensible because in all likelihood a blend of Jewish and Gentile believers attended the church at Colossae. Their music probably reflected their multicultural heritage, an identification point our pluralistic society in North America has in common with the early church.

We know, says Clint Arnold,[12] that the city of Ephesus (remember that the parallel passage of Colossians 3:16 is Ephesians 5:19) had a much larger and more pluralistic population than Colossae. Consisting of Asians, Persians, Romans, Greeks, and Egyptians, it was strongly multicultural and had at least a quarter million inhabitants, which was huge for that time. Josephus reports that many Jews who lived in Ephesus had immigrated from Babylon, not Jerusalem. Likely, they carried with them the music styles prevalent there. Since the inhabitants of Ephesus were drawn from all these scattered places, the music in the house churches and synagogues probably reflected the divergent cultures represented. Immigrants cannot easily shed their cultural upbringing.

Tracing the History of "Spiritual Songs"

Research has produced evidence regarding the meaning of "spiritual songs" that may seem strange, perhaps even touching a sensitive chord in readers. Understand, my goal is to be honest and to inform.

"Spiritual songs" may have a more focused meaning than many evangelicals might think. Many scholars relate it to glossolalia, to the influence of mystical traditions, and in a later development, to the jubilus in Catholic chant. For example, Jewish scholar Eric Werner links "spiritual songs" to the synagogue and to "the glossolaly of the Paulinian age." And Ford and Hardy relate them to mystical traditions in Eastern culture.[13]

Moreover, musicologists believe "spiritual songs" relates to the development of improvised songs on a single word like *alleluia*. The Greek phrase for "spiritual songs" is *odaes pneumaticaes* or "pneumatic odes"—that is, "songs upon the breath."[14] What could "songs upon the breath" mean?

Egon Wellesz is one musicologist who relates it to improvisation. Wellesz says improvising on a single word like *alleluia* was common practice in Near East cultures during the time of Christ and later became formalized in the jubilus of the Catholic mass. The final syllable ("ah") of the word *alleluia* was prolonged in a kind of wordless improvisation.

Jerome and Augustine spoke of the practice. Jerome (c. 347–420) described it as neither "words nor syllables nor letters nor speech." Augustine said of it:

> It is a certain sound of joy *without words* . . . it is the expression of a mind poured forth with joy. . . . A man rejoicing after certain *words which cannot be understood,* bursteth forth into sounds of exultation without words so that it seemeth that he . . . filled with excessive joy cannot express in words the subject of that joy (emphasis added).[15]

When Augustine referred to "words which cannot be understood" or songs "without words," he might have been speaking of simple improvisation or some kind of ecstatic expression similar to that mentioned in the Old Testament (1 Sam. 10:5–6; 16:13–14, 23) or even the "singing in the spirit" occurring in the Corinthian church (1 Cor. 14:1–3). The non-charismatic Jewish scholar, Werner, says,

> In church and Synagogue, extended melismatic chant was regarded as an ecstatic praise. . . . I venture to put forward my own conviction that the whole concept of the pure, wordless, melismatic jubilation should be considered the last, jealously guarded remnant of an organized musical form of glossolaly.[16]

Edie Ensley says the improvised jubilus persisted in the worship of Francis of Assisi, Bernard of Clairvaux, and Thomas Aquinas, dying out only in the sixteenth century.[17]

Clint Arnold, however, along with other interpreters, prefers to translate *pneumaticaes* as "spiritual" or "spirit" odes rather than odes "on the breath." He would apply the word *spiritual* to all three terms—*spiritual* psalms, hymns, and songs—and views the Holy Spirit as inspiring all three. Andrew T. Lincoln concurs: "'spiritual,' although agreeing in gender with only the last in the series, embraces all three terms. The songs which believers sing to each other are spiritual because they are inspired by the Spirit and manifest the life of the Spirit."[18] Peter O'Brien provides the following summary:

> As the word of Christ indwells the members of the community and controls them so they teach and admonish one another in Spirit-inspired psalms, hymns, and songs.[19]

Even if this interpretation is accepted, it still does not mitigate the possible element of spontaneous, Spirit-inspired utterance that could embrace all three terms:

> For if I pray in a tongue, my spirit prays, but my mind is unfruitful. So what shall I do? I will pray with my spirit, but I will also pray with my mind; I will sing with my spirit, but I will also sing with my mind.
>
> 1 Corinthians 14:14–15

Performing "Spiritual Songs" Today

Is any counterpart to this spontaneous praise being practiced today?[20] Yes. Liturgical and non-liturgical evangelical churches occasionally employ improvised praise as a brief "coda" at the end of choruses for ten to thirty seconds. I've heard this performed inoffensively in Lutheran and Foursquare churches. Moreover, some Assembly of God churches "sing in the spirit" for *one to two minutes* as a regular part of their Sunday morning service.

38

Even in Assembly of God practice, however, there is nothing necessarily "supernatural" about it. Many simply improvise alleluias
and other short phrases a cappella over a sustained instrumental
drone or chord.[21] The triad tends to emerge.[22] One can hear neighbor and passing tones and free material in the cloudlike textures
that arise. Since I improvise, one Sunday I felt free to join in—humming the drone and sometimes singing alleluias or short "I thank
you, Lord" or "I bless you" phrases.

The total effect did not smack of a "fervor gone wild." In fact,
what I heard was peaceful and reverential, more like the strum-
ming of many harps. Choruses like "Give Thanks" lend themselves
to this kind of treatment. Sing it as written; at the end allow some
free singing; then return to the melody to close off.[23] Moreover,
prayer of this kind is widespread in Latin American and Asian
churches and is not perceived by them as charismatic. Usually the
leader rounds off this exercise with a spoken prayer. Prayer is
closely tied in to the whole concept of "spiritual song."

A known melody can also be used for the basis of spontaneous
song. The congregation can sing their own verses to the chorus
"Allelulia," for example. Or chord progressions, each four beats
long with a pedal tone (C, G, F, G over a pedal C), are also possible.
Repeat as long as necessary.

I have also heard instrumentalists do an exclusively instrumental free improvisation after a worship chorus at Vineyard churches.
The progressions I–ii–V–IV (repeat) and I–VII♭–VI♭–VII♭–I(repeat) can
be employed.[24] This too can be a meaningful expression of worship.

For many churches, however, this form may not be appropriate
because it could be divisive.[25] It is valuable, though, to become
aware of its various manifestations. The rationale of wedding the
spontaneous with the spiritual seems to lie behind the form. But
remember, spontaneity in worship doesn't make us more spiritual
than another group.

If any aspect of this presentation interests you, don't rush or force
implementation. Allow ample time for the people to adjust. You
might want to consider having your worship group (instrumental
or vocal) model the shorter, coda version as an introductory step.
If the form becomes familiar and comfortable to all, then invite the
people to join in. Viewed in this light, Colossians 3:16 definitely gives
us a richness to think about! A whole book could be written just on
this concept of "psalms, hymns, and spiritual songs."

Moreover, this chapter does not address at all the singing and chanting of psalms, though this is a tremendous area for development. With imagination, the chanting of psalms can fit with your unique music style. It *can* be done.

The Biblical Argument for Variety

Another confirming point for employing both hymns and choruses is the model of the book of Psalms. The Hebrews preserved their old songs, sang contemporary songs, and looked forward to the composition of yet unwritten new songs. In other words, the Old Testament Psalms display the same respect for variety and tradition that the New Testament affirms. The Psalms span about a thousand years, dating back to Moses (about 1400 B.C.), to David (c. 1000 B.C.), to the postexilic period (c. 400 B.C.), and still others call for a "new song."

Some psalms are short, others long. Some are historical, many are personal. Some are structurally complex (the acrostic, the symmetrical); others, straightforward and repetitious. This scriptural precedence of allowing a variety of expression deserves attention. We also see the same passion for variety demonstrated in God's created order. God loves variety!

Does your approach to church music embody this kind of breadth? If we took all of the music lyrics you use at your church and made a book out of them, would they have the variety found in the Psalms? In short, the modeling of Scripture in both testaments supports comprehensiveness. For our practical purposes, this could mean employing tunes, rhythms, and translated lyrics from Hebrew, Hispanic, African, and Asian cultures, as well as other traditions—Taizé, for example.

To employ only choruses in worship, however, is not to commit mortal sin! No Scripture *commands* the use of hymns, nor can we assert that the form of hymns today corresponds one-to-one with the materials designated "hymns" in Ephesians and Colossians. Rather, I'm arguing that the pattern of both Old and New Testament Scripture, which manifests a variety of forms, suggests and encourages a diversity of materials and a respect for ongoing tradition. I am deeply concerned that the practice of hymn singing seems to be faltering on the West Coast and in other parts of North America. As a result, our younger generation is being impoverished and is losing a richness it should be acquiring.

Finally, what about the often heard objection that "hymns and choruses don't go together"? This simply is not true. (For a demonstration see the chart on page 53 in the next chapter.) People who say this often know few, if any, hymns and may have no fond associations with them or feel threatened by them. Guitarists find many of them awkward to play because most hymnbook harmonizations are written for keyboardists. (A recent survey indicates the piano is the dominant instrument in evangelical churches.)[26] So guitarists often feel defeated trying to play hymnbook harmonizations, which are usually too fast and unsuited for their instruments. If more hymnbooks would offer pop symbols in keys with sharps (G, D, A, E) and with slower "harmonic rhythms," that would help make hymns more accessible to guitarists. Some do.[27] Another solution is to have keyboardists play the hymns and guitarists the choruses.

One more alternative is to place hymns and choruses in different parts of your service. You could open with a chorus section and include two hymns toward the middle of your service. Or you could open with a hymn, continue with choruses, and close your worship "set" with a hymn. Hymns can even be functional within the center of a set.

Preserve the Excellent, Whether It's Old or New

Major changes have already impacted and will continue to affect our churches due to our listening habits and the conditions in our homes, schools, and churches. In Caucasian America, fewer people have a piano in their home and fewer children take classical lessons. In our public schools, there are fewer choral, band, and orchestral programs; and in our churches, fewer trained choirs. We are being reduced to performing with tapes!

In Canada, at one time there were a hundred Canadian companies making pianos; today there are none. The statistics are clear. Recording industry sales have soared since 1940, whereas instrument sales have inversely trailed off percentage-wise. Increasingly, people are not making their own music, they're listening to recordings. Synthesizer manufacturers hope that interactive music-making on computers will help reverse the trend. Churches, all of whom depend on live music for worship, ought to be concerned.

In Southern California less than 7 percent of the population listens to classical music. Of about fifty AM and FM stations on the radio dial in Los Angeles, only one programs predominantly classical music. Meanwhile, a higher percentage of guitarists, bassists, percussionists, and synthesizer players are resident in our churches. The upshot seems clear—we will have more contemporary bands. The coming young generation will perform with instruments they are skilled in and in styles they know and hear in their heads. An increasing number of churches will have organs with no one who knows how to play them. I recently heard of one Christian church that in desperation hired a Buddhist to play the organ for them and of another church whose organist travels four hours to play only every second week.

These times require the collaborative leadership of parents, pastors, and musicians. We face serious questions. Do we as parents have the force of will to do what is necessary to provide our children with quality instruments and quality instruction? Will we train them so they can perform and learn to appreciate both the classics and the new styles and be able to transmit to future generations what is best in our culture?

Will churches with adult and children's choir programs permit them to erode? I hope not. Can we as churches strike a healthier blend of the old and new?

While advancing toward renewal through worship, *be brave yet careful!* Aggressively reach out and embrace new forms, but at the same time preserve for your children excellence from the past. In this way you will be following the model of Scripture.

> I don't want you to think of art as a
> little whipped cream on the cake of life.
> It's more like steak and potatoes.
> Dallas Willard

Questions for Reflection and Discussion

1. When Paul said "let the word of Christ richly dwell within you," what do you think he had in mind?
2. What about the objection that hymns and choruses don't go together? Does it contain some validity?

3. What would be the benefits and liabilities of employing some kind of "singing in the spirit"—vocally or instrumentally—in your church?
4. Do you prefer the "three forms" view or the "full-range" view of "psalms, hymns, and spiritual songs" in Colossians 3:16? Why?
5. Can you present a persuasive case for employing a blend of hymns and choruses in two or three sentences?
6. How would you evaluate the balance of psalms, hymns, and spiritual songs in your church?

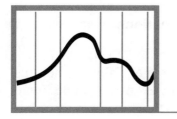

3

Free-Flowing Praise

By wisdom a house is built,
and through understanding, it is established;
through knowledge its rooms are filled
with rare and beautiful treasures.

Proverbs 24:3–4

Not long ago, I spent the better part of a year visiting one to two churches every Sunday morning in order to gain some perspective of the variety of worship practices occurring in Southern California. Three basic formats seemed to emerge:

- the liturgical service organized around the lectionary and the church year
- the thematic service, where the music and readings serve the sermon
- the free-flowing praise service, where the music and sermon are independent[1]

This last type is part of the "new worship" occurring today, and because it's quite different from the others, it is not well understood. So in this chapter and the next, I want to help us get a better grasp of it.

Discrete Events versus Continuous Sections

We can organize the first two types according to *discrete events* and the third by *continuous sections.* Let me explain. In a service organized as a list of discrete or distinct events, a single hymn might be followed by a prayer, another hymn, the choir, the offering, a solo, a Scripture reading, and the sermon—the typical evangelical format. In this sequence each adjacent item is a different type of activity and each is relatively independent and short. Several of these different items can be arranged to comprise a section and be grouped under one heading in the worship bulletin.

The free-flowing praise arrangement, however, consists of one or more uninterrupted sections of *one type* of activity. For example, sustained praise could last for ten to forty-five minutes without breaking the flow, as could Scripture reading or prayer. The sustained-section type of service is now being employed by young, emerging congregations. Both the discrete and the sustained organization can be effective, and in both cases the end result can be equally edifying. The interesting development today is the multitude of ways churches are innovating variations *within* and mixes *between* the three forms. That's where the action is.

The next two chapters will demonstrate how flowing praise can be adopted wholly or in part, in contemporary and more traditional formats. In devoting considerable space to it, the intent is to educate, not send a message that it is a "better form." It is simply *different.* It will not be nor must be the form of choice for every church.

Alarms have been sounded concerning the free-flowing praise format. Some musicians, especially organists, find the call for worship choruses threatening. The proper rhythmic feel of some choruses is difficult for them to obtain and they fear finding themselves on the periphery of musical activity. Others, especially middle-aged people, find the use of choruses repetitive and boring and the free-flowing praise format undisciplined and aimless. Some critics maintain the form invites abuse, that its proponents use it to manipulate the people into emotional highs. Yet, some pastors feel compelled to look at the form because they are afraid of losing members to the church down the road that employs a less staid format. All of these are serious worries and concerns. Can they be allayed? Yes!

It is time to seek perspective and appreciate the rationale behind both free-flowing praise and traditional formats. We need less suspicion and more informed understanding. I hope you find these pages nonjudgmental. I believe that by becoming more comprehensively skilled, however, we are better able to edify the church and reduce conflict. Consider Paul Wohlgemuth's assessment:

> [Free-flowing praise] *demands a new kind* of song leader, choir director, keyboard performer, as well as instrumentalist. . . . No worship in recent years is so dependent upon music for the heart of its expression. . . . Currently, no seminary offers training or a graduate degree program for a music leader that would be preparation for this *new, emerging role as a worship leader*. . . . The need is for trained leaders . . . who are at least informed about significant new, and even threatening worship music and practices (emphasis added).[2]

It is time to offer options for churches that may want some feeling of free-flowing praise but not the full-blown version. *The Hymnal for Worship & Celebration* (Waco: Word, 1986), which has sold more than two million copies, also recognizes this widespread desire, for it includes twenty-three brief services with a flowing-praise format. It even includes notated keyboard modulations and transitions in its "mini-services."

The Wimber Five-Phase Model

What is the rationale for this free-flowing style? Eddie Espinosa of the Vineyard in Anaheim Hills, California, where John Wimber is pastor,[3] likens it to a physical workout. He says that just as sustained periods of exercise are good for the cardiovascular system, so sustained singing for fifteen to forty minutes is good for worshipers' spiritual systems. Long, uninterrupted sections of worship allow people time to offer their whole selves (mind, will, and emotions) to the Lord without distraction. He also likens free-flowing praise to sitting down to a leisurely meal, lingering and enjoying fellowship one with another around the family table. Accordingly, this Five-Phase model contains adoration and intimacy phases that allow us to linger in God's presence. Hopefully, the weekly modeling of worship at church will trickle down into our private worship. When caught in a traffic jam or washing the dishes, we might be more inclined to shut off the radio and worship before the Lord alone or with a worship cassette.

Sustained sections of public singing also require more planning, *more* skill—not less—more insight in order to execute them smoothly. Because six to ten choruses or hymns may be selected, each must flow into the other, and transitions must be handled deftly so as to produce the effect of a seamless garment.

To achieve these smooth transitions, Espinosa and Wimber developed the Five-Phase pattern in their long worship set. This pattern did not occur to them suddenly; rather, it evolved after years of experience of leading worship—and only later consciously crystallizing in their thinking. They found that different types of choruses could be categorized and linked into a sequence. The five phases are: (1) invitation, (2) engagement, (3) exaltation, (4) adoration, (5) intimacy (plus a summarizing closeout). The need for the model probably arose because choruses are so short and their worship set was so long that a method for linking many choruses smoothly and providing a sense of progression became important. I believe the ideas inherent in the model have the potential for a broader application than even Wimber and Espinosa envisaged. That is what my particular presentation seeks to bring out. And its psychological pattern, though powerful, need not be excessively manipulative. In fact, planners must admit that any concert, any worship service, to some degree, is designed to impact people.

Five-Phase Worship Curve Respects Psychological Dimension

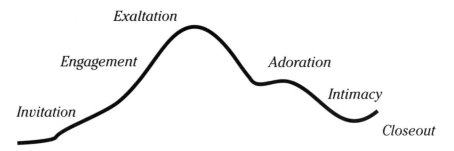

The *invitation phase* is like a call to worship. It accepts people where they are and begins to draw them into worship. The feeling of it may be celebratory, upbeat, and praise oriented, but it doesn't have to be. If appropriate, it may be accompanied with hand clapping. The key point is that the lyric is directed to the people—not God—and it tells them what they are about to do. The lyric of "Don't You Know It's Time to Praise the Lord" illustrates the idea:

> Don't you know it's time to praise the Lord,
> In the sanctuary of His Holy Spirit.
> So set your mind on Him,
> And let your praise begin,
> And the glory of the Lord,
> Will fill this place.[4]

Notice that the lyric does the inviting and focusing without your having to resort to verbal scolding ("Can we have quiet!"). For a vigorous call to worship with hand clapping, the Hebrew chorus "The Celebration Song" (Chambers) would be excellent, whereas a more mellow call could be "Let's Forget about Ourselves and Magnify the Lord and Worship Him," or "Come, Worship the Lord." Alternatively, traditional churches could use hymns during this phase and conclude it with a Scripture call to worship before beginning the engagement phase.

In the invitation phase, leaders continue until they have made contact with the people and everyone is focused. "The skillful leader woos the congregation into worship like the patient lover draws the beloved."[5] The invitation phase is particularly helpful for emerging churches that meet in high schools and other structures not designed specifically for worship. Where there is an absence of material worship symbols—no communion table, no open Bible, no stained glass windows, no inspirational banners, no burning candles, no kneeling bench, no architectural lines that soar—the environment does not assist in drawing out worship.

In the *engagement phase* the people begin to draw near to God, and the lyric is now addressed to the Lord, not one another (e.g., "How Majestic," "Come Thou Almighty King"):

> Come Thou Almighty King
> Help us Thy Praise to sing.

Espinosa likens this phase to the engagement period before marriage, for we are now attentive, serious. Some church cultures may be able to skip the invitation phase and begin here immediately.

In the *exaltation phase* the people sing out "to the Lord" with power, giving meaningful expression to the words of transcendence—words like *great, majestic, worthy, reigns, Lord, mountains,* and so on. The pitch spans are generally greater than in the other phases because high notes are needed to bring out a dynamic response and project a sense of God's greatness. Here is where the organ can be especially useful. Also, if the people stand throughout the invitation, engagement, and exaltation phases, response will be stronger.

In the *adoration phase* the people can be seated, the dynamics gradually subside, the melody range may reduce to five or six notes, and the key words may be *you, Jesus* (e.g., "We Worship and Adore You"). Notice also that in the performance of the exaltation and adoration phases, two sides of God's character have received expression: his transcendency (wholly "otherness") and his closeness to us. The expression of both aspects tends to allay contrived emotion. Also, the praise involved in the engagement and exaltation phases is *about* God, while in adoration we are singing *to* God.

Transitions and modulations can be longer and more expressive in the adoration phase; we are not in a rush. Sometimes, I pause a fraction of a second on the dominant chord (e.g., G-chord in the key of C), wait, watch, and gather the attention of the people so that a totally united response occurs on the first note of an adoration or intimacy piece. It's a matter of seizing a significant, dramatic moment of attentiveness so we can go forward together.

The last phase before the close, the *intimacy phase*, is the quietest and most personal. We address God as Abba or Daddy (e.g., "In Moments Like These" or "O Lord, You're Beautiful"). This is the "kiss." One meaning for the Greek word for *worship, proskuneo,* is "to turn toward to kiss," as in to kiss the feet, the hands, or the cheek. Since closeness is required for kissing, people need to be properly prepared for it in the phases that precede it.

Whereas the lyrics may emphasize the corporate "we" in the exaltation phase, they may now take the personal dimension of "I" ("Father, I Love You"). "Our" can change to "my" in songs like "Marvelous grace of my loving Lord, grace that exceeds my sin and my guilt!" And "him" or "his" can change to "you" or "your" in "'Tis so sweet to trust *you* Jesus, Just to take *you* at your word." The acoustic guitar is particularly effective in achieving intimacy. Percussion sounds, appropriate up to this point, may not be appropriate during the intimacy phase.

It all ends when the people stand for a *closeout* chorus or hymn (e.g., "My Tribute") that leads out of intimacy and helps them adjust to the next event in the service. Musically, I tend to like big, summarizing pieces for the closeout. Textually, songs of dedication, aspiration, exaltation, or songs relating directly to the pastor's theme or the next item of the service may be appropriate.

Tempos and Transitions

When planning your free-flowing set, be sure to test the tempo connections. If you desire the invitation, engagement, and exaltation phases to be upbeat and brisk, try tapping a pencil to check that the tempos are similar enough to ensure the necessary momentum to lead securely into the climactic exaltation phase. Faltering tempos will impede that. If you tap the tempos in the set described in the chart on page 53, you will find that "We Bring a Sacrifice of Praise" through "Glorify Your Name" are all fairly brisk; the big change to a slower tempo comes with "I Love You, Lord" in the adoration phase. "Glorify Your Name" is somewhat transitional.

To maintain this momentum, it is crucial to innovate short transitions between praise songs. Dead space between numbers kills the sense of momentum. Use common keys (note the D-majors in the chart) when possible, or fashion quick, one-to-two measure modulations. In Assembly of God churches, song leaders effectively voice short expressions of praise verbally to smooth the transitions—sometimes the people join in on that response. (I prefer purely instrumental transitions, but that is your choice.) Just remember, a number of abrupt tempo changes can be disruptive. Metaphorically speaking, we don't want to stumble or break our stride while running. Overall, think of the tempos the following way: invitation and engagement (running), exaltation (jogging), adoration (walking), and intimacy (stopping, silent communion, gazing). That is one possibility.

Hand Signals

Flowing praise demands a flexible delivery, for hymns and choruses may need an extra repetition, a change in dynamics, or benefit by a modulation. The following hand signals increase effective communication between musicians and improve the flow:

- fingers pointing up for sharp keys, fingers pointing down for flat keys
- curved thumb and forefinger in a C shape indicates the key of C
- thumbs up for a modulation up a half step
- palm up means louder, palm down, softer
- rotating your wrist and index finger means another repetition
- hand on head (da capo) means to go back to the very beginning

Arrange yourself for ease of visual contact with your musicians.

Psychological Underpinnings

A basic premise of this Five-Phase model is that *praise normally precedes adoration.* By "praise" I'm referring to upbeat songs of transcendence in the engagement and exaltation phases; and by "adoration," songs in the adoration and intimacy phases. This fundamental principle—that praise or exaltation normally precedes adoration—is strategic.[6] It's behind much of the best worship leading because it makes sense psychologically. People simply cannot come to church and plunge into adoration without preparation. People need time before they are ready to express true adoration and intimacy. And beginning with praise makes sense too. Most people need to wake up and be energized by upbeat music early in the service—especially in early morning services.

Incorporating Hymns into the Model

Hymns, I must admit, *are* more difficult to incorporate into the model. Textually, the wide range of thoughts introduced from stanza to stanza tend to spill over into more than one phase. Choruses, on the other hand, tend to fall into a single phase more easily because they usually contain only one major thought. Hymns do have their benefits, however.

When hymns are included in the set, organists can share in the worship. For example, the organ can be particularly effective during a hymn of exaltation or during the closeout. If your church organ is retrofitted with MIDI,[7] the organist can participate even in contemporary choruses. The chart below demonstrates that hymns and choruses can be effectively combined in ways that allow for variety. The supplemental disk provides a demonstration of each of the modulations in the set.

A Model Five-Phase Set

Phase	Piece	Key Word	Key
	STAND		
Invitation	"We Bring a Sacrifice of Praise"	praise	D
	"He Has Made Me Glad"	glad	D
Engagement	"Rejoice in the Lord Always"	rejoice	D
Exaltation	"Rejoice, the Lord Is King!"	rejoice	C
	"Crown Him with Many Crowns"	crown	C
	SIT		
Exaltation/ Adoration	"Glorify Your Name"	glorify	B♭/C
Adoration	"I Love You, Lord"	love	F
Intimacy	"As the Deer"	you	C
	STAND		
Closeout	"Fairest Lord Jesus"		D♭/D/E♭

Sensitively craft your worship set. In the above example, I've pitched the keys low because I'm planning for an early morning service where our voices will need to warm up. Raising the key a half or whole step between repetitions or stanzas can increase intensity (the accompanying disk explores that in great detail with examples and exercises). Try not to overuse this technique, though; determine from the text which stanza(s) will benefit most. For example, raising the last stanza of "Fairest Lord Jesus" a half step up helps to express the regality of the text ("Lord of creation") immeasurably. Key changes up a fourth or down a fifth (see "Glorify Your Name" to "I Love You, Lord"— C to F)[8] between pieces usually require no modulation material at all.

Note that the use of common words between adjacent choruses prevents patchiness and builds unity (see "rejoice" and "rejoice" under the "Key Word" column above). Charles Wesley also used this device in "O for a Thousand Tongues to Sing" to link stanzas. In the chart on the next page, the italics show how a word ending a stanza is reused in starting the next stanza. Clever! A good idea for us too.

End of stanza	1. the triumphs of his *grace*
Start	2. My *gracious* Master and my God
End	3. the honors of Thy *Name*
Start	4. Jesus, the *name* that calms my fears

Employ the Five-Phase Model with Flexibility

The Five-Phase progression has a balanced, graduated arch. Use it as a handy frame to guide your worship thinking. You can be flexible about *time;* the same progression can be used in either long or short worship sets. You can also be flexible about *content;* use all choruses, all hymns, or any mixture or weighting of hymns and choruses. And you can be flexible about *place.* Use it before the sermon as the one dominating activity of the entire worship service, or use a part of it during the prelude. Use it only at the beginning or only at the end of your service. Use it in Sunday evening services when you're collecting a bunch of favorites for a sing-along. Use any number of hymns or choruses in any phase.

You can even cut out some phases, rearrange them, or weight them differently. The exaltation and adoration phases seem to form the core of the model. Think of these two phases as mirroring the basic character of God: his transcendence and his immanence. They help us project an accurate, faithful image of God to the people—a vital concept. I *always* try to have moments of transcendence and adoration/intimacy in every Sunday morning worship service. That's always on my mind. A good place for Scripture reading is between these phases, if you want to divide a set. I've also tried moving from exaltation to adoration and back to exaltation.

Flowing Worship Options

Option One	*Option Two*
Exaltation	Exaltation
Break (Scripture/prayer/solo?)	Adoration
Adoration	Exaltation

You can also give a single phase like adoration more weight than the others. I've experimented successfully with short sets (ten minutes) toward the middle of the morning service that focus on exclusively adoration pieces. It works especially well when the set emerges out of a time of prayer or the communion service.

If you are introducing free-flowing praise into a traditional service format, begin conservatively. First, include one chorus as a "response to revelation." Extend that to two, then three continuous hymns or choruses. As your skill increases, and the people become accustomed to the change, you may want to gradually lengthen the set.

Avoid Jerkiness

One benefit of the model is that it encourages us not to jump around between categories in a worship set. This jerking about tends to be disorienting, results in a lack of direction, and distracts from the spiritual focus of the service. It's like a home decorated without integrated colors, furniture, and paintings.

Another advantage is that the performing team can have a feeling for the overall dynamic shape without knowing the exact sequence of every tune. From the phases, the lyrics, and the progression of songs over time, the group can anticipate how they should be functioning musically to achieve an ensemble effect.

Important! *If there is an abrupt change of tempo* in beginning a new song, have the supporting group gradually emerge two or four measures after the leader. That's an easy yet safe way to establish a new tempo.

What about technology? Sequenced drum machine parts,[9] MIDI files, and the use of software such as "Band in a Box"[10] may function better at the beginning where steady tempos are normative. The rubato, though, which could occur in the later adoration and intimacy phases, makes it more difficult for performers to keep in sync with a preset track.

Accumulation, not Repetition

Finally, what about the objection that chorus singing is boring and repetitious? That felt perception, more than anything, reveals a lack of musicianship. When resourceful musicians repeat a chorus over and over, it's not boring and it's not simple repetition. It's *accumulation.* On each repetition, the insightful musician will do something subtle—change the rhythm, the chords, or the dynamics—to add life and a sense of unfolding newness. In fact, there is a real danger that expert leaders may use these techniques (i.e., emotional repetitions) to manipulate the people. *Worship lead-*

ers have an obligation not to manipulate the people. They must earn and never betray the trust people put in them.

Let me further expand on the idea of accumulation. If you tell your spouse, "I love you," that means something. But if you say, "I love you! I love you! I love you!"—that's more than simple repetition! The three-fold repetition communicates a sense of intense feeling. In the same way, when the praise offered to the Lamb in Revelation is intensified by the sevenfold repetition—"Worthy is the Lamb, who was slain, to receive power and wealth and wisdom and strength and honor and glory and praise!" (Rev. 5:12)— it is far more than simple repetition. It has an extolling function. The rhythmic, climactic effect communicated in heaven is similar to the language we use in human emotion. Jesus also employed repetition for intensity when he used a favorite phrase, "Truly, truly I say unto you."

Scriptural Support: Psalm 95

Espinosa discerns scriptural support for the Five-Phase model in Psalm 95.

Invitation	Come, let us sing for joy to the LORD; let us shout aloud to the Rock of our salvation. (v. 1)
Engagement	Let us come before him with thanksgiving and extol him with music and song. (v. 2)
Exaltation	For the LORD is the great God, the great King above all gods. In his hand are the depths of the earth, and the mountain peaks belong to him. The sea is his, for he made it, and his hands formed the dry land. (vv. 3–5)
Adoration	Come, let us bow down in worship, let us kneel before the LORD our Maker. (v. 6)
Intimacy	For he is our God and we are the people of his pasture, the flock under his care. (v. 7)

How psychologically sound!

The following chart illustrates a variety of song possibilities for each phase. The assigned categories are not rigid; a song may serve more than one category. For the choruses, I chose "golden oldies" in order to communicate to readers of all ages. I use quotation marks for the choruses and italics for the hymns.

56

As you prepare your own song list, Bob Sorge suggests you divide your material into three categories—hymns, fast songs, and slow songs. (Quality fast choruses are particularly hard to find! Focus your search on them.) Engagement and exaltation songs would normally fall into the fast category, whereas adoration and intimacy songs are usually slow. Or arrange your own chorus and hymn repertoire into the Five-Phase format as demonstrated on page 53.

I have chosen upbeat choruses in the first three phases. You, however, might fill these cells with an entirely different array of choices and obtain a quite different mood and feel. Whatever you do, be guided by the same principles and techniques, namely:

- worship that has a goal and direction
- worship that respects the psychological dimension
- worship that reflects the character of God (transcendence, intimacy)
- lyrics that point to function (singing about and later to God)
- mixing of hymns and choruses (richness, variety)
- commitment to smooth transitions (linking both pieces and phases)
- commitment to avoiding distractions (not jumping around)
- use of common tempos
- use of common words
- use of common keys
- being prepared but still open to the leading of the Spirit

Notice that this model is mainly psychological, not thematic. It is designed to bring people before God, which is a great achievement in itself. It is not as conducive to the designing of thematic services, where the content of the pastor's sermon drives the whole service.

Worship in the Five-Phase model can be complementary to the sermon but is usually not strongly connected thematically to it. Why? Musically, it is difficult to achieve both thematic connection and free flow at the same time on a weekly basis. Flowing praise has a shape and structure of its own. It is hard to find thematic songs that will also fit back-to-back in a set. As the service progresses in time, however, the worship leader may introduce thematic elements that form a bridge to the sermon—not only in songs but in prayers, readings, drama vignettes, testimonies, and so forth.

Examples of Five-Phase
Hymns and Choruses

Invitation	*Engagement*	*Exaltation*
"We Bring a Sacrifice of Praise"	"Our God Is an Awesome God"	"All the Earth Shall Worship" (Tuttle)
"Don't You Know It's Time to Praise the Lord"	"How Majestic"	"Let There Be Glory and Honor and Praises"
"I Just Came to Praise the Lord"	"Rejoice in the Lord Always"	"All Hail King Jesus"
"Let's Forget about Ourselves"	"He Is the King"	"We Exalt Thee"
"Spirit Song"	"Great and Mighty Is He"	"Our God Reigns"
"Come, Worship the Lord"	"The Celebration Song"	"Thou Art Worthy"
"As We Gather"	"I Will Sing of the Mercies of the Lord"	"Majesty" (Hayford)
"This Is the Day That the Lord Has Made"	"I Shall Prepare Him My Heart"	"I Just Want to Praise You" (Tannous)
Come, Christians, Join to Sing	*O Worship the King*	*Crown Him with Many Crowns*
Praise the Savior, Ye Who Know Him	*All Creatures of Our God and King*	*Immortal, Invisible*
My Faith Has Found a Resting Place	*Guide Me, O Thou Great Jehovah*	*Rejoice, the Lord Is King!*
Let's All Go up to Zion	*Come, Thou Almighty King*	*How Great Thou Art*
Come, We That Love the Lord	*O for a Thousand Tongues to Sing*	*All Hail the Power of Jesus' Name*

58

Adoration	_Intimacy_	_Closeout_
"We Worship and Adore You"	"O Lord, You're Beautiful"	"We Are One in the Spirit"
"Glorify Your Name"	"Turn Your Eyes upon Jesus"	"In My Life, Lord, Be Glorified"
"His Name Is Wonderful"	"My Delight"	"Holy, Holy, Holy"
"I Love You, Lord"	"Alleluia, Alleluia"	"Shine, Jesus, Shine"
"Emmanuel"	"As the Deer"	"He Is Able, More Than Able"
"Lord, We Praise You"	"Sweet Perfume"	"Thank You, Lord, for Saving My Soul"
"Father, I Adore You"	"Holy Ground"	"Our God Reigns"
"Praise Song"	"In Moments Like These"	_It Is Well_
Fairest Lord Jesus	_Jesus, I Am Resting, Resting_	_My Tribute_
My Jesus, I Love Thee	_Jesus, the Very Thought of Thee_	_To God Be the Glory_
Be Thou My Vision	_Children of the Heavenly Father_	_And Can It Be_
Jesus, Priceless Treasure	_Close to Thee_	_Our Great Savior_
Majestic Sweetness Sits Enthroned	_O to Be Like Thee!_	_May the Mind_
Of the Father's Love Begotten	_Savior, Like a Shepherd_	_Fairest Lord Jesus_
How Sweet the Name of Jesus Sounds	_I Need Thee Every Hour_	_Great Is Thy Faithfulness_
He Hideth My Soul	_In the Garden_ (Miles)	_Because He Lives_

It should be obvious that free-flowing praise will not be achieved without discipline, craft, and spiritual insight. Crafting and testing a worship set can easily take two hours.

I hope this chapter broadens your thinking and offers ways to improve at least some facet of your leadership—even if to the tiniest degree! What is helpful, absorb; disregard the rest.[11]

One reminder. I have talked much about technique. I have no desire to erect methodological idols: we *use* techniques, but we don't *trust* them. We put our confidence in God! In the next chapter, I will present another tested, captivating way to think of free-flowing praise. It's a powerful image that has its roots in tabernacle worship—"The Journey into the Holy of Holies."

Questions for Reflection and Discussion

1. Should praise precede adoration? How is it psychologically valid?
2. What strengths and weaknesses do you discern in John Wimber's Five-Phase model?
3. How does the Wimber model relate to evangelism, fellowship, and worship services?
4. Are liturgical, thematic, and flowing praise the main formats in your area? What is your experience of each?
5. What is most distractive or annoying in a worship set?
6. Make a list of transcendent words. Can you find choruses or hymns that powerfully incorporate them?

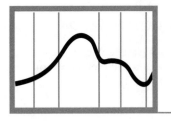

Journey into
the Holy of Holies

> Only to sit and think of God,
> Oh what a joy it is!
> To think the thought, to breathe the Name;
> Earth has no higher bliss.
>
> Frederick W. Faber

Students of worship have discovered in Old Testament tabernacle or temple worship another powerful pattern for leading extended congregational praise.[1] The basic movement is from celebration to adoration, and it begins with the people making pilgrimages to Jerusalem, entering its gates with praise, and ends in the Holy of Holies. This progression and worship model is called "The Journey into the Holy of Holies."

Imagine Jews traveling in caravans from near and far as they sojourn to the temple:

Along the trails resound the songs of pilgrims wending their way to observe the great festival. One leads a goat, another an ox, a third a sheep to offer to God at the sanctuary. There they will recite prayers and sing hymns and dance in religious procession about the altar. Speaking many dialects they come from many lands, but for all of them Jerusalem is the Holy City. Ascending while singing

61

the Hallel with ever-enlarging throngs, the pilgrims catch first sight of the temple ("that is where the tribes go up, the tribes of the Lord, to praise the name of the Lord"), its gold plates and white marble glistening in the sun. And in the swarming crowds, fathers with their sons and daughters tour the perimeter of the temple examining each gate.[2]

"Enter his gates with thanksgiving and his courts with praise," exclaims Psalm 100:4. As the people process through the gates there is joyful celebration and loud and happy proclamation of God's goodness and greatness. Brass, string, and percussion instruments accompany their singing and clapping as the people break free from the burdens of life and count their blessings.

Today we can join that journey from the altar and laver to the Holy Place (lampstand, bread, incense) and finally into the Holy of Holies in our congregational song. As we do, exuberant joy turns to mysterious wonderment and solemn adoration.

And we can reflect on the temple furniture and wonder at its meaning for us.

Close-up of the Inner Tabernacle

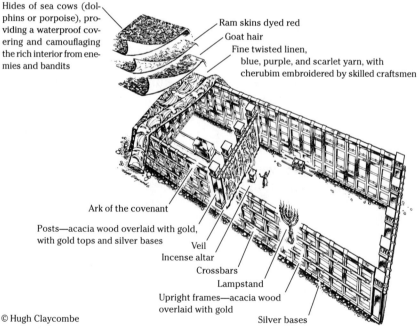

Hides of sea cows (dolphins or porpoise), providing a waterproof covering and camouflaging the rich interior from enemies and bandits

Ram skins dyed red

Goat hair

Fine twisted linen, blue, purple, and scarlet yarn, with cherubim embroidered by skilled craftsmen

Ark of the covenant

Posts—acacia wood overlaid with gold, with gold tops and silver bases

Veil

Incense altar

Crossbars

Lampstand

Upright frames—acacia wood overlaid with gold

Silver bases

© Hugh Claycombe

Overview of the Tabernacle

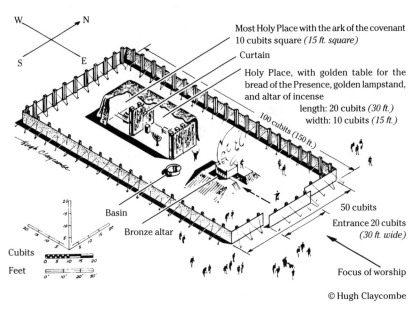

W. N

S E

Most Holy Place with the ark of the covenant
10 cubits square *(15 ft. square)*

Curtain

Holy Place, with golden table for the
bread of the Presence, golden lampstand,
and altar of incense

length: 20 cubits *(30 ft.)*
width: 10 cubits *(15 ft.)*

100 cubits (150 ft.)

Basin

Bronze altar

Cubits

Feet

50 cubits

Entrance 20 cubits
(30 ft. wide)

Focus of worship

© Hugh Claycombe

The Meaning of the Temple Furniture

As each male Israelite brought an *offering* for sacrifice, so we, too, bring a sacrifice of praise: "Through Jesus, therefore, let us continually offer to God a sacrifice of praise—the fruit of lips that confess his name" (Heb. 13:15). At the *altar* in the inner court, the offering is wholly consumed and goes up in smoke to heaven, illustrating the need for total consecration. The *laver*, the washing basin for the priests, speaks of our need for cleansing before we come into the presence of a holy God. Psalm 24:3 reads: "Who may ascend the hill of the Lord? Who may stand in his holy place? He who has clean hands and a pure heart."

Advancing into the holy place, we see the *table of shewbread*, which foreshadows the Lord's Supper and reminds us that we come as members of one body. In the enclosed space, the *seven-branched golden candlesticks* burn continually, replenished by a continuous supply of oil (Zech. 4). It symbolizes the Holy Spirit, who illuminates the Word of God and enables us to perceive spiritual things (1 Cor. 2:12). In front of the veil, now torn and open wide, stands the *altar of incense,* a symbol of prayer, the gateway into the Holy of Holies. It typifies the risen Christ offering

63

prayers on our behalf before the throne. His prayers, along with ours commingled, rise as sweet perfume before the Lord.

In stillness and awe we enter the Holy of Holies where the *adoring cherubim* guard the ark; the wooden *chest* overlaid with gold inside and out represents the presence of God. Upon the *mercy seat*, the lid of the chest, we see sprinkled blood, the price paid for our forgiveness by the completed work of Christ. We now cease from any effort to make ourselves acceptable to God. Christ has done it all, and we are clothed in his righteousness.

Inside the ark we see the tablets of stone, the pot of manna, and the budded rod. The *tablets of stone* tell of the demands of the Law, now totally satisfied by the death of Christ. The *pot of manna* points to Christ, the self-proclaimed Bread of Life:

> I am the bread of life. Your forefathers ate the manna in the desert, yet they died. But here is the bread that comes down from heaven, which a man may eat and not die. I am the living bread.
>
> John 6:48–51

When Aaron's *budded rod* comes into view, we understand that as this dead stick flowered and bore fruit, so also Christ arose and lives forever. He has obtained "a permanent priesthood" (Heb. 7:24). Because we are "in Christ" and partake in the power of his resurrection, we, too, have become a "royal priesthood" and shall one day become "a kingdom of priests" (Rev. 5:10).

The temple furniture, therefore, foreshadows how we may prepare to enter into the Holy of Holies and have a genuine meeting with God: God desires us to be totally consecrated (altar), pure in spirit (laver), unified in fellowship (bread), dependent on the Holy Spirit (candlestick), and in a spirit of prayer (incense). Access to a holy and intimate worship has been made available through the work of our Lord and Savior Jesus Christ:

> Since we have confidence to enter the Most Holy Place by the blood of Jesus, by a new and living way opened for us through the curtain, that is, his body, and since we have a great priest over the house of God, let us draw near to God with a sincere heart in full assurance of faith.
>
> Hebrews 10:19–22

Cornwall's Adaptation

Judson Cornwall suggests that the song leader can take people on a worship journey that mirrors the "Journey into the Holy of

Holies" at every point. He cites Psalm 100 as scriptural support for the application of the pattern.

The leader, he says, must know where the people are, where he wants to take them, and when they have arrived. Cornwall's "worship progression" has five phases.

First: Songs of Personal Testimony in the Camp

The first object is to meet the worshipers where they are, outside the gates in the camp. Here worshipers are concerned with people, places, things, personal needs, and have little God consciousness. The worship leader gently gets their attention and gives them something to identify with. Personal testimony hymns, gospel songs, "I am" and "I have" songs, songs of personal condition and experience all serve to accomplish this. "Let the congregation enjoy singing songs of testimony until they are sufficiently united," says Cornwall. Sound similar to Wimber's invitation phase? Yes, except that Cornwall explicitly makes reference to gospel songs. That's the new thought—songs like "Count Your Many Blessings," "In My Heart There Rings a Melody of Love," "Bless That Wonderful Name of Jesus" can be employed.

Second: Through the Gates with Thanksgiving

Says Cornwall:

The procession through the eastern gate into the outer court should be a joyful march, for thanks should never be expressed mournfully or negatively. While the people are singing choruses of thanksgiving they will be thinking both of themselves and of their God, but by putting the emphasis upon the giving of thanks, the majority of the thought patterns should be on their God. Singing at this level will often invoke a beginning level of praise, but it will not produce worship [adoration], for the singers are not yet close enough to God's presence to express a worship response.[3]

Psalm 24:7 says, "Lift up your heads, O you gates . . . that the King of glory may come in." These gates are the gates of our hearts. Our King desires to be enthroned in our hearts.

Third: Into His Courts with Praise

The emphasis changes from what God has done to who he is, to blessing his name, and to thinking less of one's self and more of God.

65

Cornwall candidly admits that "soulish worship" that is focused on the self may occur outside the gates or in the court:

> Soulish worship is *feeling* motivated and depends upon external impetus. ... If a "worship service" requires emotional stories and psychological impetus to stir it into being, it is very likely soulish worship. So much of America's "evangelistic services" and "gospel music" are soulish both in origin and in result.[4]

He would not have the people stop there, however, but push on toward the purer worship occurring in the Holy Place.

Fourth: Solemn Worship inside the Holy Place; and Fifth: In the Holy of Holies

In this phase all attention is now directed solely to God, Jesus, or the Holy Spirit. Cornwall explains: "Nothing in there speaks of man; it is in its every aspect a revelation of God."[5] In Israel's inner sanctuary, an atmosphere of quiet reverence enveloped the space: the flickering flame of the candlesticks, the smell of the incense, and the outstretched wings of adoring cherubim contributed to that. Cornwall's description of a congregation worshiping in the Holy Place reflects that same reverence, and he notes mistakes leaders often make.

> If the leader has been successful in bringing the people step by step into the outer court and on through it into the holy place, there will be a rise in the spiritual response of the people. Instead of mere soulish, emotional responses, there will be responses from the human spirit that have depth and devotion in them. Clapping will likely be replaced with devotional responses of upturned faces, raised hands, tears, and even a subtle change in the timbre of the voices. When there is an awareness that we have come into the presence of God we step out of lightness into sobriety.
>
> It is at this point that too many leaders make a serious mistake by jerking the people back into the outer court with an emotional chorus of thanksgiving. Worship takes time; don't rush the people. Let them sing: let them repeat any chorus or verse of a hymn that seems to give honest expression to what they are feeling and doing at the moment. *The mind can jump from one concept to another far faster than the spirit can.* Allow the spirit time to savor the sense of the presence of the Lord.
>
> Just worship. Cleverness is inappropriate. Talk is unnecessary. Directions for response are superfluous. Let the people worship. Silence may be threatening to the leader, but it is golden to the worshiper. A gentle sustained chord on the organ and a song of the Spirit on the lips of the leader should be more than sufficient to carry a worship response of the entire congregation for a protracted period of time.[6]

Of the worship leader, Cornwall says, "If he succeeds he will be more a leader of worshipers than a leader of songs."[7]

Rounding Off

Two options emerge for concluding this reverential worship. After the Holy of Holies phase is completed and the people have had a quiet time of worship, they may be invited to sit down "in the Lord's presence" or be led back to the outer court with a celebratory hymn in preparation for the preaching of the Word.

Sound familiar? Yes! The model in form and spirit bears a lot of resemblance to Wimber's Five-Phase model, though the terminology is different. How would they look side by side? A comparison in the following chart (see outer columns) reveals a remarkable correspondence.

Liturgical and Free-Flowing Praise Synthesis

Wimber's Five Phases	Webber's Liturgical Model: Isaiah 6	Cornwall's "Journey into Holy of Holies"
1. Invitation	[Call to Worship]	1. Personal Testimony: "outside the camp"
2. Engagement	[Invocation]	2. Thanksgiving: "through the gates"
3. Exaltation	1. Transcendent Praise: "I saw the Lord"	3. Praise: "into his courts with praise"
	2. Confession of Sin: "Woe to me"	
	3. Words of Forgiveness: "Your guilt is taken away"	
4. Adoration		4. Holy Place
5. Intimacy		5. Holy of Holies
Closeout		Rounding Off
Scripture Reading	[Reading]	Scripture Reading

(continued)

67

Liturgical and Free-Flowing Praise Synthesis   *(continued)*

Preaching	4. Preaching: "Whom shall I send?"	Preaching
	Lord's Supper	
Dismissal	5. Commitment: "Here am I"	Dismissal

Integrating Songs of Repentance into Flowing Worship

This chart reveals yet another insight. The Cornwall and Wimber models could incorporate songs of repentance and forgiveness, an important emphasis they do not overtly address.[8] Robert Webber's liturgical model (center), which emphasizes repentance, could also be synthesized into the other structures (we'll explore this model in the next chapter). Choruses like "Change My Heart, O God " (Espinosa), "Lord Have Mercy on Me" (Tuttle), "It's Your Blood" (Christ), "Create in Me a Clean Heart, O God," "Tender Mercy" (Wagner), and hymns like "Kind and Merciful God" (Leech), "Search Me, O God" (Orr), "I Hear Thy Welcome Voice" (Hartsough), "Christ Has for Sin Atonement Made" (Hoffman), and "Whiter Than Snow" (Nicholson) could express this emphasis musically. Prayers of repentance and words of forgiveness could even be *spoken* rather than sung before continuing on in the pattern.

Valuable Imagery!

The metaphor of the "Journey into the Holy of Holies" has noteworthy assets: (1) It's easy to explain in a few words to the people. (2) Its imagery connects readily. (3) It's valuable for worship leaders who, at the outset of a service, want to communicate succinctly to the people the overall pattern of praise that the worship will follow. Use it that way! Instruction may be reinforced by singing pieces like "He Has Made Me Glad," which underscore its imagery. The first line reads, "I will enter His gates with thanksgiving in my heart; I will enter His courts with praise."

It should be evident that the Wimber and Cornwall models

- relate most to a worship-oriented service, less to a fellowship service, and perhaps least of all to an evangelistically oriented service, though they are incompatible with none of the above[9]

- are somewhat resistant to a thematically conceived service, though the closeout number can tie in thematically with the sermon
- may require pastors to delegate the responsibility of choosing pieces that link together to their worship leader; each must assess his own expertise here

My objective has not been to impart a "formula" to be rigidly followed with the expectation that it can, of itself, deliver a great worship experience. Yet we all need tools to use, to modify, and to depart from. We don't need to fear structures.[10]

True worship, however, is a matter of the spirit, as Jesus explained to the Samaritan woman:

> The water I give [will become] a spring of water welling up to eternal life. . . .
> A time is coming and has now come when the true worshipers will worship the Father in spirit and truth, for they are the kind of worshipers the Father seeks. God is spirit, and his worshipers must worship in spirit and in truth.
> John 4:14–15, 23–24

In the past two chapters I've tried to show ways that free-flowing worship can have a pattern; these models should assist leaders who have not had clear goals. A feeling of progression and development is desirable in services.

The Five-Phase and Holy of Holies models have a logic to them, a sensitivity to the psychological dimension that respects the human person and the many-faceted character of God. More than a passing fad, they have been found to be demonstrably valuable. If you employ them, your mind will be influenced by their structure. Eventually, though, you may sense gaps. Address those deficiencies! (To demonstrate this, I expanded my discussion to include repentance and forgiveness.) I'll next widen the focus to consider three major ways of designing the entire order of service.

> Narrow is the mansion of my soul;
> enlarge it, that You may enter it.[11]

Questions for Reflection and Discussion

1. What are the primary merits of the "Journey into the Holy of Holies" model?

2. Cornwall seems to accept "soulish worship" as inevitable. Does that bother you?
3. What do you think of the statement, "The mind can jump from one concept to another far faster than the spirit can"?
4. How about, "Silence may be threatening to the leader, but it is golden to the worshiper"?

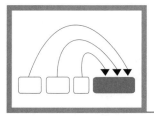

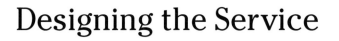

5

Designing the Service

> Strong individual leadership in worship is one way good planning
> is done, but creativity in a church will often *grow* when leadership
> is . . . [shared by] two or three persons.
>
> Wilfred J. Unruh
> *Planning Congregational Worship*

We do not find in Scripture a prescribed order of service for New Testament Christians to follow. Apparently, the Holy Spirit wisely left the designing of the service for each culture to determine. While Scripture does not offer explicit guidance, it does make clear that revelation and response are basic actions of worship. Donald Hustad has helped us all with this guiding principle:

> Insofar as we are able to conceive and achieve it, there should be
> a *full revelation* of God [Jesus Christ and the Holy Spirit], his actions
> and his will for us, and a *full response* by men and women, involv-
> ing body, emotions, intellect, and will.[1]

Worship forms should serve principles like this.

In this chapter I'm going to present three forms of worship. I refuse to stand in judgment on which form is best, because this determination is best made by the people involved. They know best their history and resources, as they wait on God. Everyone should be ready, however, to offer convincing reasons for their decisions. My intention is to promote understanding and to present each form fairly. I will begin with the liturgical perspective, then go to thematic services, and finally suggest procedures for use in open worship. The three forms are *not mutually exclusive;* they can be *blended.* Liturgical and open worship present alternative insights to the mainstream, thematic evangelical service.

Whatever style or mix of styles you choose, protect your fundamental priorities: Keep prominent the congregational song, the offering of prayers (weak in many megachurches), and the reading of Scripture (in addition to the sermon).[2] Let's begin with liturgical services, keeping in mind that liturgical worship is *not* inherently less spiritual than open or thematic worship.

Liturgical Services: Isaiah 6 Model

In liturgical services, the church year (Advent, Christmas, Epiphany, Lent, Easter, and Pentecost) and the lectionary (predetermined, systematic Scripture readings for the entire year) drive the service. The pastor does not freely select his own sermon topic; it is based and drawn from the Scripture readings from week to week (usually passages from the Old Testament and the Acts or Epistles, and always the Gospel). The theophany of Isaiah 6, termed the "Divine-Human Model," provides a profound psychological pattern for organizing the overall service:

Praise	I saw the Lord seated on a throne, high and exalted. . . . "Holy, holy, holy is the Lord Almighty; the whole earth is full of his glory." (vv. 1, 3)
Confession	"Woe to me! . . . I am ruined! For I am a man of unclean lips, and I live among a people of unclean lips." (v. 5)
Forgiveness	Then one of the seraphs flew to me with a live coal. . . . With it he touched my mouth and said, . . . "Your guilt is taken away and your sin atoned for." (v. 7)
God Calls	"Whom shall I send? And who will go for us?" (v. 8)
Commitment	And I said, "Here am I. Send me!" (v. 8)

This passage emphasizes first the transcendence of God. Once the greatness of God is established, we see ourselves as sinners in need of forgiveness. An angel takes a live coal from the altar and touches Isaiah's mouth, pronouncing his sin "purged" (KJV). God calls, "Whom shall I send"—which is the sermon—and Isaiah responds, "Send me"—the response to the sermon. In the dismissal, worship is related to life as the people are sent to live out the gospel in their communities.

Robert Webber, an evangelical Episcopalian,[3] advocates the following standard order of service based on Isaiah 6:

I. The Preparation (Six Elements)
    Opening Hymn
    The Call to Worship
    The Invocation
    The Acknowledgment of God
    The Confession of Sin
    The Words of Forgiveness
II. Reading, Preaching, and Response to the Word
III. Lord's Supper
IV. The Dismissal

Observe first that the confession and words of forgiveness occur early in the service, clearing the way for joy in worship. Second, time is given for response *after* the sermon. The offering and the announcements are part of that response.

In this format, the people sing an opening hymn. There is a call to worship (e.g., Ps. 95:1–2) and a prayer calling on God to make himself present. The acknowledgment of God extols his transcendent nature (not his intimacy). After the words of confession and forgiveness, a reading from the Old Testament, a Gospel, and an Epistle occurs. After the sermon, the responses include the offering and announcements, the recitation of a creed, the Lord's Supper, and the benediction.

By way of contrast, in thematic services the announcements and the offering usually precede the sermon, a single Scripture passage is read, no creed is corporately confessed, communion is not observed weekly, and the service comes to a more abrupt end after the sermon. Pastors like their sermon to be ringing in the ears of the people at the benediction!

In the liturgical model, revelation precedes response. The first part of the service is weighted toward revelation, the closing part to response, with various "chains" of revelation and response occurring along the way. Take for example the chains of revelation and response in the first part of the 1662 Anglican prayer book order of worship:

Revelation	Reading of Psalm
Response	Singing of Gloria Patri (Glory be to the Father)
Revelation	Old Testament Reading
Response	Te Deum (a "Glory to God" statement)
Revelation	New Testament Reading
Response	Nunc Dimitus (Now let Thy servant depart, Luke 2:28–32)

Hustad's Variation on Isaiah 6

Hustad outlines an order of service also based on Isaiah 6,[4] but he tailors it to mainstream evangelical practice. Since the confession and assurance of pardon are unfamiliar to many evangelicals, both in concept and in formality of expression, Hustad suggests that the opening prayer of confession and forgiveness come from *Scripture quotations* rather than formal liturgical language:

Confession. "Our Father, we thank you that, no matter how often we have failed you and others in the year that is past, today—and each day—we can begin afresh . . . ," or, "Father, we come to you today asking that we might receive that refreshing of forgiveness. . . . We confess that too often we have loved things and used people and we need your forgiveness. . . ."[5]

Words of Forgiveness. "If we walk in the light, as he is in the light, we have fellowship with one another, and the blood of Jesus, his Son, purifies us from all sin" (1 John 1:7), or, "If we confess our sins, he is faithful and just to forgive us our sins, and to cleanse us from all unrighteousness" (1 John 1:9 KJV).[6]

Or consider a prayer like this:

Our Father, we your children are often troubled in mind, hearing within us at once the affirmations of faith and the accusations of conscience. We are sure that there is in us nothing that could attract the love of One as holy and as just as You are. Yet You have declared Your unchanging love for us in Christ Jesus. Nothing in us can win Your love; nothing in the universe can prevent You from loving us. We trust not in what we are but in what You have declared Yourself to be. Amen.[7]

Hustad's Isaiah 6 Order of Worship

Spiritual Goals	Order of Worship
Awareness of God	Hymn: "To God Be the Glory" (Crosby-Doane)
Confession and Forgiveness	Opening Prayer (Invocation, Confession, Assurance of Pardon)
	Greeting/Welcome
	Hymn: "Break Thou the Bread of Life"
God Speaks to Us	*Scripture Reading*
	Choir: "We Praise Thee, O God"
	Sermon
We Respond	Hymn (Invitation): "Stand up, Stand up for Jesus"
	Offering (Solo): "Wherever He Leads I'll Go"
We Celebrate	Lord's Table (bread, cup)
We Pray	*Pastoral Prayer and United "Amen"*
	Doxology and Benediction

The hymn "Break Thou the Bread" foreshadows the Scripture reading, whereas the choir responds to revelation. Both Webber and Hustad place the reading of Scripture close to the sermon, which is sensible.

Note that several responses occur *after* the sermon: the congregational song, the offering, a solo, and a pastoral prayer. Though exceptional for evangelical services, the pastoral prayer placed near the end of the service observes "the normal pattern of all Christian liturgies." Responses after the sermon can build around what we have learned about God. That's a strong point. The practice also accords with the sequence in Acts 2:42: "They devoted themselves to the apostles' teaching and to the fellowship, to the breaking of bread, and to prayer."

Thematic Worship Planning

Thematic worship is the favored design of perhaps the majority of evangelical churches. The desire of pastors to be free to choose their own sermon topics or series of messages cuts to the heart of the liturgical/nonliturgical issue. In evangelical circles most choose to be free. Pastors want the planning of the service to center around and be driven by the sermon. This good intention (i.e., a thematically integrated service) can, however, be carried too far. Hustad sounds a caution worth considering.

> There is a concept of worship order held by some evangelicals, which sees "unity without diversity" as the guiding principle. If the morning sermon is about "faith," every hymn will support that subject—"Faith of Our Fathers," "Faith Is the Victory," "Have Faith in God," "O for a Faith That Will Not Shrink," etc. This practice reveals that the sermon and its response are the only significant acts of worship for those planners. The wise and humble pastor will acknowledge that on some occasions a praise hymn, or the prayer of confession or of intercession, or the choir anthem may meet the spiritual needs of some people more than the homily.[8]

Must the sermon be the highlight of the service every Sunday for every person? That is a commonly held evangelical belief.

Moreover, the following deficiencies may accompany free church worship: (1) lack of planning, (2) too little time devoted to prayer, (3) insufficiently prominent Scripture reading(s), and (4) meager congregational response opportunities.

The thematic service, however, has proven to be tremendously effective over the years and will continue to be a powerful, much-used concept.[9] Allen and Borror encourage evangelicals to really enjoy their freedom and not be locked into any necessary ordering of service events.[10]

When planning a thematic service, the pastor and worship leader need to communicate early in the week. Consider this logical and sensible sequence of questions:

1. What is the *target* of the service? Where is pastor headed? What response, what outcome is desired? Planners generally need more than the Scripture passage for the day. Allen and Borror suggest obtaining the sermon outline:

   > The best way to begin is with the sermon topic or outline . . . how can the other service components help the pastor get where he feels led to go? An obvious burden for a pastor, he must notify his other service participants in advance. But it will be well worth the trouble. The point of the hour will be so clear, even before the message, that all involved in a well orchestrated effort will be a part of the success and the blessing! . . . All musical input must help build the case.[11]

2. What are the *givens?* Congregational praise, Scripture reading(s), and prayers all seem foundational. So keep these prominent. Other considerations include greetings, testimonies, announcements, the offering, and musical expressions.
3. What *resources* are available? Would a prayer of encounter and intercession (corporately or in small groups); a fresh testimony from someone; an interview; a solo; a choir number; a letter, book, newspaper, or cassette tape excerpt; a reader's theater; a banner; pantomime; or opportunities to serve enhance the service?
4. What *sequence* of events would give the service a logical progression and be psychologically sound?
5. What *title* or *captions* would integrate the service?

To be free is marvelous, but as in all of life, greater freedom entails greater responsibility. Evangelical pastors in the free tradition must not squander this freedom. They need to be better informed about worship, more committed to clear service objectives, more aware of how worship services are dramatic events, and more open to collaborative planning with others than their liturgical brothers and sisters.

Liturgical and Free Church Formats Compared

Liturgical and free church formats have both strengths and weaknesses. Positively, the liturgical service imposes discipline and a logical framework to the weekly service and adheres to the church year. Events like the candle-lighting ceremony throughout the four weeks of Advent, for example, can lengthen and infuse with meaning the Christmas season. The liturgical service contains fixed words for confessing our sins and for receiving God's forgiveness. In contrast, the thematic service emphasizes impromptu prayer—people learn how to pray spontaneously. Prayers for needs in the congregation, outreach, and missions often predominate, whereas prayers of confession may not occur.

The liturgical service calls for short responses from the people, which underscores participative, dialogical activity. For example, the leader says, "Lift up your hearts," and the people automatically

77

respond, "We lift them up to the Lord." Other responses from the people include, "Thanks be to God" (after Scripture), "Lord, have mercy" (after intercessory prayers), and when the minister says, "The Lord be with you," the people respond, "And also with you." On the down side, these predetermined, fixed responses may feel stiff to some churched as well as nonchurched participants. In thematic services, however, spontaneous "amens" may punctuate the service. People feel free to respond at any point, not just when the worship book calls for a response.

In addition, the liturgical service employs lectionary Scripture readings, and the sermon focuses on those readings. An obvious benefit of this practice is that it discourages partisan, hobbyhorse preaching. It also prevents leaders from centering on a few favorite passages for Scripture readings Sunday after Sunday.

On the other hand, the minister in the "free," thematic tradition can choose any sermon topic for the day or prepare a series of teaching sermons on an entire book from the Bible. The pastor is free to address the people where he feels they need help the most. When the readings and music reinforce the sermon, a central theme can emerge for the day. Moreover, since the people do not have a "worship book" that contains in one place the readings, prayers, and responses for the day, the people acquire the habit of bringing their own Bibles to church, opening them for the Scripture reading, and following the passage selected for the sermon. During the sermon some make notes in their Bibles. The result? The Bible becomes more personal and believers are encouraged to get in the habit of being "in the Word" during the week.

Developing Procedures for Open Worship

In open, or *koinonia,* worship, predetermined understandings between leaders are vital—particularly in relation to the *procedures* employed in the outworking of the service. By "open worship," I mean worship where "rather than keeping strictly and exclusively to the preplanned program [note: there is preplanning], all the participants are seeking to be led creatively by the Spirit into a flow of events unique to that group of people at that point in time."[12] This sounds akin to Paul's description of worship occurring at the house church in Corinth:

When you come together, everyone has a hymn, or a word of instruction, a revelation, a tongue or an interpretation. All of these must be done for the strengthening of the church.

1 Corinthians 14:26

Graham Kendrick says, "The job is often done badly. . . . [There] is all too often a suspicion of advance planning, firm leadership and efficient organization."[13] Note again, advance preparation forms an integral part of Kendrick's leadership style. Kendrick, a guitarist, says:

I find it necessary to prepare a list of songs complete with number and key, and position it on a clip-board in front of me. This functions not only as a reminder of the numbers . . . but as a reminder of the breadth of choices available.[14]

In open worship we must "expect the unexpected" and "be free to alter or abandon the plans we have made. . . . Leading worship is leading people . . . standing before God on their behalf seeking their health and welfare. . . . It is a process of active faith to lead people by following the Spirit."[15]

Kendrick emphasizes the importance of maintaining a discerning approach: "We need to develop a sensitivity as to when something 'jars' against the spirit within us or disturbs our peace. . . . [Discernment] comes through experience and the practice of spiritual sensitivity over a period of time."[16] He urges leaders to be alert to opportunities for ministering to people the very moment they have shared. "It is remarkable how we quickly move on to the next item on the agenda, when the obvious thing to do would be to stop and take action immediately!"[17]

Moreover, in open worship, leaders need a sense of derived authority: "Jesus recognized . . . [that authority] was derived from being under authority (Matt. 8:9), and being submitted to one another (Eph. 5:21)."[18]

Leaders must also develop behind-the-scenes interpersonal trust in one another and have the security of ground rules:

It helps a great deal for there to be a set of ground rules generally understood by everybody and in detail by the leaders. For example, there are questions of who acts in a crisis. . . . I remember occasions when I have been leading and something has unexpectedly happened that was beyond my "jurisdiction" or ability to cope with. It has been a great relief to myself and to everyone else when another leader has stepped forward and dealt competently with such a situation. . . .

> The degree of genuine caring that the leader displays is crucial to the kind of response he gets back . . . the degree of care taken "behind the scenes," developing among the leadership a quality of friendship and functional interaction frees people from worry, fear, uncertainty and unhelpful interruption as they worship.[19]

Usually the problems encountered are not dramatic. A simple but sensitive redirection of the service may be needed:

> Sensitivity must be shown to the person who makes a faulty contribution in sincerity and good faith. . . . [The leader should be positive and not "put down" the person, saying rather,] "We seem to be moving toward intercession here and it is tremendously important to pray for Mr. Smith's gout, but I feel that at this moment we should be taking note of our earlier exhortation to give the Lord a rich offering of thanks and praise, so let's sing. . . ."[20]

Kendrick says, "If, however, a dangerous or hurtful thing has been said, then it should be refuted and corrected immediately or else the meeting may never recover."[21]

Kendrick would probably feel a kinship with the "managed flow" of the Wimber and "Journey into the Holy of Holies" models, viewing these as variations or close brothers to "open worship." Where a worship team is involved and slides or overheads need to be prepared and sequenced, preplanning is even more mandatory; and if the team personnel are not yet comfortable improvising, it may be difficult to abandon premade plans extensively. Yet open worship insists on the freedom to abandon plans and follow the Spirit.

Convergence Worship

Today denominational lines are not as strong as they once were, and leaders everywhere are more aware of other traditions and more inclined to draw on aspects of them, as this remarkable fusion of Protestant and Catholic traditions demonstrates.

A few years ago, a friend talked me into going to a city-wide Catholic Renewal Conference held at the Anaheim Convention Center, a stone's throw from Disneyland. About eight thousand people were present in each of the two services I attended, and the worship style combined the liturgical and flowing praise formats. I sat amazed as the people fervently sang Catholic songs, Protestant hymns, Maranatha and Integrity praise choruses, the Lord's Prayer, and—would you believe—evangelical choruses from the 1960s, with such enthusiasm you would have thought they were "hot off the press." A worship team, comprised of several singers and a supporting cast of professional quality instrumentalists playing synthesizers, guitars, and percussion, led the people. After the service I went up to the stage area and talked with the instrumentalists and discovered to my great surprise that they weren't Catholic! They said, "The singers are Catholic, but all of us playing instruments are involved leading worship at Vineyard churches. We were hired for the event." This cross-fertilization of worship styles and personnel would have been unthinkable a couple of generations ago.

The Formats Being Blended Today

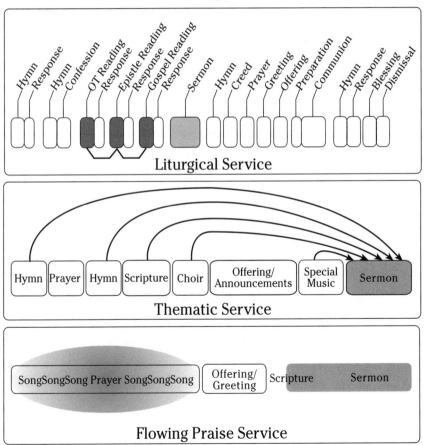

In the new worship, elements from the liturgical, thematic, and flowing praise formats are often blended. Robert E. Webber calls this "convergence worship." The chart shows these three formats, which dominate the worship landscape today.

The liturgical worship and thematic worship formats have a longer history than flowing praise. Most liturgical formats in Protestant churches today have been in continuous use since the Protestant Reformation[22] and can be derived from synagogue worship. In the chart, notice several Scripture readings are located toward the beginning of the service, a sermon toward the middle, and the Lord's Supper celebrated weekly (or at least frequently) near the end. The thematic service, in contrast, has roots in the evangelistic crusades of Moody/Sankey and Sunday/Rodheaver, which incorporated a song leader, a gospel choir situated directly behind the pulpit, and special music immediately before the message. The message was the centerpiece of the event—the items before the message were considered the preliminaries.[23]

Astonishing Variety of Pauline Worship

Many of us may have a tendency to discount open worship. But if we look at all the extraordinary variety of elements that appear in Pauline worship, it seems clear he was drawing on synagogue and temple influences as well as the body-life metaphor of the Church that so captivated him. As you look through the list of Pauline elements provided in the following chart, some may be familiar to your weekly worship practice and some may be foreign. Try to imagine attending a Pauline worship service— for many of us this would be a stretching experience! This recognition alone should teach us to be more charitable to one another.[24]

Variety of Elements in Pauline Worship

Opening and closing benedictions	1 Cor. 1:3; 16:23
Doxology and acclamation	1 Cor. 15:57
Liturgical prayer	2 Cor. 1:3
Spontaneous prayer	1 Cor. 14:14–15
Hymns, psalms, spiritual songs	1 Cor. 14:26; Eph. 5:19; Col. 3:16

Praise, singing, thanksgiving	1 Cor. 14:15
Responsive amens	1 Cor. 14:16
Physical prostration	1 Cor. 14:25
Holy kisses	Rom. 16:16; 1 Cor. 16:20; 2 Cor. 13:12; 1 Thess. 5:26; 1 Peter 5:14
Public reading of Paul's letters	Col. 4:16; 1 Thess. 5:27
Prophecy, revelation, discernment	1 Cor. 12:10; 14:6
Tongues and interpretations	1 Cor. 14:27
Instruction, preaching, edification	1 Cor. 1:17; 14:26; 15:14
Healing	1 Cor. 12:9, 28, 30
Breaking of bread	1 Cor. 11:20–34
Baptism	1 Cor. 1:13–14
Use of Maranatha, an Aramaic liturgical form	1 Cor. 16:22
Collection	1 Cor. 16:1

Suggestions for Small- to Medium-Sized Churches

The following suggestions may be appropriate for your situation, whatever your style. I offer them as something to think about.

1. When you are communicating the sermon content to the worship leaders who are designing a thematic service, merely telling them the scriptural reference is usually *not* enough. A short paragraph on the central thrust of the sermon, prepared by the pastor two to three months in advance, though, is invaluable. If such direction is unavailable, insufficiently clear, or, because of the nature of the topic, difficult to carry out, worship leaders can lead the congregation in Godward praise. Godward praise complements almost any sermon.

2. If the prelude is not meaningful (people are late, talking), there are several options.

First, retain the prelude but reorganize it. For example, five minutes before the service, stop the prelude, have the pastor announce the preparation for worship, read Scripture as a call to worship, and remain on the platform. Then continue the prelude for another five minutes before the opening hymn or the announcements. By doing this, you are placing the five-minute prelude period within the body of the service, which elevates the significance of the parishioner's preparation for worship, provides incentive for the instrumentalist(s) to prepare well, and eliminates the need for negative comment from the pulpit on talking and lateness.

Second, disband the instrumental prelude. Have a five- to ten-minute preservice of praise choruses led by an individual or worship team. Start the preservice by having your people stand (this gets their attention), then read two or three verses from the Psalms as a call to worship (have your people remain standing for at least the first number). Your worship bulletin could alert guests that the preservice sing has preempted an instrumental prelude. Or as an alternative, use this time to introduce new hymns or choruses, alert and rehearse the people on any unusual features in the service, and establish a tone of worship. A preservice is a particularly good idea if you have no evening service in which to introduce new pieces. Follow this with announcements.

Last, accept the talking and play an instrumental praise tape as background music. Begin the service with announcements and the praise with a Wimber-type invitation phase.

3. Consider placing the announcements and welcome either at the beginning or end of the service but not in the middle (it kills flow).

4. Remember, the main purpose of announcements is: (a) to create a climate for ministry, (b) to share concerns, and (c) to establish a "family" environment.

5. Introduce guest musicians during the welcome and announcements. This helps flow and prevents the guests from being perceived as entertainment.

6. If your offertory time is not meaningful—the service seems to stop or the organ or piano offertory is not being listened to—use that space for a vocal solo, a memorized congregational song, or for learning a new hymn or chorus. Play through the hymn once while the offering is being taken, then have the people join you. This works best when the words are sung from memory or shown on a screen. Then the people do not have to juggle purses, hymn books, and offering plates at the same time.

Hymn texts can reinforce the action of giving. Hymns like "We Give Thee but Thine Own," "We Praise Thee, O God, Our Redeemer," "Savior, Thy Dying Love," "The Wise May Bring Their Learning," "Come, Ye Christians, Be Committed" say in words what the people are doing. This is an elegant way of underscoring the meaning of the offering.

7. In general, discourage the practice of lengthy, flow-killing verbal introductions to special music; rather, encourage musicians to let their music do their talking.

8. If you desire but can't seem to find enough time for free-flowing praise in your service, try (a) starting a praise preservice, (b) omitting the preoffertory prayer and merging your singing into the offering, (c) lengthening the service, or (d) timing the parts of the service for a month. Where is the time going?

A pastor of a large Los Angeles church shared this story with me while we were having breakfast at a restaurant. It underscores that we learn by doing. His son came back from the library all excited:

Son: "I've learned how to swim, Dad, I can do it!"
Dad (amazed): "Great! How did you learn it?"
Son: "From a book in the library." (Son gets down on the floor and demonstrates how it's done.)

Later in the day at the pool, the pastor told me, "It was all gurgling."

That is the way it is with the material in this chapter. It needs experiential outworking. Try some of the ideas. Like learning to swim, more than one trial run may be necessary.

Questions for Reflection and Discussion

1. Are pastors more content-oriented and musicians more feeling-oriented when they approach the planning of the service?
2. How do you feel about giving time for worship response after the sermon?
3. What do you think about a time for confession and words of forgiveness?
4. How would you handle inappropriate responses in an open worship service? What procedures could anticipate these problems?
5. What are the primary merits of liturgical, thematic, and open worship services?
6. Evangelicals are criticized for being antiliturgical and antiaesthetic. Do you think this is true?

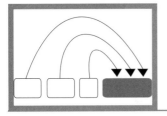

Creating Drama: Bulletins, Readings, Slides, Videos

A plan in the heart of a man
is like deep water, but a man
of understanding draws it out.
Proverbs 20:5 NASB

Without question, television, interactive computer graphics, and cyberspace are dramatically commanding our attention and impacting our society. After being immersed in these media during the week, our people come to church with quite different expectations than they did in the past. We are a more visual society. This means we must exercise more care in formatting our worship bulletins. We must be open to new ways of reading Scripture and to exploring the uses of slides and videos, especially where these media can contribute to the drama of worship. And make no mistake about it—worship involves drama!

Setting the Scene with the Order of Service

Many churches use the worship bulletin to orient the worshiper to the overall service pattern and purpose. Worship headings can be especially valuable in thematically designed services. Hustad, remember, employed the following "headings" in his order of service derived from the Isaiah 6 model:

Awareness of God
Confession and Forgiveness
God Speaks
We Respond
We Celebrate
We Pray

Headings can communicate a sense of movement and direction, and their possibilities are endless. Here are a few more to stimulate your thinking.

1. The Preparation for Worship
   The Worship of God through Praise
   The Worship of God through Giving
   The Worship of God through Guidance
   The Worship of God through Communion
   The Worship of God through Dedication
2. We Approach God Reverently
   We Praise God Gratefully
   We Beseech God Humbly
   We Hear God Prayerfully
   We Obey God Willingly
3. Expectation [the call to worship]
   Revelation [Scripture reading]
   Communication [Sermon]
   Meditation [Lord's Supper]
   Benediction

Hymns can also be differentiated by function.

Hymn of Praise
Hymn of Confession
Hymn of Meditation
Hymn of Stewardship
Hymn of Dedication
Hymn of Remembrance
Hymn of Commitment

Headings are not mandatory, however. Some free church services offer no order of service at all, or just a brief written order of service similar to this Calvary Chapel example:

We Worship in Song and Praise
We Share in Announcements
We Give Our Tithes and Offerings to the Lord
We Again Worship in Song and Praise

That's it! This order of service consists of headings only—no details—and the sermon follows it. The rationale for this undetailed order of service appears in the "credo" printed on the back of the worship folder:

We believe worship of God should be spiritual.
Therefore: We remain flexible and yielded to the leading of the Holy Spirit to direct our worship.[1]

Incidentally, when you design an evangelistic outreach service on a Sunday morning, it is a good idea not to overwhelm guests with a multitude of details in the printed order of service. Provide just enough so they can see the flow.

Let Fonts Help You Communicate

Also, since time is of the essence in worship services, one way to avoid wordy explanations is to use fonts to improve response and communicate instructions visually. Fonts are especially helpful in antiphonal readings. If the following were printed in your worship folder, what would it communicate to you, the worshiper?

Praise the Lord
Praise the Lord
Praise the Lord
Praise the Lord

Praise the Lord!
PRAISE THE LORD!
PRAISE THE LORD!

Through the different fonts alone you could probably surmise that the leader would read the plain text and the congregation the bold, and the larger the print, the louder the response. Notice, the boldface makes headings such as "Leader" and "All" unnecessary and results in a better flow. Does this take a lot of explaining to perform? Very little if any. If the tempo is brisk, you will get a dynamic response! Phrases like "Glory to God!" "He is coming!" and single words like "Amen" also work well with this technique. Consider putting responses like these in a bulletin insert.

Emphasize Themes through Patterns

Another way to help set a dramatic worship scene through your bulletin is by using patterns. Hardly a new technique, it's as old as the Psalms. We sometimes forget that many of the psalms were written specifically for public worship and contain ideas we could effectively use today. One such idea is the use of three repetitions for emphasis. Here are some threes that set a scene of praise.

> Let the heavens rejoice,
> Let the earth be glad;
> Let the sea resound, and all that is in it.
>
> Psalm 96:11

> Ascribe to the Lord, **O families of nations,**
> Ascribe to the Lord **glory and strength.**
> Ascribe to the Lord **the glory due his name.**
>
> Psalm 96:7–8

In the second example, I combined the pattern of repeating threes with the use of fonts. The boldface instructs the congregation to respond.

Reader's Theater—for Everyone!

Reader's theater doesn't have to be limited to one select team of readers. Why not have everyone in the congregation join in? Here again Israel's history can give us a few pointers. The Israelites not only traversed the wilderness in a precise marching formation but also settled in prescribed geographic regions. Moreover, twenty-four separate choirs (two per tribe?) were accorded specific stations when performing their praise in the temple. Possibly when they assembled for their festive holidays, the people and the choirs were divided into sectors (see Deut. 27). It's likely the Levites performed the third line (below) from one location, the Aaronites from another, and so on, with everyone joining in on the last line. Here's an example.

> O house of Israel, **praise the Lord;**
> O house of Aaron, **praise the Lord;**
> O house of Levi, **praise the Lord; . . .**
> **(All) Praise be to the Lord from Zion!**
> Psalm 135:19–20

We could do much the same thing as the Israelites by dividing our Sunday morning congregation into different response groups and letting the Lord's praises resound!

Heightening Involvement through Split Sentences

Another reader's theater technique that can enhance Sunday morning worship is having one reader or group begin a line and another reader or group finish it.

> Blessed are the poor in spirit, **for theirs is the kingdom of heaven.** Blessed are those who mourn, **for they will be comforted.**
> Matthew 5:3–4

A variation on this same idea is to let the bold print be performed by the choir or the congregation:

> As servants of God we commend ourselves in every way: in great endurance; in troubles, hardships and distresses . . . beaten, **and yet not killed,** sorrowful, **yet always rejoicing;** poor, **yet making many rich;** having nothing, **and yet possessing everything.**
> 2 Corinthians 6:4; 9–10

This technique not only relieves boredom but engenders a more *intimate, flexible interaction* between the leader and congregation. And it reinforces the meaning of the text. When bold type is employed in paragraph form, line headings indicating who should read ("Leader" or "All") are superfluous:

> After the death of Moses the servant of the Lord, the Lord said to Joshua the son of Nun, Moses' aide: "Moses my servant is dead. Now then, you and all these people, get ready to cross the Jordan River into the land I am about to give to them—to the Israelites. I will give you every place where you set your foot, as I promised Moses. . . . **No one will be able to stand up against you all the days of your life. As I was with Moses, so I will be with you; I will never leave you nor forsake you.**
>
> **"Be strong and courageous,** because you will lead these people to inherit the land I swore to their forefathers to give them. **Be strong and very courageous.** Be careful to obey all the law my servant Moses gave you; do not turn from it to the right or to the left, that you may be successful wherever you go. **Do not let this Book of the Law depart from your mouth; meditate on it day and night, so that you may be careful to do everything written in it.** Then you will be prosperous and successful. Have I not commanded you? **Be strong and courageous.** Do not be terrified; **do not be discouraged,** for the Lord your God will be with you wherever you go."
>
> Joshua 1:1–3, 5–9

By using this technique, the people focus on the unfolding text with less distraction. The congregation or choir can be included in any segment of a reading. With a computer, a bulletin insert with the text is easy to prepare.

One important note: Where there is punctuation, instruct everyone to take a breath. This will improve congregational reading by keeping everybody together.

If you want children to read Scripture and understand it, then consider using the International Children's Bible occasionally. It has short sentences:

> So then, get rid of all evil and all lying. Do not be a hypocrite. Do not be jealous or speak evil of others. Put all these things out of your life. As newborn babies want milk, you should want the pure and simple teaching. By it you can grow up and be saved.
>
> 1 Peter 2:1–2 ICB

Character Lines

Another technique employed in reader's theater involves *character lines.* Employ a different reader for each character in a story—

for example, Mary, Pilate, Christ, and angels in the Easter story. Or use two readers for one person—one for the outward dialogue lines, another for inner thought lines. "He said/she said" lines can be left in and spoken by a separate reader (narrator).

Echoing the Meaning

Lines, phrases, or key words in any script can be *echoed* or repeated in various ways to bring home the meaning of a passage. In the example below, Reader 2 anticipates and Reader 3 follows the phrase, "but have not love," of Reader 1 (R1):

Reader 1:	If I speak in the tongues of men and of angels . . .
Reader 2:	but have not love (anticipates R1)
Reader 1:	but have not love
Reader 3:	but have not love (follows R1)

In this technique, Readers 2 and 3 can echo Reader 1 at a variety of points—anticipating, doubling, or following one another in a spoken counterpoint. Subtle effects can result as the readers work through the remaining text of 1 Corinthians 13. Here's another option: while this is going on, someone could be singing a solo on the love of God—for example, "The Prayer of Francis of Assisi" ("Lord make me an instrument of Thy peace").

Reader's Theater for Pentecost Sunday

Unusual effects can be created that startle and surprise. In the example below, have the choir enter only on the bold print in the last paragraph. This results in an arresting, rapid-fire effect, which wakes up everybody and conveys a feeling of the unexpected. Roman numerals refer to Readers 1, 2, and 3.

I. So when the disciples met together, they asked Jesus,

II. "Lord, are you at this time going to restore the kingdom to Israel?"

I. He said to them:

III. "It is not for you to know the times or dates the Father has set by his own authority. But you will receive power when the Holy Spirit comes on you; and you will be my witnesses

93

in Jerusalem, and in all Judea and Samaria, and to the ends of the earth."

I. When the day of Pentecost came, they were all together in one place. Suddenly a **sound** like the blowing of a **violent wind** came from heaven and **filled** the whole **house** where they were sitting. They saw what seemed to be **tongues** of **fire** that separated and came to **rest** on **each** of them. All of them were **filled** with the **Holy Spirit** and began to speak in other **tongues** as the **Spirit** enabled them.

Acts 1:6–8; 2:1–4

Read the last paragraph briskly. Test and experience it during a choir rehearsal. Congregations or choirs will perform the bold print *without straggling readers* if you instruct them to read silently the plain text (moving their lips) and give voice only to the bold print. This piece takes a minimum of rehearsal but has a maximum effect.

Reader's theater is flexible in regard to time and space; it can take two or ten minutes. It is especially useful for heightening interest on festive or special occasions. Readers may be placed in any configuration and located in any place—at the front or in the audience—in the worship space. Fashion your own homemade material. My previous book, *People in the Presence of God* (Zondervan), contains two ready-for-performance examples in the appendix with permission to reproduce. One is "The Easter Story for Six Readers" (which lasts about five minutes); the other is a congregational reading of the entire book of 1 Thessalonians (lasting about twenty-five minutes). An excerpt from the first example, provided below with accompanying instructions, offers more ideas for your consideration.

The Easter Story for Six Readers

Instructions. The reading requires two narrators and four readers. The narrators should stand at opposite sides of the stage area, facing each other but slightly turned toward the congregation. The four readers together serve as a crowd. Suggestion: Use a pen highlighter on your headings to cue your speaking parts.

Reader 1: (Man) Christ; member of the Sanhedrin
Reader 2: (Woman) Mary, the mother of James
Reader 3: (Man) Pilate; angel at the tomb
Reader 4: (Woman) Mary Magdalene
Narrator 1: (Man)
Narrator 2: (Woman)

Narrator 1:	At the conclusion of three years of ministry, Jesus of Nazareth, the Christ, turned his eyes and thoughts toward Jerusalem. Accompanied by his disciples, he traveled to Bethany. He entered Jerusalem on the Monday before the Passover.
Readers 1, 2, 3, 4:	(simultaneously as a crowd repeat cries of acclamation at least two or three times)
Reader 1:	Peace in the heavens, glory in the highest!
Reader 2:	Hosanna to the Son of David!
Reader 3:	Hosanna to the King of Israel, David's seed!
Reader 4:	Hosanna to the Messiah!
Narrator 1:	Four days later, the cheers and hosannas had turned to jeers and curses.

In all the examples of reader's theater, including dramatizations, improvised background music can help set the mood and smooth the transitions.

Enriching Worship with Slides

If you plan to project the words of hymns or choruses on a screen each Sunday, my recommendation is *don't use overheads*. Invest in two projectors, and use slides with nature backgrounds instead. Slides of lyrics are clearer, easier to manage, and when combined with nature slides, their total effect is much more aesthetic. I now go into some detail concerning a setup employed by a church of 150 with an average church budget.[2] Their equipment outlay was modest.

Their screen is 10' by 7.5'. Their nature slides have been collected from many sources—photography buffs in their church supplied the initial batch. The slides are divided into categories—ocean, trees, lakes/streams, sunsets, flowers, mountains, space (planets, stars, galaxies)—and are stored in clear plastic pages holding twenty per page. When they are preparing and choosing slides for the service, a light box in the sound booth helps the viewing process. All nature slides are horizontally oriented (not vertically), and come in two sizes (15/16″ and 1–1/4″). They mix them; it's not a problem.

Their song slides are made by printing the lyrics on a laser printer, using Helvetica 24-point font in all capital letters. They begin with the underlined title and omit all but the most necessary punctuation. The margins are: left 1″, right 2″, top 1″, bottom 1-1/2″. This allows about 17 lines of text. Long choruses need more than one slide. For hymns, they put each verse on a separate slide for greater flexibility of verse selection.

The printed lyrics are then photographed using high contrast slide film, which gives a black background with white printing. This technique allows the superimposed nature slide to show through. Each printed page is placed on a document stand and photographed one page per slide. When the film is developed, the slides are labeled with the song title, a notation (1/4 means one of four slides), and arranged alphabetically in a three-ring binder.

Two carousel slide projectors are in the sound booth—one for the song lyrics, the other for the nature slides. Both are equipped with a Sestar zoom lens (100- or 200mm, f/3.5). The lyric slides are loaded with a blank slot between each song, whereas the nature slides (in the second carousel) have no spaces between—usually one slide per song. During worship, the nature slide is shown during the introduction and the lyric slide when the singing begins. Multiple slide songs are combined with the same nature slide.

Using this technology, the worship leader flows from song to song without stopping to announce pages or verses. The congregation is conditioned to expect a soloist or instrumentalist when no lyric slide is showing. A welcome slide is shown at the beginning of the service, as well as definitions of worship (Leafblad, Hustad, Temple, etc.) that encourage the people to focus on worship.

They have special slides for Christmas and other holidays. One Easter, they showed borrowed slides from a university art department that depicted quality, classic paintings of Christ's birth, life, death, and resurrection, while recorded classical music played. For presentations like this, a fader unit, which fades from one projector to the other, is helpful.

An alternative to this setup is to load and sequence songs with computers. When your worship leader spontaneously selects a piece, it can be found immediately on the computer by using the "find" command.

Nature slides show much better when the house lights are dimmed. House and stage lights should be controllable from the sound booth. Lighting changes are effective in setting the appropriate atmosphere (e.g., darker lighting for intimacy).

Having Fun with Video Announcements

A large church in Los Angeles gives its announcements through video presentations each week. When the screen comes down, it's like a two or three minute "commercial."

One Sunday I was sitting beside two elderly women during the prelude and overheard them whispering back and forth about the latest scoop—would you believe—the announcements! They were wondering out loud what creative thing the video team would come up with next! Obviously these presentations spark interest—and they conserve time by avoiding rambling announcements. Even medium-sized churches will employ the technology as multimedia becomes better understood and more affordable.

I've outlined some innovations in this chapter, but I'm not advocating that church leaders inundate their people with creativity at every worship service. That quickly becomes boring. Yet we do need to make some adjustments to culture, and where technology serves our goals we should seize every opportunity. When you look at it carefully, doesn't worship in the Book of Revelation have the trappings of a media event?[3]

Questions for Reflection and Discussion

1. Are headings more essential in thematically designed services than free-flowing praise services?
2. Does a detailed, printed order of worship make for better worship?

3. Locate other examples of patterns such as threes or "group responses" in the Psalms.
4. What special configurations could you imagine for reader's theater presentations?
5. Have you found that when worshipers have their eyes on the screen—not buried in hymnbooks—they sing better?

Inspiring the People's Song

But this I know: when the Holy Spirit of God comes among us with
His anointing, we become a worshiping people.

A. W. Tozer

This chapter is about improving response, particularly
congregational response. All around the country there
are pastors and musicians who really care—care enough to
make the effort to do the things advocated in this chapter.
Devotion to our Lord impels them to go the extra mile, do
the psychologically sensitive thing, and learn the strategic
techniques.[1]

Leading worship requires both practical skills *and* spiritual perception. But Graham Kendrick rightly cautions us
concerning the limitations of technique:

It is impossible to draw rich worship from poverty-stricken hearts.
... Worship should develop alongside spiritual growth, both expressing it and stimulating it, but if we merely impose new styles and
methods on top of a dead situation we will end up with nothing better than a beautifully decorated coffin.[2]

I don't expect all worship leaders to agree with *everything*
here: again, take what is helpful. In this chapter, I will inquire

first what pastors can do, then what musicians can do, and finally urge leaders to protect each other in carrying out ministry.

What Can Pastors Do?

A worshiping pastor will seek to develop a worshiping church. Worship is not just the business of musicians; the pastor's responsibility (which is so important!) is to oversee, to set the tone and atmosphere, to create the proper attitudes and conditions, and to be visibly supportive. Pastors also need to encourage the elders to model worship. Zealously protect the practice of reading Scripture and offering prayers. In the area of music, protect the following goals.

1. *Ensure that the people's song gets priority over individuals or group performers in worship services.* The people's praise is paramount; protecting that ought to be one of your fundamental responsibilities. Most music directors would subscribe theoretically to the idea that the congregation is the first and most important choir. But if you look where they actually put their energy, you'll find it seldom goes into improving congregational response.

Don't be fooled! You can't expect to develop a strong singing church if you don't work at it and allow sufficient time for it. When we fill up the service with choir and special music to the point that we de-emphasize congregational response, we are teaching the people to be spectators. And as a church becomes larger, competition between individuals who want to perform mounts.[3] With all these factors, time for the people's song can be easily eroded.

2. *Communicate the purposes of congregational song to all.* Hymns and choruses serve to unite the congregation, link belief to feelings, express and inspire prayer, instill fundamental doctrines of the faith, and draw people into the presence of God. Faithfully reinforce, underscore, state, and restate these and other purposes until they take hold in the people.

3. *Insist on a variety of musical materials.* "Let the word of Christ dwell in you *richly* . . . as you sing psalms, hymns and spiritual songs" (Col. 3:16, emphasis added). If the early church had a variety of materials, why should you or your people accept the poverty of *only* hymns, *only* choruses? Give your people the opportunity to learn new pieces, even those from different cultures.

4. *Nest new hymns and choruses*—that is, work on and continue to review them for several weeks in a row until they take hold. Then move on to another cluster of materials. Make a list of pieces that are "new," "fairly familiar," and "very familiar."[4] If you find a new piece that you are really committed to, reinforce it every Sunday until it acquires the status "very familiar." Once learned, place new hymns and choruses into your rotation. Continuity of this sort is superior to a scattered approach where *all* hymns are chosen because they fit the theme of the day and then are dropped for months or years. Strive for a balance between sensitivity to the theme of the day and the need for reinforcement. Nesting also aids memorization. Introduce no more than one new song in a given service.

5. *Paraphrase hymns during prayers and in congregational readings.* Paraphrasing a hymn (just before singing it) is often more effective than just reading the stanzas. Meanings can be exposed and embellished in fresh ways; abstruse language can be clarified and feelings brought out. Here is a paraphrase of "Jesus, the Very Thought of Thee" (Caswall-Dykes) to be read by the congregation:

All:	Jesus, just to think of you brings the Adoration of our inner beings. But, far greater will be our adoration When we see you face-to-face And can rest in your presence.
Women:	It is impossible to sing with our voices, To hold you in our hearts, or even to remember Having heard a sweeter sound than The blessed Name of Jesus, our Savior.
Men:	You are the hope of every repentant heart, The joy of all those who yield to you. Your kind compassion is known to all who fall; Your goodness is felt by anyone who seeks you.
All:	Jesus, be to us our only source of joy. You, Yourself, are our great reward! And Jesus, we want you to be our glory Now and throughout eternity.[5]

Write your own paraphrase as a spiritual exercise! The above reading (essentially a written prayer) could precede the singing of the hymn "Jesus, the Very Thought of Thee." Another option is to paraphrase the hymn during an improvised prayer. For "Jesus, the

Very Thought of Thee," your lead line could be "Jesus, when we [I] think of you. . . ." The hymn "Immortal, Invisible" could also benefit from a paraphrase.

6. *Arrange for testimonials.* Incorporate a "What this hymn means to me" feature occasionally in your service. Invite someone to share.

7. *Share hymn stories.* Evocative hymn stories are valuable motivators. Buy a copy of Kenneth W. Osbeck's *101 Hymn Stories* (Grand Rapids: Kregel Publications, 1982). It's also a great resource for sermon illustrations. Also see *The Worshiping Church: A Hymnal,* Worship Leader's Edition (Carol Stream, Ill: Hope Publishing, 1990). It contains a number of valuable helps and a biographical sketch of each hymn (865 in all).

8. *Encourage the purchase of hymn and chorus books and CDs for home use.*

9. *Eliminate wordy, intruding hymn announcements.* I have been in services where the music stops after *each piece* and the leader explains how each song fits into the theme. I have not found this practice enticing in an evening service and even less appropriate for a morning service. Use words sparingly. Ways to avoid the intrusion of announcing hymn numbers include listing the hymn page numbers on a hymn sign (like those used for Sunday school attendance), on an overhead, or printing the lyric in the worship folder.

Short, road-mapping comments, however, can be helpful. Pastor Paul Anderson says his leaders continually encourage him to tell the people what is happening. Paul suggests the following:

> Take them there, but tell them as they go where they are going. Not a lot of words, just a line to connect two songs together, or a sentence before singing in the Spirit. It can help lift the fog and give people permission to enter.

10. *Educate! Motivate! Model Spirituality!* When I was a teenager, from time to time I'd bicycle to church to practice on the church piano during the weekdays. As my pastor went in and out on appointments, he'd often stop and say, "Hi, Barry!" or wave and continue on his way. I noticed he was often singing a hymn as he left. When he came back I would again hear his voice—singing a tune. That impressed me. His voice and presence invariably communicated a sense of well-being. And I noticed that he quoted hymns extemporaneously just as he did Scripture when preaching. That's musical leadership. Pastors, I suggest you share those

intimate parts of your day-to-day life with your people. Have hymns and choruses nurtured you? Let your people know.

This excerpt from *Wesley's Rules for Congregational Singing* (1770) may be valuable for inspiring response. Display it on an overhead or slide or print it in your bulletin and read it together. Brace yourself, the text is "salty." Imagine gapped-toothed miners hearing these words and falling in line! Says John Wesley:

> **SING ALL.** See that you join with the congregation as frequently as you can.
> **SING LUSTILY,** and with good courage. Beware of singing as if you were half-dead or half-asleep; but lift up your voice with strength.
> **SING MODESTLY.** Do not bawl, so as to be heard above or distinct from the rest of the congregation—that you may not destroy the harmony—but strive to unite your voices together so as to make one clear melodious sound.
> **SING IN TIME.** Whatever time is sung, be sure to keep with it. Do not run before and do not stay behind it; but attend close to the leading voices, and move therewith as exactly as you can; and take care not to sing too slow. This drawling way naturally steals on all who are lazy; and it is high time to drive it out from among us, and sing all our tunes just as quick as we did at first.
> **SING SPIRITUALLY.** Have an eye to God in every word you sing. Aim at pleasing Him more than yourself, or any other creature.[6]

You can be sure your efforts will be appreciated by your worship leader. "What a team we are!" she or he will be thinking as you read "Wesley's Rules" to the people.

What Can Musicians Do?

I can think of at least five things musicians can do to inspire the people's song.

1. Make Learning Hymns and Choruses Enjoyable

A critical issue! Most young people have no acquaintance with hymns, and the older people do not know the new choruses. So there is much learning to be done by all. Most people learn tunes by rote; therefore *repetition* of the tune is vital, and planning ways to provide interesting repetition in a variety of settings *before* attempting to engage congregational performance is invaluable.

Let me explain. Effective learning may occur by listening (not performing) and then later by direct performance (having the people sing it). Since people are not disposed to learn new pieces, listening first can be particularly helpful. If I want to introduce a new hymn or chorus, I play it the week before during the offering. When the congregation hears a new hymn or chorus sung or played gorgeously with conviction and imagination, they become aroused and their readiness to learn increases. When they start thinking, "Isn't that a beautiful tune!" that's a turning point. So do everything possible to make the tune enticing *before* the people actually begin to sing it.

Learning by listening. (1) Have a keyboard person or instrumentalist play the tune as beautifully as possible as part of the prelude, offering, or postlude for one or more Sundays; (2) have a singer or vocal group sing it during the offertory or as special music; (3) have the choir perform it in an attractive form; (4) have a skilled reader read the lyric or, better yet, a paraphrase of it; (5) communicate interesting details relating to its composition verbally or in the church bulletin; (6) have a singer or choir sing the first two stanzas and then invite the congregation to join in. Again, the goal is for the congregation to have such a positive experience of the tune that they will *want* to sing it.

Learning by direct performance. Think through your performance strategy of presenting new material. Practice at home first how you're going to do it. Then do a trial run; talk it through at home just as you plan to do it at church. Anticipate problems. "Winging it" at church could be disastrous, so don't try teaching a song you don't know well! Try to memorize all hymns and choruses. Close the book and test your memory—where is your memory weakest? When lining out hymns or choruses, reduce verbal explanation to the minimum; maintain the musical beat, tempo, momentum; and repeat difficult phrases. Keep your presentation flowing. Say, "Repeat after me," and have them echo you. You may not want to use any accompaniment at this stage or you may have the keyboardist play in simple octaves. Consider pitching the tune lower than the published key for ease of performance in order to maintain a relaxed atmosphere and prevent people from having to strain their voices or worry about cracking on a high note.

Introduce no more than one new song at a time. It is better to teach a new song at the beginning of a set and reinforce it at the end than to teach it in the middle when the people have already entered into worship. That's distracting and breaks the flow.

104

The learning of new songs by the congregation may occur (1) in a small group setting (Bible study, praise/prayer group, or Sunday school class); (2) during an arranged "congregational practice"—one Sunday evening a month given over to praise; (3) during the evening service (two to five minutes during preservice warm-up time); (4) during part of the Sunday service proper (i.e., offering).

2. Pitch Songs Intelligently

Find the right pitch for every congregational song. The right pitch is the pitch that (a) fulfills the function of the song *at that moment*, and (b) results in a solid response from the people with *high and low voices* in your congregation. No one key can suffice for every situation. Many factors enter in, such as the acoustics of the worship space, the confidence level of the people, the time of day, the context (are the people coming out of prayer or has the focus been on transcendence?). Guitarists, use your capo if necessary.

Some hymnbooks (e.g., *The Baptist Hymnal*) pitch tunes in different keys. An annotation is made at the bottom of the page, which is a clever feature, where the lower or higher version may be found. Photocopy and tape these versions together so you have a choice Sunday morning. Then learn how to fashion one-measure modulations that rise a half-step for when the people would benefit from such a modulation. Not to be concerned about these factors is to be insensitive.

If your church chronically sings feebly, consider pitching the key lower for a time. This makes the singing less strenuous and more inviting. A leeway of two to three semitones often exists on the lower end. The pitches A and B-flat below middle C are possible for most voices, providing the piece does not require these notes to be sung forcefully. If you need to transpose down more than a half-step, you may have to write out the entire transposition, *but do that.* Do *what* needs to be done *when* it needs to be done. (Electronic keyboards can transpose with the flick of a switch. Try that.) Experiment. It's worth it!

Allow for early service warm-up. If your service begins early in the morning, allow the congregational voices to limber up by lowering the key one to three semitones for the opening hymn(s). Be sensitive to human realities.

■ *Modulate to build forward momentum.* Pitching the song lower than written and raising the key a half step once or twice can add a sense of forward direction and excitement. Use this device with discretion on the stanza(s) where it will have the greatest effect; for example, with "May the Mind" (Wilkinson) modulate on the words "May I run the race." But don't overuse this technique! Songs pitched high require the expending of tremendous energy.

Once the upper range has been reached and the people are singing well, a further half-step up modulation may make a tremendous difference. Energy may surge from a congregation determined to sing!

Seek restful feelings during times of prayer and adoration. Songs pitched lower can evoke a sense of adoration. If your song emerges gently out of a time of corporate prayer, a relaxed tone quality at low volume is often desirable. *Lowness equals restfulness.* It makes no sense to require people to strain for high notes when you are trying to communicate restfulness on a piece like "Jesus, I Am Resting" (Pigott). Under these conditions, attentive, soft singing is much preferred to loud singing. (Try the piece in F or even E-major, instead of G.) If you have a digital keyboard, switch on the chorus button for more ambience, or choose a darker piano sound (or Rhoades preset) that has an unobtrusive, blending quality.

Avoid vocal fatigue. Again, do all you can to be sensitive! If the tune has several high notes in a row (a high tessitura) and few compensating low notes in the immediate context, vocal fatigue after several stanzas may set in, particularly for the men. They may resort to singing an octave lower. Pitching the tune lower initially and then raising it for the last stanza can reduce fatigue measurably. For example, worshipers may weary in singing four stanzas of "All Creatures of Our God and King" in E-flat because of several high E-flats. Encourage your accompanist to learn this piece in C, D-flat, or D, and raise the pitch to E-flat only for the last stanza. This magnificent tune may then be more serviceable for everyone.

Obtain feedback and evaluate. Listen to the congregational response as you lead. Stop singing occasionally and evaluate. When did the best response occur? Why? Are men singing an octave lower? Are they cutting out on high notes? In general, people are afraid of letting someone hear their voice crack. Work in partnership with your musicians and pastor to obtain feedback on these questions.

3. Get the Men Singing

Motivate the men. Instill in them that it's not sissy to sing. David, Israel's greatest warrior, was also their greatest singer. Men should sing for the sake of their children. Men should sing for the reputation of God's name. What does listless singing communicate to our children? Are we not telling them through our voices that we don't really believe in God? That the God we serve is flat and bland—nothing to be reckoned with? How false! Our God lives! Our God is a God of unsurpassed surprise, of unimaginable gentleness, and—above all—a God to be feared and respected. Transcendent worship should reflect that.

The response of men can be improved by dividing male and female response. Rehearsing women and men separately for two to five minutes before morning or evening services can be invaluable. Keep the rehearsal short; if you accomplish only a little each time, be happy with that. Avoid negative comments; always find something positive to say.

Since it is more difficult to get men singing than women, concentrate on the women first. When the men hear the women's singing improve, that will give them incentive to match it. Two women or men from your worship team can further assist motivation and model response. Here are some ideas for getting a joyful noise out of the men in your congregation.

- Choose a song everyone likes, for example "My Tribute." Rehearse, having the women sing the second stanza alone ("Just let me live").
- Rehearse choruses in which the men sing the melody and the women a descant—for example, "Seek Ye First the Kingdom of God," "Sing Alleluia to the Lord," or "Glory to the King." Rehearse the women first, then add the men. Men will enjoy hearing the women singing and be moved by it. By having the women sing first, you are laying the foundation for the men's response. "All I Need is You" seems like an unpromising chorus, but when the women echo the men, it comes alive.[7]
- For a more complicated and prolonged project, try "All Hail the Power of Jesus' Name" (Diadem). Teach all the men to sing the bass part located in the refrain. Say, "Repeat after me," and then sing (line out) measures 13^3 through 17^1:

107

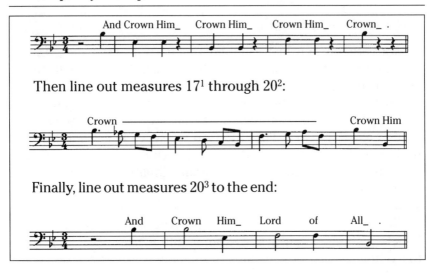

Then line out measures 17^1 through 20^2:

Finally, line out measures 20^3 to the end:

If the key of B♭ major is too high for the sopranos, try it in A or A♭ major. Breaking down the learning into three segments like this makes it easier. Practice this for two or three minutes each Sunday for a month with the men seated. Response may be poor at first; but then have them stand.

I tried this. The men blinked at the instruction to stand. It came as a surprise. Some women smiled and, laughing, poked their husbands in the ribs! But what a change it made as men all over the church stood: response improved dramatically. The next Sunday we had the altos sing their own part. The Sunday after that we had everyone sing the piece in three part harmony (the bass part was miked with males in the worship team performing it). The result was fantastic! People were buzzing about it after the service. That effort, though, took six weeks of practice. Follow the same procedures with "Wonderful Grace of Jesus" and "God of Great Wonders." The men in your worship team can sing and demonstrate the bass part.

Remember, it takes time. Don't force or labor it. If you need to, back off and pick it up a little later. Having an initial success is the important thing! Here's another insight: Having worked with seminarians, I've observed that men often sing better when tunes are lowered one or two semitones from the hymnbook key.

4. Employ a Worship Team to Improve Response

Worship teams provide stability for the worship leader and support for the congregation. When worship leaders are "down," the enthusiasm of fellow team members can inspire them. Team members also often improve on the worship leader's ideas during rehearsal and provide valuable critiques after the service. By the way, leaders should model an attitude of calmness and confidence before the service, so avoid hurrying about.

I see many churches that do not use their worship team effectively. We need to work at congregational song as hard as we do "special music." One problem I've found is that often there's little musical contrast. To obtain contrast, have your worship singers occasionally sing four-part harmony a cappella on selected hymns. Also, perform a sound check on every mike at every service. When I attend churches, frequently the voices and instruments in the worship team cannot be heard and have little impact. Another suggestion, meet during the week for rehearsal if possible.

Practicing the congregational songs with your team *before* the service begins is vital. Meet separately an hour and a half before the service with your core musicians—the keyboardist, guitarist, and percussionist. Check for agreement on all the chords and review the tempos. Practice the rhythmic feel where necessary and rehearse the transitions between songs. Then invite the other musicians and singers (an hour before the service) to do a run-through, on the platform, of the key pieces, focusing on the basic shape as well as specific details, including the synchronization of the overheads or slides. Break for prayer at least fifteen minutes before the service. When worship teams pray together, they bring power and unity to the service.

Use your singers and instrumentalists to impart musical shape and variety to the music. You could have the singers function variously as duets, trios, or quartets. Or have the whole team sing a stanza alone. Or have someone solo for one or two verses with the option of the congregation joining on the refrain.

This works particularly well when the congregation is engaged in a section of sustained singing. One stanza sung or played by the worship team can tremendously inspire a congregation, especially if the text has some great theology that needs underlining or some drama or personal content in it (e.g., "I Heard the Bells on Christmas Day"—"and then in *my* despair . . . there is no peace on earth I said"). You can also make slides of a solo or choir anthem text and project it on the screen as the piece is being performed (one line per slide, with nature scenes backdropping). Consider choosing a person who can identify emotionally with the content: for example, have a woman who has recently given birth sing stanza two of "Because He Lives" ("How sweet to hold a newborn baby").

You can place a piece in the order of worship or even keep it as a surprise. As the singer steps to the podium, say "Congregation on stanza three" to indicate the soloist will sing stanza two alone. Without missing a beat, the singer will begin on time and the congregation will enter on stanza three. Incisive instructions are important. After your congregation experiences this technique several times, they will immediately "read" the situation when someone solos and feel comfortable.

Having a performer sing or play one or two stanzas alone accomplishes several functions. A mood can be skillfully set and emotion injected. This also gives time to the congregation to meditate on the text. People can relax their voices. The same stanza can be repeated if the text is dense with meaning. If the piece is one of several in a section, the performer can smooth the transition to the next piece by singing while the congregation finds the page, thus contributing to a sense of flow.

Moreover, by integrating your soloist into the congregational song, he or she has functioned as a servant and a worshiper and is less likely to be perceived as an entertainer.

5. Employ Choreographed Hand Movements

Getting people's bodies into worship can add an entirely new dimension to worship. "Won't the people resist?" you ask. I have yet to find any resistance to the hand actions accompanying "Holy Holy Holy."[8] That is why I offer it to you (see endnotes for text and music). When we communicate the *meaning* of the hand gestures, the people become quite receptive. When they sense there is a reverential purpose to what they are doing, a positive response ensues.

For the piece "Holy Holy Holy," line out the melody first in a low key ($B^\flat$). Then teach the hand movements. Say to the people, "Try for gentle, flowing movement. Do what I do." Have them speak the words (not sing) as they perform the actions the first time.

I've included both the text and accompanying comments so you can get the idea of how you might talk your way through the meaning of the actions as you do them.

110

"Holy Holy Holy is the Lord of Hosts. By putting our hands over our chest we are saying, 'Lord apply your holiness to my life. I want to be holy.'

"The whole earth is full of your glory. Feel the downbeat on the word *whole* [demonstrate that a couple of times]. Now we raise and circle our arms. Three times. The glory of the Lord embraces the whole earth. Can you feel that?

"Holy is the Lord. Gradually raise your hands above your head. Now form praying hands. Look up. Our eyes are looking up to God. He is our source of holiness. Let's linger for a moment, arms extended [pause]. Now, let them gently fall."

Then proceed to the next stage. "Now, let's sing the tune twice *with* the actions." Sing the tune first in B♭: For the repeat, modulate to C. "We'll begin *very* softly. On the repetitions of the line *The whole earth is full of your glory* let the volume build, then let it subside on the last line." The surging bass part in the endnoted music arrangement will help that building and subsiding effect.

The result should be one of real reverence, and the movements should help release other dimensions of experience. I've used this piece just before the closeout of the Wimber model. For other examples, see my book *People in the Presence of God* (Zondervan).

Here are a few more guidelines for encouraging the people's song:

- Present a positive attitude.
- Welcome or acknowledge God's presence.
- Stand for praise, sit for adoration.
- Conduct praise with your hand, adoration with your voice.
- Don't close your eyes too much while leading—seek to be aware.
- Keep a spirited tempo for praise songs.
- Perk up dragging hymns with a percussive or staccato keyboard touch.
- Vary organ registrations and articulations.
- Seek contrast: all singers or instrumentalists shouldn't perform all the time.
- Practice the hymns during the choir rehearsal.
- Have the choir stop and sing in the aisle with the people during processionals.

- Use the choir and congregation antiphonally.
- Plan a "Hymn of the Month," a "Hymn Sunday," or "Hymn Festival." On "Hymn Sunday" (morning or evening), the pastor can preach on the text of a hymn. A good series of messages can result.
- Keep records. Record the date each hymn or chorus was sung.[9]

"I'm Outta Here!"

Jeff Baxter, a highly sought after, triple-scale studio musician, was called in for a three-hour recording session. (Triple scale is $225 an hour.) He looked over the music, took the money, and without performing said "I'm outta here."

Evidently, Baxter, after looking over the score, felt it was worth $675 to the producer when he concluded that the recording would be better off *without* his instrumental input. His experience in hundreds of studio sessions led him to that judgment.

We need more of this kind of insight in worship. It would be a good thing if church musicians could impose self-discipline and say from time to time, "I'm outta here" and *not* perform on every number. The malady is widespread in our churches: everyone wants to play all the time.

Talk to your musicians! Educate them. Point out that in symphony orchestras not everyone plays all the time.

Employ all your musicians only for loud, exalting pieces, and use just a few on intimate songs. The same instruments, the same organ registrations, the same dynamics for each number is a deadly combination. Mindless performance breeds mindless singing! On the other hand, purposeful performance encourages purposeful singing. People need contrast!

Leaders, Protect Each Other!

Each of you should look not only to your own interests, but also to the interests of others.

Philippians 2:4

Let's look at an area where pastors could understand musicians better—and musicians, pastors. Let's compare the task of delivering a twenty- to thirty-minute sermon with leading a twenty- to thirty-minute worship set in the free-flowing style.

Imagine a contemporary format: the worship leader is leading from a keyboard (pianist or organist with MIDI) or a guitar, assisted by two or more vocalists, another instrumentalist, and a percussionist or someone employing a drum machine. (If this does not describe your worship group, imagine your own situation.)

For the pastor, the sermon is a solo effort; but for the worship leader, the worship is a team effort. The pastor has control over every part of his delivery, while the worship leader is dependent on the skill level of volunteers who may perform wrong notes and rhythms; show a lack of phrasing and articulation, an insensitivity to dynamics, an inability to find the rhythmic groove, an incapacity to modulate between stanzas or create transitions between pieces; or be unable to improvise in different music styles. Obviously, the skill level of members in the group may vary greatly.

While many pastors are minimally dependent on technology, many worship leaders are dependent on an array of technology: the management of synthesizer patches and cards, overheads and slides and their proper sequencing and timing.

The miking, mixing, and sound levels of monitors, particularly, often cause untold frustrations for the musician. I hear these voiced continually and emphatically. Musicians need to hear each other in the worship space in order to be a good ensemble.

The Sound Booth and Church Acoustics

Imperative! *Seek in your sound booth a person who technically knows the sound board and has a musical ear.* That combination is rare. Individuals are often strong in one area but not in both. Take off the headphones when determining the volume level and equalization. Consider hiring a person (if you're a large church) to ensure that the sound quality is consistent from service to service.

Church acoustics are another often unrecognized but divisive factor. Preachers can be relatively comfortable in any number of minimally reverberant spaces, but a good music space requires a longer reverberation time than speech. Good acoustics result from informed, architectural designing.[10]

The following conditions generally make life difficult for musicians: thickly carpeted floors, cushioned seats, curtained backdrops, low ceilings, seats positioned under balconies, and acoustical tile. They stifle the natural resonance and amplification of the human voice and can discourage (even cripple) congregational response. Musicians end up not being able to hear one another. Sounds do not sparkle, blend, and fuse. Feeling alone and missing the supporting sound around them, people sing more self-consciously, tentatively. There is little joy in corporate singing. Such acoustics dampen the energy people bring to the service. *In such spaces, worship leaders labor against unyielding, enormous odds.*

Pastors, do you want a preaching space? That's simple. Or do you want a worship space? That's complex. Consider that when you are building or renovating. Your chief musician does—or should!

Feeling Inadequate and Vulnerable

As for the matter of response itself, the preacher usually does not require an overt response every Sunday, but the worship leader's task requires one each and every time. And that response is measurable by everybody. That puts extra pressure on the worship leader! The people can *pretend* to be interested in the sermon, while in the privacy of their minds be thinking of the grocery list or the lawn that needs watering. But for worship leaders, there are *no pretensions.*[11] Feeble singing is observable by all, and it is unsettling! It directly reflects on the musician's inability to spark interest. Further, if attendance is sparse or full, the seating scattered or dense, response is affected more adversely.

Many other factors work to break down the confidence of worship leaders. Opponents may criticize their music style (timing, pacing, tempos, amount of chorus repetition, the amount of talking done), and how their personality is exerted (in dominating or less obtrusive ways). On the question of personality, the real issue is not how much but when.

In general, worship leaders must establish control at the outset. As the people settle into worship, however, you need to relinquish some control so as not to be a dominating visual object. As the service moves toward intimacy, let the congregation focus on God without distraction. You may need to reassert yourself again for the closeout number.

Recognize also that the worship leader is uniquely subject to the immediacies of the moment, the collective consciousness of the congregation—sometimes they're up, sometimes down for apparently unaccountable reasons. The result? This often-repeated soliloquy: [The worship leader sits down and reflects] "It wasn't happening today. I may have led them in singing, but I did not succeed in leading them to worship. Response was really off. . . ." When Ismael Gurrola, a pastor, read this quote, he responded that pastors often feel the same way: "Sometimes, Barry, I'm thinking this through my sermon—'I'm not connecting. Boy, the people are down today.'" Pastors take congregational response very personally too!

For worship leaders, the shaping of congregational song (and choir music) is uniquely *embodied* in their personality and style. They need to be covered—not left open to the criticism of the congregation. You can protect and channel your musicians' self-esteem with words of encouragement. Keep your worship leader from being destroyed. Worship leaders cannot help but fail at some services.

And musicians, return the favor—protect your pastor! What pastor, coming down from the platform, does not feel vulnerable from time to time. What pastor does not think about illustrations and transitions that could have gone better—not to mention his awesome accountability before God to help the people grow spiritually. What pastor doesn't receive criticism for long sermons, redundancy, and alleged insensitivity. Because of your inside understanding as a musician of the pressures of performance and ministry, your support can be particularly comforting.

Most musicians (and I suspect many pastors too) are perfectionists. Keyboardists spend their time practicing, trying to perform passages more smoothly and with better phrasing. Soloists try to improve their tone. Choir directors constantly refine and polish diction and attacks and releases within the pressing time constraints afforded them. So self-criticism can be tremendously tenacious, because musicians always feel they could have done it better. Often they are happy (satisfied) with a tiny portion of their work—a few measures—and disappointed (perhaps even disgusted!) with the rest. This is the real life of many performing musicians.

In some congregations there is undue pressure for leaders to produce emotional highs every time, the "Can you top this?" syndrome. No matter what happens in the service, it is not enough! We need some healthy realism. Worship involves response, but not necessarily an emotional catharsis every Sunday!

The worship leader should not attempt to create, induce, or worse yet, command the presence of God. That is what the prophets of Baal tried to do on Mount Carmel. Who are we to think we have the power to order around the Almighty? If the worship leader succumbs to this pressure and begins to manipulate the people, apply loving correction. A worship committee member or the pastor can intercede where there is honesty and insight. Again, pastors often feel subject to similar pressures.

Body Language

The body language that both musicians and pastors display publicly is terribly important. It can support or undercut everything. Reviewing music scores and shuffling papers or sermon notes should be left for some other time, for they undermine the respect for leaders and detract from the sense of transcendence we so much want to obtain in our services. Gum chewing, fidgeting, slumping in seats, and gawking at the congregation during worship services is also inappropriate. Musicians should set a good example in sermon listening—and pastors in hymn singing. Total attentiveness and delight in God's presence should be our constant intention. Leaders must model good churchmanship.

> I hope in the Lord Jesus to send Timothy to you soon. . . . I have no one else like him, who takes a genuine interest in your welfare. For everyone looks out for his own interests, not those of Jesus Christ.
>
> Philippians 2:19–21

Questions for Reflection and Discussion

1. Do you take criticism of your preaching and worship leading personally?
2. What hymn could you paraphrase in a prayer or congregational reading?
3. How should pastors become involved in improving congregational song?
4. Is there one correct key in which to sing any one hymn or chorus? Discuss and demonstrate, if possible.

116

5. "The worship leader is uniquely subject to the immediacies of the moment, the collective consciousness of the congregation—sometimes they're up and sometimes they're down." This statement is true for pastors too. Share examples and discuss.
6. Use your hymnal in your devotions this week.

PART TWO

PRESSING ISSUES

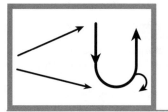

Is Worship a Performance?
The Concept

To perform is to do something complicated or difficult with skill in public with a view toward serving and ministering.

Tom Keene, a studio musician, shared his concerns about evangelical musicians with me at a coffee shop after a Sunday night church meeting. He's turned off by the "Hollywood" kind of performance he sees in Christian concerts and evangelical church worship that exalts individuals and individualism.

I see worship leaders and music directors doing things just to be clever; they really haven't thought through it. I've heard arrangements in church of "Just as I Am" with a bossa nova beat and a big band sound. I even heard one church do a bluesy arrangement of "Swinging in the Sheaves" ["Bringing in the Sheaves"]. Can you imagine that?

Music directors are "pushing buttons"—not leading worship, but drawing attention to their own expertise and exceptional skills. In the evangelical scene we've gone through this phase of big endings, high notes. The "in" thing is long, thirty-two-bar introductions.

Christian professional artists are trying hard to be hip. *"[name omitted]"* puts on "fun" concerts. "____" makes all the funny faces, does all the gyrations of the rock stars, bumps into the bass player, does all the "accepted" rock and roll gestures. "_____" hits all the high notes and delivers an emotional high for every concert.

These Christian artists have painted themselves into a terrible corner, pandering to the self-indulgences of their audiences. What will be the next high point? When you take your clothes off? Performer egos are rampant. It trickles down, and now we have the local church clones infected with the "Can you top this?" attitude.

Then they wonder why the pastor is upset! This stuff is meeting nobody's needs. It's amateurish to the pro musicians, and the older people are mortified by it.

When will music directors, worship leaders and Christian music artists learn to feel as much rewarded by having a standing ovation as having nothing at all? If you have one standing ovation after another, you have no standing ovations.

I'd just like to sit down at the piano and share some music with the people, listen to each other and God, not necessarily expecting, or having the people expect from me, a tremendous high.[1]

The reality is, though, people *are* attracted in great numbers to hear the good performers, the skilled speakers and musicians. We *are* inclined to buy into the entertainment syndrome and to exalt the Christian performer, preacher, or musician. This ought to make us uneasy.[2]

When performers are exceptionally good, it is not easy to distinguish the genuinely motivated from the fraudulent:

People think they may be able to discern if a minister or musician is genuine, but they probably cannot if that person is highly skilled. They need to ask if he lives what he preaches and inquire how he is doing in his home life.[3]

Reloading the Word *Performance*

The idea of "worship as performance" is troublesome! A right attitude to performance, therefore, is *foundational* to ministry. Pastors, musicians, and the people perceive the word *performance* differently. For example, the people distrust it, musicians value it, and pastors deny it (deny that they are performers). The people are right in wanting sincerity. The bad associations the word connotes has caused many Christian leaders to jettison the term from the pulpit altogether. Most leaders would use the words "participating in" worship rather than "performing" worship. Similarly, many pastors feel more comfortable using the terms "executing" or "delivering" the sermon rather than "performing" the sermon. Even more unacceptable, however, is to call a Christian concert or a musical at church a "show." Concern for the appropriateness of this kind of language (especially in the context of worship) is proper.

Pastors, nevertheless, need to understand that in their relationships with musicians, the word *performance* simply will not go away. For musicians, it's a word they have used throughout their training and they will *continue* to use it in their conversations with choirs, soloists, and worship teams—and perhaps even in the pulpit. It's also a word employed in our most recent and widely read Bible translations, and it has something positive to teach us. Not to acknowledge this is to impoverish ourselves.

How is it used in the Bible? What does it mean to musicians? How did Kierkegaard use it? What would be a proper perspective to "performance"? Let's look at each of these.

Speaking as a musician, let me state boldly that when the word is properly understood and applied, I believe that worship has a strong performance dimension. Performance reaches to the roots of responsible leadership. I know this may sound like heresy to many leaders, but hear me out. Since the word will not go away, I propose to *reload* its meaning for the purpose of forming bridges of understanding between musicians and pastors. We need a level playing field where we all understand what is meant by different terminology. Often, we fight without understanding what we fight about.

Kierkegaard and Performance

Although evangelicals would not endorse all aspects of Kierkegaard's theology, in recent days they have been influenced by his statement that in corporate worship

- the people should be the *performers* of worship
- the pastor and worship leaders the *prompters* of worship
- God, the *audience*

To grasp his concept, consider a football stadium in which the people perform worship on the field, the pastor and worship leaders coach or prompt the people (act as player-coaches), and God is the audience in the stands. The value of this formulation is that it stresses active, major participation by the people. It is a wel-

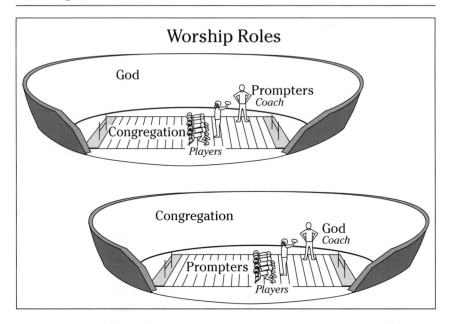

come corrective to the situation in many churches in which the people take their seats, drop some coins into the offering, sit back and expect to be entertained and edified by the choir, the special music, and an interesting sermon. It also corrects contemporary praise formats where the band leads and the audience listens and enjoys. The two football illustrations above depict the typical evangelical view (congregation as audience) and the preferred view of Kierkegaard (God as the audience).

Did you notice that the way Kierkegaard uses the word *perform* creates no problem for us at all? Why is that? It is because in this context we are performing "to God." We are not performing for human applause. God is the audience, and that changes everything. The "to the Lord" principle is Kierkegaard's exclusive focus.

Helpful though this focus is, it is an oversimplification of the actual dynamics involved. In reality, there are *two audiences* (God and the people) not one. God is not only the audience, he also *initiates* the worship process. God reveals himself to us and we respond to him. Scripture clearly teaches that worship is response. The picture becomes even more complex when we consider the worship leaders. They bear the added complication of being both *performers and prompters* of worship—again, more like player-coaches—and that makes everything immeasurably more difficult.

The Unseen Prompter

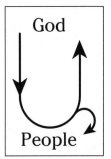

The role of the prompter is crucial in the weekly leading of worship, as the following remarkable story illustrates. The opening of San Francisco's opera season was an hour away when disaster struck. The lead tenor, about to sing the demanding role in Verdi's *Othello,* lost his voice. A worldwide search began to see if one of a half dozen tenors who knew the role could come and save opening night.

Curtain time was delayed three hours. Rumors were rampant that none other than Placido Domingo was being flown in from New York by private jet. They proved true, and Domingo sang, without rehearsal, an opera he hadn't sung for a year.

When asked how he did it, he said, "I couldn't have done it without the help of the prompter."

The prompter sits hidden from the audience in a tiny box attached to the stage floor. His head and upper body are above the stage; his lower body is below floor level but above the orchestra pit. At times he comes close to being trampled by the performers.

His job is arduous. He cues every singer and knows the mind of the conductor, the weaknesses in each opera, and the individual stumbling blocks of each performer. If trouble comes he must unscramble it. *When his job is well done, it normally goes completely unnoticed by the audience.*[4]

This description of the prompter relates closely to the role of keyboardists, worship leaders, and pastors. Their leadership style should not be obtrusive or distractive. What is important is the meeting of the people with God. The prompter works to secure that meeting by removing distractions so that the people can respond to God. Worship prompters perform "up" to God and "down" to the people, simultaneously.

Performance in Webster's Dictionary and the Bible

Note the many dimensions of the word *performance* that Webster's dictionary underscores. To perform means "to carry on to the finish . . . to

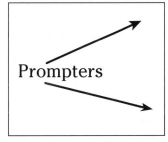

carry out or execute some action, engagement, or the like; to do something with special skill; also, to show off; as, to *perform* on the piano. . . . Perform usually refers to processes that are lengthy, exacting, or ceremonial, or to deeds that are striking."[5] The components of this definition relate strongly to new worship practice.

Although Webster's refers to "showing off"—the negative aspect—more importantly it brings out an additional aspect that interests artists: skill. Whereas the people are particularly sensitive to one's motivation in performance, on the other hand, musicians are particularly focused on the details that make a performance noteworthy. *Musicians equate performance more with quality and excellence than "showing off."* They cannot easily "turn off" this orientation. Listen to conversations among musicians and you will find they keep circling back to the issue of quality and standards.

But how does the Bible use the word *perform* in relation to worship? Does it reveal any additional dimensions? Yes. In the Old Testament the word translated *perform* is often associated with obedience in carrying out or executing some work, duty, or command. The context often takes the form "they *shall* perform":

All that is to be done, they *shall perform.* . . . All their work, *shall be performed* at the command of Aaron and his sons.

Numbers 4:26–27 NASB[6]

It is also associated with artistic skill:

See, the Lord has called by name Bezalel . . . to make designs . . . and in the cutting of stones for settings, and in the carving of wood, so as to *perform* in every inventive work.

Exodus 35:30–33 NASB

A unique biblical emphasis not found in Webster's is the association of performance with "serving" and "ministering":

[The priests] shall *perform* the duties . . . to do *the service* of the tabernacle.

Numbers 3:7 NASB

Now these are those whom David appointed over the *service* of song . . . and they *ministered* with song . . . and they *served* in their office according to their order.

1 Chronicles 6:31–32 NASB[7]

[The levitical priests] are to come near my table to *minister* before me and *perform* my *service.*

Ezekiel 44:16

Notice in the last quote that the words *minister, perform,* and *service* occur together in a single verse. Here is the most important point in the chapter. I believe these three words in the last quotation—*performing, serving, ministering*—are practically interchangeable and that the idea of connecting serving and ministering with performance is immensely helpful in clarifying the biblical attitude toward performance.[8] When we picture these three words together, a healthy perspective to performance emerges. So when you use the word *performance* in public worship, include the words *serving* and *ministering* in the immediate context.[9] The negativity associated with this term will be muted . . . hopefully.

Operational Definition of Performance

Drawing from Webster and the Scriptures, then, here is my attempt to *reload* the term *performance,* and to offer an operational definition for corporate worship:

To perform is . . .
to do
something complicated or difficult
with skill
in public
with a view toward serving or ministering.

The two new parts to the reloaded definition *not specified* in Webster's and unique to Scripture are "in public" and "serving and ministering." Now let us examine in sequence the parts of this definition, bearing in mind three groups of people—the pastor, the worship team, and the congregation.

To Perform Is to Do

Worship is a verb; it's active. There is a task to do, a service to render:

> Come, let us worship and bow down;
> Let us kneel before the Lord our maker.
> Psalm 95:6 NASB

127

> Ascribe to the LORD the glory due his name;
> bring an offering and come into his courts.
> Psalm 96:8

These are clear-cut performance statements, showing that we are powerless to effect inner transformation in ourselves, but we can place ourselves before God. We can bow, kneel, give glory, and bring an offering. We can wait before him.

Shachad, the primary word for worship in the Old Testament, means literally to "bow" (politely or respectfully), to "prostrate oneself."[10] It has a definite physical dimension to it. It is not a propositional word.

Proskuneo, the primary Greek counterpart for worship in the New Testament, has the same overtones of "submissive lowliness and deep respect." *Kuneo* means "to kiss" and *pros* means "to turn toward."

The Hebrew word for the hand, *yad,* provides the root for some fifty praise words. *Yadah,* its extended form, means "to throw, to cast, or to shoot." It means "to worship with extended hands, to throw out the hands, to give thanks to God."[11]

Clearly, the biblical roots for words of praise and worship strongly accent the physical dimension of worship. They strongly emphasize the visual, gestural aspects—what the body *does* (see chapter 10 for a more detailed discussion).

The chart below summarizes the kinds of prayer postures found in the Bible. Notice, the greater the body movement, the greater the frequency of occurrence. This is the opposite of mainstream evangelical church culture.

Prostration and Raised Hands Top List of Prayer Postures

Posture	Meaning	Frequency
Bowing the head	Submission	4
Standing	Respect	6
Lifting the eyes	Looking to the source of blessing	9
Kneeling	Humility	12
Hands lifted	Expectancy, servitude	14
Prostration	Awe in the divine presence	28

We should not think of these postures as merely symbols from a bygone era. They're of timeless value. Fall on your knees! I challenge you to test their relevance to your personal worship. See if your prayer is not advanced.

Some evangelical worship traditions, when analyzed, stem more from European than biblical tradition. Nowhere in Scripture, for example, do worshipers close their eyes and fold their hands in prayer—that's unbiblical (I'm teasing!). On the other hand, forms of worship that are modeled in Scripture (i.e., raising of hands) can raise eyebrows and become objects of controversy. But the data is incontrovertibly clear: the raising of hands is a normal part of Hebrew practice, not a Pentecostal phenomenon. We need incisive teaching on this from the pulpit—or even a paragraph in your bulletin would be helpful.

What does the raising of hands mean from a biblical point of view? What did it mean to the ancient Hebrews who performed it? Scripture tells us that lifted hands were symbolically related to lifted prayers:

> *May my prayer be set before you like incense;*
>   may the lifting up of my hands be like the evening sacrifice.
>   Psalm 141:2, emphasis added

When the Hebrews prayed at the evening sacrifice, they offered incense. As their prayers rose to God, the incense also rose to him. Their lifted hands indicated that their hearts were rising to God just as the incense ascended. Their lifted hands gave concrete expression to the worship in their hearts: "Let us lift up our hearts and our hands to God in heaven"(Lam. 3:41).

The raising of hands also expressed the meaning of yearning and thirsting for God:

> I meditate on all your works
>   and consider what your hands have done.
> I spread out my hands to you;
>   *my soul thirsts for you like a parched land.*
>   Psalm 143:5–6, emphasis added

You get the picture! The psalmist imagines himself like the ground (or perhaps a plant in the ground) that needs watering. As the plant stretches and strains to receive the rain from heaven, so worshipers lift their hands to say symbolically, "Let your dew fall on me. Water me, Lord. My soul thirsts for you." Without the dew or rain of heaven, the plant would shrivel and die. It's a powerful image of the worshiper wanting, needing God.

Moreover, recall that the wings of the cherubim in the Holy of Holies hovered over the mercy seat. For some, their raised hands image those wings. An evocative passage in 1 Chronicles says the Lord "dwells between the cherubim, where His name is proclaimed" (13:6 NKJV).

Should everyone raise their hands in worship then? No. The practice of raising hands is *modeled not mandated in Scripture; permitted, not forced or coerced.* The Scriptures don't command it; they permit it—even encourage it by modeling it. Shouldn't we then permit it too?

- Test it in your closet prayers first before performing it in public. See if it aids your personal prayer.
- Be patient with yourself and give yourself time to become comfortable with it.
- When you become comfortable privately, you may feel more at ease publicly.

But remember, raising your hands in worship doesn't make you a more authentic worshiper. Rather, it points to the fact that the body is an important element in worship expression. Even Paul refers to the principle:

> I want men everywhere to lift up holy hands in prayer, without anger or disputing.
>
> 1 Timothy 2:8

There is also a profound *ongoingness* to the statement "O come, let us worship." Our worship must be renewed, repeated each week. So sincere motivation in the doing of worship must be strong because last week's worship will not suffice for this week.

To Perform Is to Do Something Complicated or Difficult

As Webster's has indicated, to perform means to do something complicated, lengthy, and exacting.[12] The drama of worship in the tabernacle and temple actively involved the people. For example, the worshiper presented, placed his hands on, slaughtered, skinned, cut the lamb into pieces, and washed it for the burnt offering; but today, defined and prescribed tasks for the people are often sorely missing. The pastor's role is absorbing, the choir's role exacting, but rarely is much attention given to what the people do. How can the people be true performers when they do not have a striking, active, and involved role to play?

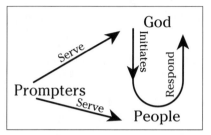

Worship activities that involve the entire congregation in sustained, disciplined participation are essential. How can this issue be addressed? The congregation could participate in sections of praise for ten minutes or more and perform extended dramatic readings and prayer responses. Aggressive participation can be encouraged by teaching the people to become a *congregational choir*. Through rehearsing unfamiliar hymns before the service begins—or teaching a descant, practicing a bass part with the men separately, rehearsing a new hymn for Easter Sunday, practicing antiphonal singing, selecting a hymn or chorus or Bible verse for memorization and practicing it by memory—the people can acquire the expectation that they have real (not token) work to do each Sunday. In your planning, why not consider establishing achievement goals for the congregational choir as well as the sanctuary choir?

Congregations need to be truly *exercised* with solid tasks that focus their attention on God, that place them before him, so that he really has them and can minister inner transformation to them. The Scriptures say, "exercise yourself rather to godliness" (1 Tim. 4:7 NKJV). That is our part. As leaders we need to ask ourselves, "Am I truly placing myself and my people before God this morning? Am I *training* them to attend to God?" Our concern should not be to achieve a perfect performance so that we can talk about it after the service, but we should work to engage our entire person (heart, soul, mind) before God, to be fully involved in ministering to him, and to be in a state of readiness to hear from him.

The Challenge: Two Audiences, Not One

While the congregation's role is too often trite and undeveloped in worship, the pastor's role fully meets Webster's criteria. It is invariably lengthy, exacting, and personally absorbing.[13] What makes this role absorbing? Well, many factors are at work, but consider this: pastors have *two* audiences to attend to—God and the people. This complicates matters. It's difficult to focus on the Lord and at the same time focus on the preaching assignment, as Pastor Ben Patterson painfully shares:

> I can get so preoccupied with trying to get the congregation to worship that I don't worship. . . . Instead of the sermon being itself an act of worship, it becomes a performance . . . that succeeds or fails, . . . in either case a *performance for the people.* Whatever the reason, Sunday mornings before worship are often the least prayerful day of the week for me. I hope what I have done Monday through Saturday will make up for that lack. . . . The more thought my staff and I put into planning worship . . . the better able I am not to worry about worship details on Sunday. The less worried I am, the more able I am emotionally to worship as I lead in worship.[14]

Pastors, talk about this tension with your worship team. Scripture readers and those who pray publicly will identify with you. Teach them to become aware of and responsible to both audiences: God is (or should be) the primary audience, yet the congregation by their physical presence can be a very real and even intimidating secondary audience. Similarly, choir directors will want a choir that truly worships during the Sunday morning service and yet communicates vividly with the people. However, as many choir directors have learned, the rehearsal time during the week may provide the best time for authentic worship. Why? Worship may be offered directly to God without the complication of the second audience, the people.

Sometimes the way overheads or slides are managed is distracting. I often say to individuals working these media, "Watch me. Don't get lost in worship; attend to me first. It is more important that the whole church worships *without distraction* than that you and I worship. We are giving ourselves for the people."

In fact this is a good idea for every leader. Worship in private first. You may not be able to do so satisfactorily in public, because when you are a leader you must first and foremost give yourself for the people. I can't stress this enough, especially for the musicians. Undistracted worship by the congregation depends on your reliability as a musician. You must be prepared to sing the first word in the next chorus, beat the next beat, or play the next chord. If you have excess energy and attention, then worship! This may seem callous, but it is a practical reality. Again, in this sense, worship is a performance. Leaders must be seeking and wanting God as they lead, but at the same time, they must be aware.

By all means, worship as completely as you can. Obviously, leaders who want their people to be hungry for worship must also eat!

Furthermore, encourage the worship team to model worship in their facial expressions and demeanor. In short, the better prepared you are, the freer you will feel to worship.

One way pastors may worship more genuinely during the service, in addition to thorough preparation, is to delegate to others tasks they often perform, such as the reading of Scripture, various prayers, the announcements, welcome, or the offering. Pastors can then focus on the Lord for an uninterrupted period during the earlier part of the service before the sermon. They are then able to relax and enjoy God before preaching.

Developing a Sense of Flow

Those who read the Scripture, pray, and preach need to be aware of how their part contributes to the larger whole. When participants understand they are coming out of and going into something, they can learn to contribute to the *flow* of the service—another performance dimension. Boldfaced headings in the order of service can underscore that direction for everyone. When the entire congregation is attuned to this larger rhythm, the people grow more attentive and spiritually sensitive.

Services that have an improvisational feel are, if anything, more demanding. Leaders must select and rehearse their songs to the point that their performance is fluent, not strained. They need to have enough reserve energy left to perform their role and yet be aware of what is happening with the people. Keyboardists must not only play but listen.

Keyboardists and worship leaders cannot close their eyes in worship for extended periods of time. They must be alert, aware. This is absolutely vital! How well are the people singing? Precisely where is their point of greatest need? In order to be able to listen carefully, keyboardists may need to cut back their dynamics occasionally. Leaders also need to be free to adhere to all or only part of their preplan, be able to adapt to the real-time momentum generated by the people, and follow the leading of the Spirit. Where such spontaneity is valued, keyboardists need to cultivate flexibility and a sense of timing and proportion. A particular number may be dropped, a chorus added or repeated, or silence may be required, depending on the real-time situation.[15]

We have now dealt with two parts of our operational definition:

1. To perform is to do.
2. To perform is to do something difficult or complicated.

We are unequally gifted and cannot equally achieve. . . . But all artists can be better than they once were. This is excelling.[16]

Questions for Reflection and Discussion

1. Should the word *performance* be avoided in the pulpit?
2. How could a sense of flow be improved?
3. What achievement goals have you established for the congregational choir?
4. Are you able to worship while you preach or lead worship? What helps the process for you?
5. The act of worship is formidable because last week's worship will not suffice for this week. What are your thoughts about this?

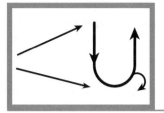

Is Worship a Performance? The Implications

> To perform is to do something complicated or difficult with skill in public with a view toward serving and ministering.

So far I have discussed Webster's definition of *perform* and the unique dimensions Scripture brings to the word, and I have offered an operational definition of worship. We learned that the Hebrew word for *worship* has a strong "doing" dimension. I underscored the need for solid congregational tasks, the challenge of two audiences, and the importance of maintaining a flow to the service. I'll now continue with the operational definition, which highlights additional critical dimensions of the word *perform*—skill, service, ministry, and the public nature of performance.

To Perform Is to Do Something with Skill

The word *performance* contains the dimension of *skill*. *Skill,* a word frequently used in the Old Testament,[1] has a New Testament counterpart—*giftedness.* And in the church, gifted people are capable of skilled work.

When selecting people to read Scripture, choose gifted readers. Choose people who have the gift of communicating what is on the page and who value God's Word enough to do the reading well. Time spent coaching individuals in public reading and prayer is time well spent. Recall the request of the disciples: "Lord, teach us to pray." It's a less overt form of discipling.

As designated people rise to read and pray, a process of modeling occurs from which everyone in the church benefits. It's also a tangible witness to the nonchurched that not only the pastor but the people have a living, demonstrable faith.

Television Has Upped the Demands on Quality

Lyle E. Schaller, well-known church consultant, says to midsized churches (churches in the 100- to 250-people range), "Act your size!" A church of 150 people is in reality a complex organization. When churches reach this critical mass, *growth is strongly tied to excellence in performance.* But the sad reality is that unchurched persons stepping into our churches are bored with our worship. For many of them, worship is sheer monotony. Unconsciously, people compare what they experience in church with television—wanting quick-paced newscasts and sound bites assembled by slick production crews.

Consider for a moment the concerted effort required to produce a single newscast. The weatherperson, for example, spends the entire day prepping for a four-minute appearance. Gone are the days when the weatherperson "lectured" with chalk in hand; now the public is treated to a "presentation" (note the difference) with computer graphics, nature scenes backdropping the temperatures, moving satellite pictures, and a running dialogue interspersed with humorous one-liners dreamed up by staff writers. The next time you see the credits scrolled at the end of a news program, remember that people come to your worship service with similar professional expectations.

We might not like this state of affairs, but it's a reality we must face. These performance expectations unconsciously permeate our thinking when we come to church. Television has imposed its professional standards on our worship practice. True, there is no way a small- to medium-sized church can fully compete in this arena (and I don't think people's expectations are *that* high), but we must

136

make *some* cultural adaptation. We can employ reader's theater and other techniques in reading Scripture. We can *strive* for excellence. I am disturbed, for example, when I hear musicians say when a musical number is ragged from inadequate rehearsal, "It doesn't matter, the people will never know the difference."

This kind of talk is destructive. First, it simply is not true. *People notice and appreciate quality.* They know when something has been properly rehearsed, though they may not be able to analyze the details that made a performance good. Second, when we are sloppy and careless, we are the losers. We suffer a loss of personal integrity. How can carelessness be offered to the Lord? How can we say our worship is costly when we do not at least strive for quality? Third, carelessness undermines faith. Our work, because it is not an honest effort, cannot be truly offered in faith.

Exercising Our Skill with Wisdom

The Old Testament concept of skill is broader than we usually take it; it keeps in mind the big picture and includes *wisdom.* I learned something about this during my teens when I was the pianist for evangelistic teams doing citywide campaigns. Being young and exuberant, I would perform dazzling runs on the keyboard during the congregational singing. One day an evangelist took me aside. "Barry," he said gently, "have you noticed the people have been a little lost?" That hurt a little, but I got the point. What I was doing was distracting.

We need wisdom in the area of exercising our technique. Good technique is not so much virtuosity as it is being responsible or *response-able*—having the ability to do *what* needs to be done *when* it needs to be done.[2] Under certain conditions it's appropriate to exercise the full range of our technique; but there are other times when *restraining* our technique may be wiser. For example, during songs of adoration and intimacy, playing too many notes on the keyboard or on percussion instruments only distracts; what is important is delicacy of touch and beauty of tone and phrasing. On the other hand, passages of awesome transcendency may demand many notes and wide spacing that cuts through to the people with authority, power, and energy. My goal in the crusades should have been to *help the people sing!*

In a worship service, our goal should be to help bring people closer to God. When the sermon, prayers, and song service function properly, we should not be conscious of the prompters. Remember our football analogy—the coaches are on the sidelines, only secondarily "players." I like to think that the song service, if done well, will blossom like a rose. It will open up so naturally and develop so easily that the people might be inclined to say, "I could have led that! There's nothing to it!" It's a marvelous feeling when services appear to take off on their own; and more than anything else, we are aware of the presence of the Lord with us in power and beauty. Amazed, we exclaim in awe to ourselves, "I couldn't have done this! This is not my doing!" Is this not precisely what Paul valued? Listen carefully to Paul—he did not put his *confidence* in technique:

> And when I came to you, brethren, I did not come with superiority of speech or of wisdom, proclaiming to you the testimony of God. For I determined to know nothing among you except Jesus Christ, and Him crucified. And I was with you in weakness and in fear and in much trembling. And my message and my preaching were not in persuasive words of wisdom, but in demonstration of the Spirit and of power, that your faith should not rest on the wisdom of men, but on the power of God.
>
> 1 Corinthians 2:1–5 NASB

> We . . . who worship by the Spirit of God . . . put no confidence in the flesh.
>
> Philippians 3:3 NASB

Does this mean we should not pursue excellence? Parts of Paul's writings, such as the eighth chapter of Romans and the thirteenth chapter of 1 Corinthians, contain passages of soaring eloquence. Is he contradicting himself? Not at all. The key is not to *trust* in eloquence. Place your faith in God, not technique! Nonetheless, C. S. Lewis contends (and I think Paul would agree) that "When Christian work is done on a serious subject there is no gravity and no sublimity it cannot attain."[3] "Trembling," as Scripture says, we offer our work to God, and trust him to bless and empower it, *as he pleases.*

Technique, however, does contribute to sublimity. The writer of Psalm 45 was conscious of possessing technique:

> My heart is stirred by a noble theme
> as I recite my verses for the king;
> my tongue is the pen of a *skillful* writer.
>
> verse 1, emphasis added

Evidence of extensive technique and craftsmanship is also apparent in the design of acrostic psalms and psalms displaying elaborate symmetry.[4]

To Perform Is to Do Something in Public

I have asked mature Christians who do professional concert work and also play in services, "What is the difference between performing at a concert and playing at church?" A thought-provoking response I repeatedly hear runs something like this: "I see no difference. As a Christian performer, all of life should be an offering of worship." Along this vein C. S. Lewis said: "Boiling an egg is the same process whether you are a Christian or a Pagan."[5] Insightful analogy! Yet in the church we must insist on a further word of clarification. In a worship service, performers must see their piece of the service as not standing alone, but as integrated. The piece must not distract, but serve the whole. And the force of human personality must also serve the goal.[6] Consider Peter:

> Clothe yourselves with humility toward one another, because,
> "God opposes the proud
> but gives grace to the humble."
>
> 1 Peter 5:5

Performers must humble themselves before the presence of God; this is only proper. Only then can he, by his grace, feel free to work powerfully through us. When we humble ourselves in the act of performing, we may actually experience our spirit and those about us being lifted up.[7]

Performance: A Function of Size

That corporate worship is public also leads to the consideration of *size*. Size makes for differences in performance standards. The larger the church, the higher the performance standard required. The larger the membership, the greater the need for a *great* ministry of music.[8]

The tabernacle or temple liturgy, for example, was conducted by "professionals," specialists called priests and Levites. They had only one job; fortunately, they had sufficient numbers so that they could specialize. On the other hand, small churches with fewer than a hundred regular attenders have meager resources and often require one person to do several jobs. As a result, they are more people-oriented than performance-oriented. Generalists do the work, so people have a greater tolerance for uneven skill.

But we must be sensible. *As your church grows, be prepared to specialize.* Some don't, and they plateau. Schaller addresses this problem frankly:

> The biggest barrier to mission and outreach . . . is the tendency for the members of the middle-sized congregation to see it as a small church and to engage in counterproductive behavior.
>
> This widespread tendency has three common results: (1) first, and most serious, it creates a self-perpetuating low self-image of modest expectations based on a perception of inadequate resources and limited potential; (2) it offers a limited range of programs, often experiences an excessively high turnover in ministerial leadership; it rarely challenges the members to reach their full potential, and it frequently is underorganized; and (3) the combination of these first two tendencies has turned out to be the most effective single approach to turning the middle-sized congregation into a small church.[9]

Schaller has a good line for midsized churches: "In a congregation as large as this, surely with God's help we can do it."

Viewing Pastors and Musicians as Fellow Performers

Pastors and musicians *are* performers. I contend that musicians and pastors have both a performance temperament and a performance orientation. Both are bitten by the "bug"! I've repeatedly heard pastors say something like this during the course of the service, "I don't feel ready to preach yet; let's have another hymn." Yet they deny they are performers! And they sorely miss preaching when they don't do it for several weeks.[10] To be on the sidelines is painful for both musicians and pastors. In this sense pastors have more in common with musicians than, say, Christian education directors.

Moreover, both musicians and pastors minister publicly and must learn to expect public criticism—sometimes withering criticism.[11] Weekly public scrutiny exposes their warts to all. And both suffer by being compared to every TV evangelist and recording

140

artist. Both may also err (in a given service) in their sense of dramatic timing: The musician needs to place the correct hymn or solo in the correct place; the pastor must release the appropriate illustration at the right moment. Both must find ways to transition smoothly.

Ego problems also go with the turf. Musicians and pastors, in my opinion, tend to be compulsive. After performing, their eyes glaze over. They try to "stop the tape" running in their heads— "this could have gone better; that was good"—as they mentally rehearse how their part in the service went.

Jealousy is for each an insidious, ever-present temptation, especially when comparisons are made of pastors to pastors, music directors to music directors, and when the pastor is compared to the worship leader in the same church. *We are so sensitive.* A pastor related: "The lowest blow is when a layperson hands a preacher the cassette of another pulpit person."

What if the music tops the sermon? This may happen on occasion. When musicians receive rave compliments, they should take the initiative to clarify to the pastor that they are not trying to upstage him or the Word; but they would like to feel free to contribute strongly. A pastor will greatly appreciate your sharing your heart on this matter humbly but frankly. For reasons like these, pastors and musicians put a high premium on securing someone to work with who is emotionally secure.

To Perform Is to Serve and Minister

In the biblical perspective, to perform is to serve and to minister. How can pastors and musicians train themselves toward unsullied service? Perhaps if musicians and pastors would regularly engage in forms of service that are completely hidden, little esteemed, and concealed from public view, they would not only become aware of their true state of humility but go a long way in learning genuine godliness.

Hiddenness is a rebuke to the flesh. Richard J. Foster has observed, "The flesh whines against [true] service but screams against hiddenness. It pulls and strains for honor and recognition."[12] Accordingly, Dallas Willard encourages leaders to place their public relations department in the hands of God:

If you want to experience the flow of love as never before, the next time you are in a competitive situation, pray that the others around you will be more outstanding, more praised, and more used of God than yourself. Really pull for them and rejoice for their successes.[13]

I love that quote. It's easy to read, but difficult to practice in everyday life. We musicians and pastors frequently find ourselves in competitive situations.

Service in *small things* can also discipline ego urges. Showing tiny courtesies, learning to listen attentively, visiting shut-ins and the elderly, driving individuals without rides home after practice, helping with the church janitorial chores occasionally, and being willing to assist others with trifling matters can help prevent inflatedness. Jesus said, "Whoever wants to become great among you must be your servant, and whoever wants to be first must be your slave" (Matt. 20:26–27). Recall the reason why Paul said he was given "a thorn in the flesh": "to keep me from exalting myself" (2 Cor. 12:7 NASB).

Yet have you observed how the phrases "anointed preaching" and "anointed worship leading" are employed today? The reckless use of the word *anointed* trivializes the concept and exalts individuals—not the Lord. Moreover, some leaders use the phrase "do not touch the Lord's anointed" to place themselves beyond the pale of criticism, thus rendering themselves unaccountable to anyone.

Self-Examination for True Service[14]

Self-Righteous Service	True Service
comes from human effort	comes from divine urges
frantic, anxious	dependent on God
seeks titanic, impressive ministry (big crowds)	welcomes all opportunities (large or small crowds)
craves applause	content with hiddenness
concerned with results	leaves the results with God
concerned with reciprocation	delights only in service
picks *whom* to serve (the high and powerful)	serves *enemies* as well as friends (servant of all)
serves when the "feeling" is there	serves when the "need" is there

uses technique for ego enhancing	submits technique to function
must perform (even if destructive!)	can withhold service, wait in silence
exposes frailties of other leaders	covers frailties of others
fractures community	builds community

On the flip side, though, is unjust criticism and, even worse, innuendo and slander. These can destroy people. Therefore, refusing to be party to gossip is an elixir of true ministry (and longevity!). In fact, guarding the reputation of others is a form of ego training. Richard Foster tells of serving at a church where the staff had a policy of not allowing any individual to speak disparagingly of one pastor to another. "Gently but firmly," he said, "we would ask them to go directly to the offending pastor."

As we discipline ourselves this way, true ministry to the Lord can gradually become a part of our identity:

> Therefore, since we receive a kingdom which cannot be shaken, let us show gratitude, by which we may offer to God an *acceptable service* with reverence and awe; for our God is a consuming fire.
>
> Hebrews 12: 28–29 NASB, emphasis added

Summary

To perform is to do something complicated or difficult skillfully in public with a view toward serving or ministering. Musicians will continue to use the word *perform,* even though it is a troublesome concept in worship practice. Biblically, to perform is to serve and to minister: the terms are practically indistinguishable.

Leaders serve two audiences, God and the people. Not only pastors and worship leaders but the people need solid performance tasks. Performers should *exercise* their technique but not put their trust in it. Good technique involves being "response-able." Size makes for differences in performance standards. As you grow, specialize. Pastors and musicians have performance temperaments and are particularly vulnerable to egoism. Service in small things can discipline ego urges and encourage true godliness.

Questions for Reflection and Discussion

1. Would you feel a "pang" if you do not perform music or deliver sermons regularly? Are you by nature a performer?
2. To what extent should worship prompters exert their personality into the worship service?
3. How do you define excellence?
4. How have you made your personal worship more costly lately?
5. Is the notion of combining performance with serving and ministering significant? Why or why not?
6. How can we give the congregation a more significant role?

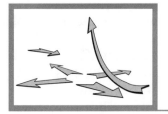

The Danger
of Cosmetic Change

If we merely impose new styles and methods on top of a dead situation, we will end up with nothing better than . . . a beautifully decorated coffin.

Graham Kendrick
Learning to Worship as a Way of Life

They devoted themselves to the apostles' teaching *[kerygma]* and to the fellowship *[koinonia],* to the breaking of bread and to prayer *[leitourgia].*

Acts 2:42

C hurch music leaders have recently called for something new, a *theology of church music.* Church musicians do not know what they are about. Because church music "has not been subject to deep perspectival scrutinies," we are lacking "bedrock theological perspectives."[1] David B. Pass has attempted to provide a coherent, comprehensive model of church music, and this and the next chapter draw from his book *Music and the Church: A Theology of Church Music,*[2] which lays down a theoretical framework, an ordered set of principles.

What is church music? I've heard it defined as broadly as "whatever music is used in the church." Pass, though, maintains that church music should be "determined by the nature of the church" (p. 55). The Greek terms *kerygma, koinonia,* and *leitourgia* characterize his model of the New Testament Church, and he presents a survey of ten theologians which establishes a consensus for it.[3] I assume in this chapter that this model substantially addresses what the church should be doing.[4] The Greek terms have the following meanings:

- *kerygma*: to proclaim
- *koinonia*: to fellowship
- *leitourgia*: to worship[5]

In this model, people hear the gospel proclaimed, respond to it and form a loving community, and offer praise and prayer to God. Pass notes that, in using these terms, the scope of church music is wider than "Sunday morning worship." It includes teaching, evangelism, fellowship, and worship inside and outside the church building—and any music that serves these goals, including recordings.

What would a *kerygma* service look like? How would it differ from a *koinonia* service? How would congregational song, choirs, contemporary bands, and other specialized groups function in each of these settings? What about the issue of performance and stylistic and cultural diversity? How do the Greek terms relate to biblical models of worship? Is there a danger of making cosmetic changes only? These are questions I will address in this and the next chapter.

Let's first outline in nontechnical language some of the central aspects of Pass's model, taking a close look at the three Greek terms.

Clarifying the Terms *Kerygma, Koinonia,* and *Leitourgia*

Kerygma

Kerygma has to do with preaching, proclaiming the message of Jesus Christ. It includes teaching and evangelism and relates to the essentials of the Christian faith—the Christ-event and its significance: "For what I received I passed on to you as of first importance: that Christ died for our sins according to the Scriptures, that he was buried, that he was raised on the third day" (1 Cor. 15:3). Here are two passages that employ the Greek word *kerygma* (translated in italics):

> He [Jesus] said to them, "Go into all the world and *preach* the good news to all creation."
>
> Mark 16:15

> Jews demand miraculous signs and Greeks look for wisdom, but we *preach* Christ crucified.
>
> 1 Corinthians 1:22–23 (see also 2 Timothy 4:17)

The term is also used of John the Baptist "*preaching* a baptism of repentance," and of Jesus "*preaching* the gospel of the kingdom." The Sermon on the Mount reveals the dimensions of *kerygmatic* preaching. Recall Christ's preaching as found in Matthew 5 through 7, and his recurrent phrases, "You have heard . . . but I tell you."

Kerygma calls people to faith, to conversion, to discipleship. It declares a gospel "revealed," not man-made: "What do you have that you did not receive?" says Paul (1 Cor. 4:7). *Kerygma* originates with God. Its communication system is hierarchical, a message originally passed on through apostolic authority; whereas *koinonia* stresses equality of expression, and *leitourgia,* integration of expression. Boldness and fearlessness are essential for *kerygma. Kerygma* convicts and calls for repentance and change; it can threaten the status quo, cause division. The messenger must be willing to experience separation and to suffer persecution and distancing from the audience. In brief, *kerygma* confronts and provokes, whereas *koinonia* comforts and *leitourgia* emphasizes praise and prayer.

An insightful means for differentiating *kerygma, koinonia,* and *leitourgia* is to note who is being addressed in each situation. *Kerygma* is communication from the one to the many (God to the people, or the pastor to the people); *koinonia* is one to another (person-to-person), and *leitourgia* highlights the many to the One (the people to God) and also subsumes *kerygma* and *koinonia.*[6] *Kerygma* is demonstrated when Peter preaches at Pentecost: "Then Peter stood up with the Eleven, raised his voice and addressed the crowd" (Acts 2:14). *Kerygma* conditions are described by Cornelius, when he says to Peter, "Now we are all here in the presence

147

of God *to listen* to everything the Lord has commanded" (Acts 10:33, emphasis added). *Kergyma* is monodirectional, *koinonia* omnidirectional, and *leitourgia* bidirectional (God initiates and then receives worship).

The scope of the *kerygmatic* mode can be extended to include not only preaching but teaching and evangelism.[7] This means that church music extends to evangelistic services—even street parades. Moreover, *kerygmatic* communication can merge with the nonverbal. Music, when combined with words, can embody a declarative function.[8] So can gestures such as acts of bowing and prostration in worship.

Koinonia

The concept of *koinonia,* the second Greek term, involves communicating one with another and maintaining and enhancing relationships, of establishing community and unity. In Scripture, *koinonia* is not only translated as fellowship but also as partnership:

> I always pray with joy because of your *partnership* in the gospel.
> Philippians 1:4–5, emphasis added

Shared feelings, giving and receiving, equality and reciprocity all characterize *koinonia*. It encourages, nurtures, comforts, and affirms:

> If you have any encouragement from being united with Christ, if any comfort from his love, if any *fellowship* with the Spirit, if any tenderness and compassion, then make my joy complete by being like-minded.
> Philippians 2:1–2, emphasis added

Moreover, the word *koinonia,* translated as "participation," expresses the meaning of the Lord's Table—"Is not the cup . . . the bread that we break a *participation* in the body of Christ" (1 Cor. 10:16). Translated as *contribution,* it is used in reference to giving financial help to the Christians in Jerusalem (Rom. 15:26). Other renderings include "sharing" and "communion."

Koinonia is conducted in an informal, relaxed, family atmosphere. It flourishes in a forgiving community: "Be kind and compassionate to one another, forgiving each other, just as in Christ

God forgave you" (Eph. 4:32). Touching—greeting someone with a handshake or a hug, affirming someone with a pat on the back—is a nonverbal means of expressing *koinonia*. *Koinonia* addresses the needs of those who are "hurting, lonely, who find it hard to trust others and God."[9] It is epitomized in the Pauline metaphor of the church as a living body in which each person is a full participant, ministering and receiving ministry:

> Its parts should have equal concern for each other. If one part suffers, every part suffers with it; if one part is honored, every part rejoices with it.
>
> 1 Corinthians 12:25–26

Koinonia recognizes a plurality of leadership and exercises the gifts of the spirit for the common good:

> When you come together, everyone has a hymn or a word of instruction, a revelation, a tongue or an interpretation. All of these must be done for the strengthening of the church.
>
> 1 Corinthians 14:26

Most naturally expressed in small, intimate groups, *koinonia* is where maximum participation prevails.

Leitourgia

In *leitourgia* (i.e., worship or service), a larger group is often envisioned, as the many address the One in "vertical" praise and prayer responses. *Leitourgia* presents the public face of the church to the world and itself. The word *leitourgia* is used in the New Testament when the *group* of leaders at the church of Antioch were worshiping together with Paul and Barnabas:

> While they were *worshiping* [ministering to] the Lord and fasting, the Holy Spirit said, "Set apart for me Barnabas and Saul for the work to which I have called them."
>
> Acts 13:2, emphasis added

Leitourgia is also used in reference to Moses, Zacharias, and Christ carrying out priestly service, ministry, or "liturgy":

> He [Moses] sprinkled with the blood both the tabernacle and everything used in its *ceremonies* (Heb. 9:21, emphasis added).

149

And it came about, when the days of his [Zacharias's] *priestly service* were ended, that he went back home (Luke 1:23 NASB, emphasis added).

But the *ministry* Jesus has received is as superior to theirs as the covenant of which he is mediator is superior to the old one, and it is founded on better promises (Heb. 8:6, emphasis added).

We do have such a high priest [Christ], who sat down at the right hand of the throne of the Majesty in heaven, and who *serves* in the sanctuary, the true tabernacle (Heb. 8:1–2, emphasis added).

In these verses tasks are performed on behalf of the people before the Lord.[10]

Relating to a life of service, *leitourgia* also expresses sacrificial help rendered by one person to another—in this case Epaphroditus to Paul:

> . . . because he [Epaphroditus] almost died for the work of Chirst, risking his life to make up for the *help* you could not give me [Paul].
> Philippians 2:30, emphasis added

Of the three modes, *leitourgia* is the most comprehensive and climactic. It is "the summit toward which the activity of the Church is directed. . . . For the goal of apostolic works is that all . . . should come together to praise God . . . and to eat [observe] the Lord's supper."[11] The most integrative of the three modes, *leitourgia* involves everyone; whereas *kerygma* especially activates the specialized communicators, and *koinonia* galvanizes the people in "one-to-another" sharing. While each mode affects the other, in a unique sense, *leitourgia* both includes and subsumes *kerygma* and *koinonia*. That is, aspects of *kerygma* and *koinonia* may be integrated into its expression.

The Issue of Sequence

The three modes are also sequentially interdependent. *Kerygma* is foundational to the other two modes: "no one can lay any foundation other than the one already laid, which is Jesus Christ" (1 Cor. 3:11). *He* is foundational. What believers share in Christ makes true *koinonia* possible. Without *kerygma,* there can be no *koinonia*. The apostle John states it with authority:

We proclaim to you what we have seen and heard, so that you also may have *fellowship* with us. And our *fellowship* is with the Father and with his Son, Jesus Christ.

1 John 1:3–4, emphasis added

What could be clearer? "Our fellowship is with the Father and with his Son, Jesus Christ." And only when *koinonia* between individuals is established can true *leitourgia* be acceptably offered to God. Without *koinonia*, we can't have *leitourgia*. The instructions of the Lord Jesus to us graphically emphasize the identical point in the strongest possible terms:

Therefore, if you are offering your gift at the altar and there remember that your brother has something against you, leave your gift there in front of the altar. First go and be reconciled to your brother; then come and offer your gift.

Matthew 5:23–24

This is not easy! But again, what could be clearer? Are we really listening? The picture is unmistakable: No gospel and no fellowship yield no authentic worship. One follows the other. In other words, *no kerygma—no koinonia—no leitourgia*. Far and away this is the most crucial principle in this book. *The centrality of the Lord Jesus Christ to everything we do can never, never be overemphasized.*

Consider further Joseph Gelineau's insightful observation: "It is probably no accident that Acts put *koinonia* before the prayers and the breaking of bread."[12] Here is the verse:

They devoted themselves to the apostles' *teaching* and to the *fellowship [koinonia]*, to the breaking of bread and to prayer.

Acts 2:42, emphasis added

For Dietrich Bonhoeffer, too, the passage "is no accident, for fellowship always springs from the Word [teaching] and finds its goal and completion in the Lord's Supper. The whole common life of the Christian fellowship oscillates between Word and Sacrament." For Bonhoeffer, Word-fellowship-sacrament corresponds to *kerygma-koinonia-leitourgia*. Many evangelicals have not looked at the passage this way.

Yet the sequence has immense practical significance. Reforms in public worship without reference to *kerygma* and *koinonia* are certain to be superficial. Dependence on aesthetics results in a church that "celebrates itself more than it celebrates God,"[13] a church that "worships worship." Changes in the order or style of worship, though highly significant, can deliver only so much by and of themselves. Our mutual grounding in Christ Jesus is what gives rise to authentic fellowship and worship.[14]

> He who abides in Me, and I in him, bears much fruit; for without Me you can do nothing.
>
> John 15:5 NKJV

The Issue of Priority

A growing number of evangelical pastors, musicians, theologians, and researchers of worship are taking the view that worship should receive priority over teaching, evangelism, and fellowship. This seems to be a relatively new emphasis for evangelicals. Let's listen to what these leaders have to say. What place should worship have in the overall ministry of the church?

Bruce Leafblad writes, "If God comes first in our lives and first in our churches, then worship must come ahead of everything else we do. Worship is that process in which we make God first in our lives."[15] He reasons as follows:

1. The great commandment—"Love the Lord your God with all your heart" and "your neighbor as yourself" (Luke 10:27)—puts the love of God first.
2. Our referents for God describe him in terms of worship. The biblical words for God—both the Hebrew word *Elohim* and the Greek word *Theos*—mean "an object of worship."
3. Worship is a priority in the Old Testament. The first four commandments of the Decalogue have to do with worship (Exod. 20), and one of the chief struggles of the Old Testament prophets was to keep Israel's worship uncorrupted from foreign gods.
4. The Westminster Shorter Catechism answers the question, "What is the chief end of man?" with, "To glorify God and enjoy Him forever."
5. Worship is the central issue in the book of Revelation. When teaching and evangelism are ended in heaven, worship continues.[16]

Jack Hayford also places worship before fellowship and evangelism: "Our first sacrifice ought to be the sacrifice of praise . . . our first work ought to be the humbling of ourselves in His presence."[17] He sees evangelism as a "by-product . . . nourished through worship and fellowship"[18] and views worship "as a key to the release of the Church's power":

> We present ourselves in worship purposing to provide a place for God to make an entrance among us, to shape us, to work among us and through us.
> God's revealed will in calling His people together [in worship] is that they might experience His presence and power—not as a spectacle or sensation, but in a discovery of His will through encounter and impact. . . .
> I am troubled because, for the most part, believers gathering for worship generally do not expect God to be present in a distinct and profound way or do anything especially discernible. He [God] wants a place to display His presence, His love, His power, and *Himself.*[19]

Hayford's priorities are clear. Ministry to the Lord comes first, then ministry to the saints, and finally ministry to the world.[20]

Wayne Peterson, a layman, echoes these ideas. He asked me, "Barry, has anyone put forward the thought that perhaps worship was intended not only to bless God but to be the means by which the Holy Spirit is to empower us for ministry? Doesn't true worship direct our focus and center our lives in the Father? If true worship is so chronically absent in the evangelical church, could this be the root of our failure to live holy lives, to serve, and evangelize? If contact with God energizes us, should not worship be our primary energizing contact?"[21]

On the other hand, Ronald Allen and Gordon Borror place the stress on balance—*parity rather than priority.* They visualize worship, edification, and evangelism the following way: (1) love God, (2) love one another, (3) love the world.[22] God, they insist, must be at the center, or we will fall out of balance.

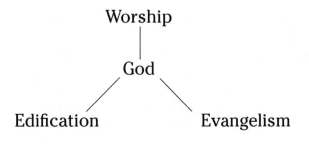

In true evangelical fashion, Hustad disagrees with the emphases of Leafblad and Hayford. He does not see the issue of priority as a productive question:

> Worship is any and every worthy response to God. There is no point to a question raised by some evangelicals, whether it is more important to "express adoration of God" or to "witness and evangelize" in our communal gatherings. One act gives corporate voice to our inner commitment; the other is our outward expression of our love and obedience to Christ's second great command, "You shall love your neighbor as yourself" (Mark 12:31).[23]

Another angle with which to look at this issue is to see what kinds of churches are growing. Five typologies lend themselves to church growth, according to Daniel Reeves and Ronald Jenson:

1. Soul-winning churches
2. Classroom churches (forty minutes of expository preaching)
3. Life-situation churches (meeting needs, emphasizing fellowship)
4. Special-purpose churches (charismatic leader; single issue dominates)
5. General practitioner churches (equal attention to evangelism, teaching, relationships, and social action)[24]

Moreover, they believe that charismatics are growing rapidly because "they have learned how to praise." Praise "unlocks all sorts of potential in people" by building into congregations "a positive attitude toward God."[25]

In summary, evangelicals clearly differ on the issue of priority. My greatest concern is that none of these emphases—evangelism, fellowship, worship—be neglected. We must insist on a balanced church! I hold that the music ministry can and should serve them all. I would like to see worship receive parity with evangelism—and evangelism with worship!

Worship: No One Definition Will Suffice

After noting the different emphases in the worship definitions by Leafblad and Hustad, it's obvious that no one definition can completely suffice. So I will conclude by suggesting definitions that emphasize the physical dimension of Christian worship, continuing to differentiate authentic worship from the cosmetic.

The worship definitions of both Leafblad and Hustad are short and memorable. They strongly relate worship to all of life, not just Sunday morning worship, and strike valuable yet different emphases:

Worship is that process in which we make God first in our lives.

Worship is any and every worthy response to God.

William Temple's attitudinal definition, on the other hand, offers more specific guidance and powerfully invokes reflection.

To worship is to quicken the conscience by the holiness of God, to feed the mind with the truth of God, to purge the imagination with the beauty of God, to devote the will to the purpose of God.[26]

Memorize that—it will be extremely helpful! Are any of these purposes being accomplished in your corporate worship?

Yet it could conceivably apply to other religions. Ralph P. Martin's trinitarian construction, though more objective and theological, brings out the uniqueness of *Christian* worship:

Christian worship is the adoration and service of God the Father through the mediation of the Son and prompted by the Holy Spirit.[27]

Each of these definitions can serve to guide us away from shallow conceptions of Christian worship. If you use slides or overheads, consider displaying a variety of worship definitions during the prelude as people prepare for worship. Here's one last definition of worship:

The outpouring of a soul at rest in the presence of the Eternal God.

The Primary Word for Worship Is Gestural

Another emphasis can orient us away from the superficial and the cosmetic. It's an area where evangelicals are chronically weak. The symbolism of the body can powerfully point toward authentic worship. In fact, the primary word that defines worship in the Old Testament makes explicit reference to the body.

Shachad, translated "worship" in the NASB eighty-one times, means literally to "bow" politely or respectfully, to "prostrate oneself," to "make obeisance," or to "bend low."[28] Worship has a profound physical dimension in Hebrew culture. It "emphasizes the way in which an Israelite fittingly thought of his approach to the holy presence of God. He bows himself down in lowly reverence

155

and prostration."[29] Prostration means to touch one's nose to the "ground" (see Gen. 42:6), a gesture representing *absolute submission*—hardly cosmetic worship![30] The Old Testament word for *worship* is not primarily propositional; it is visual, gestural, attitudinal, and often involves the relinquishing of rights.

Proskuneo, its Greek counterpart in the New Testament (translated "worship" fifty-one times in the NASB), has the same basic meaning with the same overtones of "submissive lowliness and deep respect." *Pros* means "to turn toward," and *kuneo* means "to kiss." Kissing involves closeness, intimacy, as in kissing the feet (prostration), the hands, or the cheek. We simply cannot do better than to meditate on these words. To worship is to fall down before God and to serve him.

> O come, let us worship and bow down: let us kneel before the LORD our Maker. For he is our God; and we are . . . the sheep of his hand.
>
> Psalm 95:6–7 KJV

The dominant prayer posture in the book of Revelation is prostration. For example, the apostle John sees Jesus Christ and falls down in worship:

> Among the lampstands was someone "like a son of man" . . . His head and hair were white like wool, as white as snow, and his eyes were like blazing fire. . . . When I saw him, *I fell at his feet* as though dead.
>
> Revelation 1:13–14, emphasis added

Hardly a superficial act! Another Old Testament word, *abodah,* is translated as "worship" (thirteen times in the NASB); it means to "serve" or "work." Its Greek equivalents, *latreia* and *latreuo,* are translated as "worship" (six times) and "service" (twenty times) in the NASB.[31] *Latreia* also makes explicit reference to the body in this well-known passage:

> I urge you therefore, brethren, by the mercies of God, to present your bodies a living and holy sacrifice, acceptable to God, which is your spiritual *service of worship.*
>
> Romans 12:1 NASB, emphasis added

Worship involves all of life. Sacrificing ourselves for the flock and extending ourselves for our families is a demonstration of authentic worship. Are you motivated to serve?

156

The Hebrew root *yad,* used for many praise expressions, also refers to the body. The lengthened form of *yad, yadah,* means "to throw, to cast, or to shoot." It means "to worship with extended hands, to throw out the hands, to give thanks to God."[32] *Yadah,* the second most frequently used word for praise, occurs ninety times in reference to praise and is translated in the King James Version as "praise" (fifty-three times), "give thanks" (thirty-two), "confess" (sixteen), and "thank" (five).[33] Given this frequency of scriptural usage, we must conclude that worship involving the body must be as meaningful as verbal proclamation. In the chart below, it is clear that the gestural pair of words *(shachad* and *proskuneo)* occur more frequently than the propositional pair *(abodah* and *latreia).*

Hebrew and Greek Words for Worship and Praise Accent the Physical

Word	*Frequency*	*Meaning*
Shachad (Heb.)	81	to bow, prostrate
Proskuneo (Gr.)	51	to turn toward, kiss
Abodah (Heb.)	13	to serve, work
Latreia, Latreuo (Gr.)	26	to serve, worship
Yadah (Heb.)	90	to throw out the hand

A Comprehensive Worship

When individuals worship comprehensively, both verbally and gesturally, worship takes on an added dimension and significance from a psychological standpoint:

> Meaning involving several senses is obviously more vital than meaning involving only one.... Normally, the meaning of a thing thought is less powerful than the meaning of a thing heard, which in turn is less powerful than the meaning of a thing seen as well as heard.[34]

Ultimately, God will require a comprehensive form of worship. Worship expression involving "seeing" and "hearing" will be unmistakably clear and integrative, involving both symbolic and verbal communication:

> That at the name of Jesus every *knee* should bow,
> in heaven and on earth and under the earth,
> and every *tongue* confess that Jesus Christ is Lord,
> to the glory of God the Father.
> Philippians 2:10–11, emphasis added

157

Worship in heaven eschews anything suggesting the cosmetic. It encompasses the total person. Heavenly worship clarifies that *kerygma,* foundational to worship, merges with the symbolic.[35] Both knees and tongues preach and proclaim.

> Almighty One! I bend in dust before Thee;
> Even so veiled cherubs bend;
> In calm and still devotion I adore thee,
> All-wise, all-present Friend.[36]

The Issue of Compatability

Is it possible for evangelism and worship to be combined in the same service? Can non-Christians find worship attractive? I believe so. Worship strikes a longing chord in all humans everywhere. It's built into us: all nations and tribes worship in some manner. We have witnessed this coupling of worship and evangelism in churches for decades, and Hayford's church is one where individuals find Christ as Savior at the conclusion of what is a true worship service. Hayford believes "vibrant worship is the key to vital evangelism."[37] Note: *vibrant* worship!

The term "worship evangelism" expresses this approach.[38] Sally Morgenthaler commends the Willow Creek Church for their commitment to excellence and cultural relevance in their seeker services, but she asks what would happen if churches applied their dogged, whatever-it-takes-we'll-do-it attitude to worship services?[39] Good question. The success of the Willow Creek Church is partly due to sheer hard work and commitment.

Though worship and evangelism may be combined, I'll argue in the next chapter that the *communication systems* of worship and evangelism services are different. Let's have a look at that. But again, don't view *kerygma, koinonia,* and *leitourgia* as necessarily antithetical. Paul says that as the people testify during the act of worship, the unsaved person may be "convinced by all that he is a sinner . . . [and] fall down and worship God" (1 Cor. 14:24–25). Harold Best puts it cogently, "Witness is overheard worship."[40] Evangelicals must maintain their most significant distinctives, their passion for evangelism and foreign missions. *Leitourgia* includes service of this kind. A blend between seeker-sensitive services and more traditional formats *is* possible.

Questions for Reflection and Discussion

1. Is *koinonia* worship more naturally expressed in small groups? Explain.
2. What is the significance of no *kerygma*—no *koinonia*—no *leitourgia?*
3. Have you any reservations with the Pass church model? Explain.
4. Can musical instruments express *kergyma?* How?
5. Compose your own definition of worship. Share why you framed it that way.
6. Why is it important for musicians to have a biblically balanced view of the church?

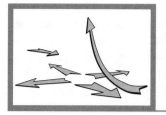

The Look of Music in Evangelism, Fellowship, and Worship

Music is the most context-friendly of the arts. It attaches itself quickly, spongelike, to whatever surrounds it. And by repetition, it is eventually perceived to equate with the context.

Harold M. Best
Music through the Eyes of Faith

The *Kerygma*-Dominated Worship Service

What does the service look like when one-way *kerygma* communication predominates and overrides the whole? What are the outcomes of *kerygma* communication?

By itself, the concept has both strengths and flaws relative to worship. On the negative side, *kerygma* does not tend to result in a true worship service per se. On the plus side, great motivation and integrity can emerge in the act of proclaiming the truth.

Kerygma tends to result in a strong performance orientation. The pastor comes to preach, the soloists and choirs to sing, the instrumentalists to play, and the organist to render a prelude, offertory, and postlude. Skilled staff members lead public prayer, read the Scriptures, take the offering, and make the announcements. The look of excellence and professionalism pervades the service as it unfolds dramatically—there is a script (order of service) and a performance of that script. The people face forward: factors such as lighting and "staging" may receive attention. A Max Lucado reading or reader's theater could occur. The intention is to engage the visitor and the church member totally.

However, a performance orientation also brings with it a passive "audience mentality." The people come to listen and receive a *kerygma* communication. As in a formal concert, everything is done *to* them. In *kerygma* services, more often than not, the people are entertainment-oriented. The order of service is impeccably laid out but without overwhelming detail; and the service, smooth and efficient, contentful and stimulating, begins and ends on time. The people (including guests) witness the proceedings in relative anonymity; interaction between them tends to be cordial but formal.

Kerygma communication, it appears, is more suited to evangelism or a classroom-teaching service than a true worship service. Because they have a professional look, *kerygma* services do not embarrass either the inviter or the invitee. In the *kerygma* communication model, the concept of response to God is not at the forefront, is not articulated as a goal by the leadership, and is not well perceived or well practiced by those present (especially guests).

Head musicians often function more as music directors than worship directors. The drive for high performance standards and the selection of music of the highest quality occupies their attention. The response of the people in congregational song is not a top priority—the organist and choir and other musicians can carry it. In their passivity, many people mumble or do not sing at all. When the people leave they talk about what they got from the service, how they were inspired, and how well the pastor, choir, and musicians performed.

Not all of these features characterize all churches employing the *kerygma* model Sunday mornings. But clearly, the *kerygmatic* model typifies *many* middle- to large-sized Protestant churches.

Kerygmatic *Music*

How can church music be related to *kerygma?* To help our understanding, let's first consider its communication system in the act of preaching (see figure on page 171). In the Sunday morning preaching, the pastor stands before the people and proclaims the Word. The people listen to a formal address in a formal setting. Due to his seminary training; his "calling"; his specialized knowledge of Greek, Hebrew, and theology; and his giftedness in the art of communication, he is uniquely credentialed, set apart, and paid to perform this service. With an acute sense of that calling, he exegetes the passage, consults commentaries, gathers illustrations, and prayerfully delivers a message in which he stands as God's representative speaking God's words boldly to the people. An implied hierarchy informs the event. Few if any in the congregation could replicate his sermon in terms of its quality and authority.

Can music-making correspond to the act of preparing and delivering such a sermon? Yes, very closely. Think of the music specialists as tied in with or alongside the pulpit—in fact, choirs are often positioned right behind the pulpit.

Musicians can preach and proclaim with the same sense of high calling as pastors. Clearly, the concert format—where a soloist, specialized group, or choir performs monodirectionally to an audience—corresponds closely to the pastor's format. Due to their training and talent, soloists and choirs are expected to perform pieces at a difficulty level the congregation would not attempt and with a precision the people cannot attain. They, too, have their specialized music scores they've learned to read. What they deliver in music quality and innovation cannot be replicated by the listening congregation.

One of the most beneficial insights that Pass's model uniquely captures is that it is precisely in the mode of *kerygmatic* communication that *a convincing rationale for the role of the choir* can be established. That is, Pass argues that choirs function best when they "address the congregation *kerygmatically.* "[1] Choirs are meant to be listened to and their message can have prophetic impact. Their specialized abilities in innovation, in performing a diversity of styles, and in embellishing the text are meant to be heard. This goal is best realized when they are used as "specialists," when they are functioning in a hierarchical setting, when they are freestanding and unencumbered from involving the congregation in their music-making process. This implies a certain *separation* from the congregation. The choir performs; the audience listens and interprets the meaning of the music. Thus freed, a greater diversity of style and genre in performance is naturally expected from the choir.

But this needs to be stated yet more strongly if we are to catch the attitude of Scripture toward *kerygma* communication. Boldly stated, *whatever* style communicates the gospel should be acceptable, so that, as Paul says, "by all possible means" we "might save some" (1 Cor. 9:22). It follows, then, that the faithful should be taught to accept styles or service formats somewhat unusual or even uncomfortable on *kerygma*/evangelism Sundays in order to win the nonchurched with a service relevant to their cultural inclinations.

Moreover, *kerygma* need not be narrowly defined as confrontation only. Choirs express the full range of human emotions. They can both confront *and* comfort. But the point is that they do so supremely when they retain their separate voice in the communication setting of "the one to the many." In *koinonia* music, characterized by equality and reciprocity, a choir's specialized abilities may not be as fully utilized. (What has been spoken here concerning choirs could apply to any other specialized performance groups—orchestra, contemporary band, bell choir, quartet, trio, etc.). The vocal solo is also a powerful means of communication and often is placed just before the sermon for maximum effect. Preferably, the congregational tunes chosen will already be known by the guests (e.g., Bunessan Gaelic melody of "Morning Has Broken") or easily learned.

Another point in favor of musical "specialists" is that choirs, soloists, and instrumentalists can contribute to the *richness* of expression that Paul advocates—"let the word of Christ dwell in you *richly*" (Col. 3:16). Recent research has revealed that words sung are processed differently in the brain than the same words spoken or preached.[2] This different processing results in different kinds of knowing, perceiving, and experiencing.

Music does not diminish faith! Rather, the multidimensional medium of music enriches and extends the communication of *kerygma, koinonia,* and *leitourgia* to multiple levels of human perception. Through music, *kerygma* (objective truth) is related to color (timbre, resonance), to space (sound movement, localization), to movement (choreographed hand movements), to time (clock and psychological time, proportion/mathematics, altered states of consciousness), to drama, and to specialized forms of language (poetry).

Moreover, it is precisely the *fundamentals* of the faith that need continual reinforcement. They need to be brought home with fervor repeatedly. Specialized music performers can do this in endlessly interesting ways. Let all the techniques of art serve content.

164

The *Koinonia*-Dominated Worship Service

If the *kerygmatic* service resembles a concert, the *koinonia* service resembles a TV talk show. It's a hands-on service. To learn something about *koinonia* service possibilities, study the techniques (not content!) used in talk shows.[3] The brightest minds are paid to devise ways to draw the maximum share of the market.[4] The *koinonia* service could feature open sharing from the entire congregation utilizing a wireless roving mike. No one person overtly predominates; communication is omnidirectional. People dress informally. A happy, family atmosphere prevails as people enter the service. If a music prelude is being played on tape or by live performers, the people talk to one another until called to order. (A sense of reverence may be lacking as the service begins.) A detailed order of service is not printed because much of the service features improvised interaction. The public prayers, Scripture readings, and the announcements are usually performed by the people. The people might be seated in a half or full circle and share prayer requests, or they might break up into small groups and pray for one another. Frequently there is no choir. The pastor, usually not wearing a robe, comes up from the audience and delivers the sermon. In black churches the sermon is a cooperative effort. The people interact spontaneously with affirming and inspiring amens and responses throughout the sermon. In liturgical churches, when the people come forward for communion, they may line up at the railing, their hands placed on each other's shoulders, emphasizing togetherness.

Concerned with meeting people's needs, some traditional churches have developed the concept of "ministry time." One pastor describes its function within their "traditional" format:

> Apart from the sermon, it is the single most significant thing that happens in our morning worship service. Ministry time is different from an "altar call." There is a process that goes on. There is a sharing of the need—a finding out of the need, before the praying and laying on of hands by the team member(s). The ministry team becomes involved. There are other benefits to our service from "ministry time." On the pastor's side, it breaks down the "Thou-I" distinction between the pulpit and the people. It allows for a body-feeling in the service. On the people's side it allows an opportunity for a one-on-one encounter. Most importantly, it has strengthened the faith of our entire congregation as our people have seen God work in answer to prayer.

165

In Jack Hayford's "Church on the Way," the people split up into small groups of three or four and pray for one another during the middle of the morning worship service for three or four minutes. In other churches, ministry time is effectively placed at the conclusion of the service.

A Lutheran pastor explains how a ministry time "healing service" was instituted in his church. Fearful that it might be perceived as "kooky," he prepared the way with an article in the church bulletin defining healing in a broad way (i.e., body, mind, and spirit). He related to me:

> That first Sunday I preached a cautious sermon on how God heals in different ways, using the Greek word *soteria* (salvation-health) as the central thought. Then my assistant and I invited people to come forward to the altar railing for prayer. To my complete surprise, 95 percent of the 275 people present came forward! Our healing service is now one of our most popular services. A team of eight ministers and people invite their friends and neighbors. Total strangers have come forward. The service occurs regularly on the fifth Sunday of the month (four or five times a year), and we print a clarifying statement in the church bulletin for that day.

Another possibility is to have a short sermon, the Lord's Table, and then a time of congregational sharing utilizing a roving mike. After communion, the people seem particularly disposed to sharing personally.

Koinonia worship tends to have a strong ministry orientation; a less professional look; and may involve small groups, employ improvisational procedures, and be led by leaders with a concern to be spirit-directed. *Koinonia* worship is done *for* the people. A primary question the people ask is, "Did I give and receive ministry?"

Koinonia *Music*

Koinonia music tends to be more congregational. Pass admits: "Very little true *koinonia* church music" is composed by great composers.[5] It is usually produced by ordinary ministers who love their people and know what it is like to sing congregationally. Congregational texts that are clearly *koinonia* include "We Are One in the Bond of Love," "Blest Be the Tie That Binds," "Sweet Perfume," "We Are One in the Spirit," "Song of Community" (Mark Hayes), "We Are God's People" (Leech), and "In Christ There Is No East or West." *Koinonia* music comforts, affirms, promotes unity.

166

Beyond specific examples of music, however, a larger point needs to be made: the act of music-making itself is inherently *koinonian.* For example, hymns unify congregations. Part of the definition of a hymn is its unifying capacity.

But let me explain in more detail. As music groups keep to the tempo, perform rhythms, accelerandos, retardandos, rubatos, crescendos, decrescendos, build phrases, breathe together, and artfully blend their voices in harmony, such a collaboration of mind and spirit is required and such an intensity of listening and responding to each other is drawn out of individuals that a baseline for *koinonia* experience is virtually established. Furthermore, *improvising* in an ensemble—like a four-way telephone conversation—requires extra sensitivity because performers, if they are not careful, can easily "talk over" each other, clutter the texture, or overplay instead of waiting for the appropriate moment to make "fills."

This precise reciprocal nature of the ensemble relationship led James I. Packer to exclaim, "The best representation of New Testament *koinonia* I know of is New Orleans Jazz. Everybody gets a chance to solo, and when they come together—it's magic, a real oneness. Unity-in-diversity. No one person predominates."[6] My guess is that it would be hard to play New Orleans Jazz superbly and not feel affection for the other performers. First Corinthians 14:26 is the biblical model for this kind of activity.

Moreover, while *kerygma* communication inherently delineates a *separation* between the performer and the audience, *koinonia* communication *brings the performer closer to the listener.* For example, the worship leader, a soloist, or specialized group (without robes) may sing the verse and invite the congregation to respond on the refrain by singing, humming, or clapping on beats two and four. Or the performer may "call out" to the audience during a piece, inviting an echoing response from the people. Or the performer(s) may sway to the beat, inviting the people to sway also or link hands across rows. Sometimes the performer walks into the audience and sings and plays there. Or, utilizing multiple locations in the lower sanctuary and balcony, the brass group or the choir can establish a connection with the audience by their physical presence there. The leader may also call for "favorites" from the people.

167

In some Alaskan churches, when the "favorite" is sung, the person who requested it stands, and the song is sung as a means of personally ministering to that person. This is not much different from David's ministering therapeutically to Saul. All these examples are ways of establishing relationships and ministering. Descants and rounds can further establish relationships between sectors of the congregation itself.

In the above cases, the music text itself may not have specific *koinonia* content, but the structure of the performance presents these values. *Koinonia* music is by nature free-flowing, user-friendly, and culturally relevant in style. In western music, *koinonia* melodies, technically speaking, will have curved rather than angular shapes. Simple harmonies may be evident. In complex music, *koinonia* textures may contain intertwining suspensions, emotional appoggiaturas; and the soft resonances of added seconds, fourths, sevenths, and ninths may replace straight triads and the bolder dominant seventh chord. Dissonant seconds in third inversion seventh chords may suggest pain. "Tension" notes in complex chords may be brought out, and inner chromatic lines may be evident.

Music may also serve *koinonia* activities in an accompaniment role. While ministry time is occurring or prayers are being offered, the people may be softly singing or instruments playing.

The *Leitourgia* Worship Service

Recall that *leitourgia* is the most comprehensive and integrative of the modes: it includes and subsumes *kerygma* and *koinonia.* It is the most satisfactory form for obtaining true worship. In *leitourgia,* the many address the One; praise and prayer are directed "to God." That is its primary sense. Foundational concepts in Old Testament worship support this orientation. In more than one hundred references in the Psalms, worshipers sing "to" the Lord. In another one hundred references, the people are described as "approaching" and appearing "before" the Lord. A strong dialogical nature is also characteristic of the service: God speaks to us, and we respond to him.

In *leitourgia,* the people want God; they wait on God. There is reverence and silence. In the *kerygma*-dominated service, the congregation sings *about* God; in the *leitourgia* service, the congregation sings *to* God.[7] This is costly worship, marked by a strong desire to respond with the total person. More time is given for worship, and the sermon length may be shorter than in the *kerygma*-dominated service.

In this type of worship, leaders see to it that the people have an active role. There may be prayers of confession, of adoration, guided prayers, "bidding" prayers. Prayer requests may be read from the pulpit area, but all actively engage in the intercessory prayer. Hands may be lifted in prayer; eyes may look up to God; knees may bow before God. Multiple passages of Scripture may be read by the people, from the pulpit, or in the audience, and a creed recited or sung. A reader's theater could occur. Communion is often practiced more frequently. Worshipers most likely follow a rudimentary order of service.

Leitourgia is usually large-group worship, and it tends to require more vision, more drama, more mystery, and more symbolism.[8] Whereas *kerygma* is done *to* the people, and *koinonia* is *for* the people, *leitourgia* is primarily response *by* the people.[9] The primary question the people ask themselves is, "Did I meet with God?" Secondary questions the people ask are: "What thought did I get from the service?" and, "Did I give and receive ministry?"

Leitourgia *Music*

Leitourgia music is directed to God, emphasizes prayer and praise, and tends to be group dominated. In an evocative passage, Joseph Gelineau expresses a powerful vision of worship music:

> [It is] music not necessarily new and surprising in its language, not necessarily too difficult to perform, but so suited to what it is celebrating that it would be an inexhaustible source of prayer, meaning and feeling. . . . A music that was not full of itself but the bearer of silence and worship as Mary bore the incarnate Word.[10]

What evocative thoughts—"a music that was not full of itself," a music that would be "an inexhaustible source of prayer, meaning and feeling." Also, what about the meaning of his phrase, "the bearer of silence and worship"? How provocative!

Nicholas Temperley also has something to say along these lines about hymns. "Hymns," he says, "exist for the singers, not for an audience, still less for a critic."[11] Whereas in *kerygma* a separation exists where the choir performs and the people listen and interpret, in *leitourgia* the people both perform and interpret. The meaning of the hymn is interpreted by the performing congregation and their bodies are the musical instruments.

Because hymns and choruses exist for the congregation, it is time that we devoted more energy to the congregational choir, more care to cultivating a full-bodied response. This involves sitting down and thinking through *all* the details that can help improve that response. I agree with Paul Westermeyer that the title "cantor" (from "cantare," meaning "to sing"), which refers to the chief singer/leader of the people in song, is valuable because it underscores the primary obligation of the director of music or worship. He is correct in noting, "There is both a symbolic and a practical value in being called what you are."[12]

In *leitourgia* we often tend to undervalue the importance of the congregation's song and their capacity (collectively) to minister powerfully to one another and to God. Most congregations are capable of singing much better and of being more open to learning new hymns and new choruses. Many congregations, however, are resistant to unfamiliar songs and styles. We can, though, find ways to make the learning process less threatening, and even enjoyable (see chapter 7).

I find that congregations will readily warm up to Hebrew and other ethnic melodies and accompaniments. If we are gentle and loving in our presentation, the people will also take to choreographed hand movements that bring out the meaning of the lyrics and focus attention on God. Congregations can be exciting to work with—more open to change and innovation than we tend to give them credit for, provided adequate preparation is taken in thinking through the process required to advance them.

As for the choir and specialized groups, Pass rightly notes the differentiation of *leitourgia* from *kerygma.* In *kerygma* the choir and congregation are more separate, whereas in *leitourgia,* "the choir joins the congregation as an indivisible part of that congregation in its prayerful and praiseful address of God."[13] For this reason, in many liturgical churches the choir is positioned to face

What Transpires during Worship Services

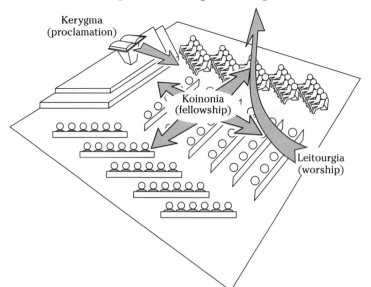

each other in right angles to the side of the pulpit—or even placed in the balcony, out of the view of the people. In *kerygma*-dominant situations, the choir is often centered behind the pulpit; positionally this emphasizes their declarative function. *Kerygma* is performer oriented; *leitourgia*, participant oriented. *Kerygma* emphasizes specialized groups, while *leitourgia* includes specialized groups but underscores the nonspecialized group: the congregation.

In *leitourgia* worship services we want a richness and variety of expression that reflects the character of God and of his Son, Jesus Christ. Let us have moments of transcendent majesty and of adoration and intimacy. Turn the choir loose! Turn the congregation loose! Turn the soloists, the bands loose! Turn the preacher loose! But most of all, let us meet God!

How Do These Modes Relate to Biblical Models of Worship?

Of the biblical models of worship, the synagogue comes closest to *kerygma.* Corinthian or Pauline worship most closely images *koinonia* worship. Tabernacle or temple worship and worship in the Book of Revelation best express *leitourgia* worship. None of the biblical models contain any one mode in its pure form; combinations and different weightings of each occur. The same should also be true in our churches; this is why I chose the terms "*kerygma*-dominated" and "*koinonia*-dominated" in my earlier headings.

The local church's mission is to incarnate all three modes "regularly, creatively, systematically, and carefully."[14] Each church will have its own mix that may change from Sunday morning to Sunday morning. And services and activities at other times during the week, inside or outside the church building, can address the imbalance. We need to seek balance over a period of time, however, for imbalance results in impoverishment. Preferably, all three modes will be functioning to some extent in a true worship service. When this occurs, a sense of *dialogue* emerges. God speaks to us, and we respond to him. The entire figure on page 171, then, models the *leitourgia* mode. Recall that *leitourgia* includes and subsumes *kerygma* and *koinonia*. I want to underscore this quality of dialogue as essential!

Summary of *Kerygma, Koinonia,* and *Leitourgia* Music

Kerygma *Music*	Koinonia *Music*	Leitourgia *Music*
proclaims forgiveness through Jesus Christ	communicates belonging	celebrates God and his presence with us
call to faith, discipleship	call to love, care	call to pray, praise
confronts with message	comforts the people	praises and petitions God
soloist, specialized group to congregation	semi- or nonspecialized group to congregation	both specialized group and congregation to God
hierarchical relationship	egalitarian relationship	integrative relationship
boldness	warmth, togetherness	desolation to jubilation
formal format	informal format	formal format
people face forward	half or full circle seating	either
monodirectional	omnidirectional	bidirectional

172

one to many	one to another	God to many, many to God
one sings, all listen	all can sing, all listen	all sing, God listens
stylistically diverse (innovative)	stylistically relevant (midway)	stylistically familiar (learnable)
low replicability by audience	medium replicability	high replicability
performer and listener separate	performer and listener close	performer and listener merged
performer-oriented	relationship-oriented	participant-oriented
singing "about" God	singing to one another	singing "to" God
"A Mighty Fortress Is Our God"; "Our God Reigns"; "I Know Whom I Have Believed"; "Low in the Grave He Lay"; "Tell Me the Old, Old Story"; "Freely, Freely"; "Because He Lives" (Gaither)	"Blest Be the Tie That Binds"; "We Are One in the Spirit"; "We Are One in the Bond of Love"; "Does Jesus Care?"; "In Christ There Is No East or West"; "We Are God's People" (Leech)	"O God, Our Help in Ages Past"; "Majesty"; "All Hail the Power of Jesus' Name"; "Holy, Holy, Holy"; "Fairest Lord Jesus"; "I Love You, Lord"; "Our Great Savior"; "My Tribute"

And this is the happy life, to rejoice to Thee, of Thee, for Thee: this is it, and there is no other.

Augustine

Questions for Reflection and Discussion

1. How would you respond to this statement: "While purporting to be worship services, in reality most Protestant services are *kerygma*-dominated"?
2. Do choirs function best when they address the congregation *kerygmatically?* Explain and discuss.
3. "In *koinonia* worship no one person predominates." Explain and discuss.
4. Is *leitourgia* worship the most comprehensive and integrative of the modes? Explain.

Resolving Tensions over Musical Style: Peter

> Why is the church so reluctant to enjoy the rich variety of style, vocabulary, process, shape and medium that issues from every quarter of the globe?
>
> Harold M. Best
> *Music Through the Eyes of Faith*

The greatest revolution in the area of modern church, says Elmer Towns, is erupting in worship.[1] The worship revolution is also the source of the greatest controversy. "The music of the baby boomer generation [predominantly rock 'n roll]," writes Doug Murren of Eastside Foursquare Church in Kirkland, Washington, "is likely to dominate the culture of our society well into the next century."[2]

This chapter and the one following are devoted to reducing divisiveness over music style.

Why Is the Issue of Musical Style So Divisive?

Churches today are grappling with what is "proper" in worship. Pastors I've talked to find music to be the major, divisive issue; for some reason, music uniquely brings the issues of change to a head.[3] Why is that? My answer, colored

175

by my evangelical upbringing, will introduce some of the issues presented in this chapter.

First, we all have preferences, which is not a problem; however, we all too often *think of our self-interests first.* This reveals several truths about us: (a) we are entertainment oriented; (b) we are not mature; (c) we are not willing to die to self; (d) we don't ask the primary questions: Is the mission of the church being well served by this music? Does it advance the kingdom? If we did, we would begin walking the road toward grace and statesmanship in our sphere of influence.

Second, we *listen* to sermons, but we *perform* hymns, choruses, and anthems. Because we are personally involved—including our bodies, self-image, and even our identity—we are more sensitive. We want the music to suit *our* personality and temperament. We want to be comfortable with what we are performing.

Third, music is a language—which is another cause for divisiveness. We know some music languages better than others. For example, when we learn through repeated exposure to appreciate the meanings and nuances of a certain style of music, we have exquisitely rich, pleasurable experiences. And we want those experiences! Also when we are young, our lack of perspective frequently makes us impatient and intolerant of anything not contemporary. Then, as we become older, we somehow grow less open to acquiring new musical languages and becoming intimate with them. Both young and old need God's grace.

Fourth, some music languages offend our aesthetic sensitivities. Some styles go against the grain of our upbringing and training. For musicians, even playing with others who lack musicianship—though we know they are offering their best—can bother us. These critical feelings can undermine relationships and ministry.

Fifth, we often equate or imbue music style with moral qualities and values. Weighty point! More about this later.

Sixth, music triggers associations, good and bad. It has the ability to set our emotions vibrating; to stir unconscious, evocative memories; to awaken tender (even guilty) consciences. Rap music may suggest bad language, ghetto blasters polluting the environment, and gangs. A saxophone may evoke a dance floor or erotic feelings. A hymn may trigger memories of a loved one, a gospel song a conversion experience, a symphony a glittering "establishment" audience dressed with tuxedos and bow ties.

Seventh, what about the loud volume associated with new music? Younger people can listen to more volume than those with "menopausal ears." As one bumper sticker puts it, "If it's too loud, you're too old!"[4]

Eighth, and more deeply, music carries forward *traditions.* To tamper with these traditions is to stir up values close to the heart.

When Traditions Are in Transition

When we read the Book of Acts, we become conscious of the early church wrestling with culture. The church was being transformed from a Jewish phenomenon into a supranational body, and this was not at all easy. At first there were mighty miracles and incredible responses to preaching; but as we follow the church's development, we see objections arise and issues becoming more complex, not amenable to simple solutions. This is the life we know so well in contemporary churches. I am totally convinced, however, that if we could apply the biblical principles found in this and the next chapter, much of the infighting we experience relative to music style would dissipate.

"Much" but not all. Let's be realistic. Music style is relative (I'll support that later), not absolute, and until Jesus returns people will continue to prefer one style over another and to dispute the merits of one over another. Though some styles are more widespread than others, there is no one universal music style. The music of distant cultures can be as meaningless to us as ours is to them. But we can work on and improve our attitude and understanding.

Music style, in my opinion, falls in the area Paul calls "disputable matters." Concerning these matters, he says, "Each one should be fully convinced in his own mind" (Rom. 14:5). So the responsibility is ours. Admittedly, we are forging into difficult water. All I ask is that you give chapters 12 and 13 a fair hearing. Let iron sharpen iron.

Could I suggest a way to receive the most from this and the next chapter? Read Acts 2; 10–11; 15; Romans 14; 1 Corinthians 8–10; and Mark 7 first in the privacy of your own home or study. Ask yourself: "What could these chapters have to do with musical style?" After a week of reflection, see what perspectives this chapter adds. That way you will have your own point of orientation and can build on it or challenge it. I suspect readers will need time to think over and process the issues in this chapter. If you decide to forge ahead now, study the matter privately later.

I now invite you to feel Acts 2; 10; and 15 unfolding as a unit. See connections that can be related to music style. See real people coping and, under the inspiration of the Holy Spirit, learning to grow through live confrontations into *sensitive, nurturing individuals.* These individuals are totally inspiring! The early church underwent enormous change, and we can learn from them. Intolerance and entrenchment does not characterize their behavior.[5]

From there we will go on to ask some practical questions—What about musical style in the Old Testament? Why were instruments banned in synagogues and the early church? Is church music a functional art? Our overall method will be to set forth Scripture passages and draw out applications.

A Case for Diversity: Acts 2

The following passage from Acts 2 is the harbinger of the "church of the nations"—the contemporary church in full bloom. Luke cites more than a dozen language locations. From this outpouring of the Holy Spirit, we learn something about *the acceptability of a Pentecost of music styles.* At the end of the passage, Peter addresses the crowd, proclaiming the gospel *kerygmatically*[6] (the one to the many).

> When the day of Pentecost came, they were all together in one place. Suddenly a sound like the blowing of a violent wind came from heaven and filled the whole house where they were sitting. They saw what seemed to be tongues of fire that separated and came to rest on each of them [on their heads?]. All of them [the 12 apostles or 120 disciples?] were filled with the Holy Spirit and began to speak in other tongues as the Spirit enabled them.
>
> Now there were staying in Jerusalem God-fearing Jews [note: only Jews] from every nation under heaven. When they heard this sound, a crowd came together in bewilderment, because each one heard them speaking in his own language. Utterly amazed, they asked: ". . . How is it that each of us hears them in his own native language [dialect]? Parthians, Medes . . . ; residents of . . . Asia, . . . Egypt . . . Libya . . . ; visitors from Rome . . . ; Cretans and Arabs— we hear them declaring the wonders of God in our own tongues!" Amazed and perplexed, they asked one another, "What does this mean?" . . .
>
> Then Peter stood up with the Eleven, raised his voice and addressed the crowd: "Fellow Jews and all of you who live in Jerusalem, let me explain this to you; listen carefully to what I say. . . ."
>
> Those who accepted his message were baptized, and about three thousand were added to their number that day.[7]
>
> Acts 2:1–12, 14, 41

This multitongued Pentecost of intelligible languages (not "tongues" as the term is commonly used today) has important implications for music,[8] since musical style is tied to the nuances of language.[9] Music *tracks* language. The rhythms embedded in individual words; the pitch patterns in which people talk; the pitch glides in speech indicating surprise, disappointment, or questioning; as well as the syntactic patterns of language—all are aspects of one's native language which are intuitively "memorized" by composers. They are captured (sometimes more, sometimes less) and become meaningful parts of musical expression. Inescapably, the feel of each dialect and culture eventually becomes patternized in indigenous music.

If you listen carefully to instrumental black music, like the blues for example, you can "hear" blacks talking in the music itself, without any words. The melody mirrors the way black speech inflections are performed in everyday life.

Here is my key point. If a multilingual approach for propagating the gospel is revealed as normative in Acts 2, then a multistylistic Pentecost of music languages must necessarily follow as normative—providing missionaries and other leaders don't suppress the possibility. I don't think the church has appreciated this point sufficiently.

From the example of Acts 2, I find at least two other applications. First, local musical dialects should not be despised or avoided in the church. For example, expressions of Nashville "country music" should be allowed in American churches where that music dialect pervades local culture, just as much as a southern drawl or a Bostonian accent should be accepted in the pulpit.

And second, Acts 2 specifies fifteen languages. But at the present time, more than eighty-five language groups exist in Greater Los Angeles. Obviously, there will be significant differences in music and worship practice, not only because of the different cultures involved but also because some churches are in various stages of transitioning into American culture. We need to be sensitive to this process and these people's needs.

A *Parallel* Kerygma

Kerygmatic features are evident in this God-designed event of Pentecost. It is highly innovative (wind, fire), performance oriented ("choir" of voices), hierarchical (apostles, disciples speaking), monodirectional (Peter preaching), and confrontive ("repent and be baptized"). There is a separation between the performers and listeners. The wind sounds and the speaking in foreign languages serve to *attract* the large crowd. The speaking in native tongues makes the event *culturally relevant and personal.* Of the fifteen language locations listed, some represent small districts (Phrygia, Pamphylia)—the speaking extends to the fiber of local culture. So remarkably diverse is this amazing outpouring!

Can music and drama also function in these ways in a *kerygma* event? Definitely. T. W. Hunt, a leading authority on music in foreign missions, says it is reported worldwide that music is "one of the most significant and characteristic expressions of the nature of a given culture . . . [that] music has a speed factor in attracting attention . . . [that] the sung gospel often gives the preached gospel a chance to be heard . . . [that it] often breaks barriers nothing else can break."[10]

Drama and pantomime are also used increasingly in *kerygma* services in our churches. To my mind, at least, a major function (if not the proper function) of drama is to set a scene, pose a situation, raise questions, present issues, establish tension and relevancy to life situations—just like the wind sounds and tongues of fire did in Acts 2. Then, with this irresolution established, let the pastor talk out the explanation and preach, just as Peter did.

A Limited Vision

A curious development follows Peter's sermon though. Only Jews and Jewish proselytes are present in Acts 2. Though Peter cites Joel concerning the Spirit being poured out on "all people" (2:17), apparently the release of the Spirit and salvation in Christ are not *perceived* at this time as being for Gentiles. Only a worldwide harvesting of Jews is imagined (Acts 11). Similarly, when Peter speaks of the promise of the Spirit being for "all who are *far off* " (v. 39, emphasis added), that is interpreted by them to mean Diaspora *Jews* living in far-off lands, not Gentiles.[11] In other words, for the time being, Acts 2 is a Pentecost for the Jewish world, as Acts 10 and 11 make abundantly clear.

Similarly, when we consider music style, are we not often myopic in our vision and provincial in our thinking, just as the early Jewish Christians were? Don't we often forget to think of the non-Christian entering our church for the first time having to contend with hymns and other things that are unfamiliar? Question: Is your preferred style a "musical Pentecost for Jews only"—a style for the comfortable pew, the "home crowd"?

With our twentieth-century hindsight, we now see the fuller picture of Acts 2—God was initiating a brand-new direction for both Jews and Gentiles. Symbolically, through the image of the "tongues of fire," he was inaugurating a plan whereby the good news would be intelligibly imparted worldwide through a multitongued witness. Inevitably, in the course of time, this would also come to mean the development of a multitongued musical witness.

A Voice Confronts Peter: "Kill and Eat"

Then, suddenly, a remarkable Pentecost for Gentiles occurs![12] The overall story of Acts 10 and 11 begins with Cornelius, a nonkosher, God-fearing Gentile, who receives a vision from God instructing him to send for Peter. So he dispatches three men, who arrive the instant that Peter also receives a vision (the sheet of nonkosher foods). Note that Peter puts them up for the night—a taboo action for Jews. Then he leaves the next morning with six Jewish Christian companions for the house of Cornelius, where a large gathering of Gentiles is waiting to hear him preach. While Peter proclaims the gospel, the Spirit comes on them the same way he did on the apostles. Peter stays on at Cornelius' home for a few days. The news of that soon reaches the Jerusalem church, whose members *criticize* Peter and demand to know why he went into a house of uncircumcised Gentiles and ate with them.

Now let's back up for the crucial details. Peter goes on the roof to pray at noon, becomes hungry, and falls into a trance. A sheet comes down from heaven with nonkosher animals, reptiles, and birds. A voice—not once but three times—urges Peter to eat:

> "Get up, Peter. Kill and eat."
>
> "Surely not, Lord!" Peter replied. "I have never eaten anything impure or unclean."
>
> The voice spoke to him a second time, "Do not call anything impure that God has made clean."
>
> Acts 10:13–15

Note the insistence of God's voice. He does not say, "You *may* eat," but "EAT!" It's a command. How unready Peter is to hear this!

It totally goes against his conscience and years of ingrained habit, tradition, and training. I don't think we have sufficiently appreciated how difficult this confrontation was for Peter. These are powerful components in anybody's life to break, in Peter's time or ours. They are extremely similar to the tensions and insecurities musicians face in adapting to new music styles.

For just as there are varieties of foods, there are varieties of music styles. Some styles, for example, can be as difficult for us to accept and may feel as "foreign" and "wrong" to us as did the foods to Peter. This is a broad statement, and, admittedly, one difference between us and Peter needs noting: Peter was commanded to eat, whereas we are not. God is more gentle with us.

But just as no foods were to be unclean for Peter, so for us (theoretically) no music styles need be unacceptable. This also means that no melody, scale, chord, texture, rhythm, instrument, or timbre is theoretically off-limits to the Christian composer.

Accepting People

A most remarkable transformation occurs in Peter's thinking over only a few days. Until the sheet with the foods descends in Acts 10, Peter works on the assumption that he should not associate, eat, or visit with Gentiles.[13] To do so would be scandalous, unbecoming conduct for a spiritual leader—especially an apostle. But notice the "leap" that transpires in Peter's thinking when he processes the meaning of the descended sheet. For Peter the issue is not only eating nonkosher foods, but even more fundamentally and deeply it is *accepting the Gentiles as equals.* And that is the fundamental issue pastors and musicians need to consider relative to musical style.

The issue of style involves not only music but, more importantly, *accepting people.* Listen as Peter addresses the crowd at Cornelius's home:

> You are well aware that it is against our law for a Jew to associate with a Gentile or visit him. But God has shown me that I should not call any *man* impure or unclean [the issue is larger than food]. So when I was sent for, I came without raising any objections. . . . I now realize how true it is that *God does not show favoritism but accepts men from every nation* who fear him and do what is right.
>
> Acts 10:28–29, 34–35, emphasis added

Who Underwent the Greater Conversion?

Peter's amazing transformation has caused Harold Dollar (of Biola University) to ask who underwent the greater "conversion" experience—Peter or Cornelius? The central challenge, he argues, was "not the reluctance of the Gentiles to respond to the gospel, but the reluctance of the Jews to preach to them."[14] It is Peter who must drop his standards; it is Peter who is forced to go to the home of Cornelius.

Peter's reaction makes him an incredible model for all musicians and pastors. He was not concerned about his own preferences; he was concerned with ministry to others, and that involved theological and cultural change as well as accepting others at a deep level.

Analysis may prove that, like Peter, the experienced, trained musician (or any older adults) may undergo far more trauma during change than the young people. A radical "conversion" or reorientation may be necessary. This may surprise you. I've found pastors more open to change than trained musicians.

Also, when we reject a person's music style, there is a danger that we may reject the person. Educated musicians, like myself, the musical elite, look down on certain styles as unworthy. Often we do not want to associate or be identified with the people who play them.[15] We make fun of them. Young people do the same thing with older people.

I know firsthand what it feels like to be rejected musically and (consequently) personally. I once attempted to improvise alongside young people in a style that was unfamiliar to me. It was obvious to everyone (including myself) that stylistically I was out of sync. I had underestimated the difficulty. The result? I was ostracized by the group. But I'm glad I experienced that feeling!

The opposite has also occurred. There have been other times when I have had to set my preferences aside and get on my hands and knees and humbly work with people with limited skills who liked music I considered trite. Feeling something like Peter in Galatians, I said to myself, "I hope my professorial colleagues don't catch me doing this. It could be embarrassing."[16] Ugh! It's like playing something that doesn't suit your image. Or it's like Peter objecting, "Surely not, Lord! Nothing impure or unclean has ever entered *my mouth*" (Acts 11:8, emphasis added).

If we are to engage in renewal and reconciliation, we must make contact with people and their styles (like the early church did) and be willing to involve ourselves and to risk a little embarrassment. Harold Best echoes similar thoughts:

> We must learn to move from anger and frustration to an attitude of redemption, nurturing, and helpful intrusion, even when we are in the presence of a musical rip-off, crass commercialism, and exploitation. And in the presence of those who make music haltingly and fearfully, we must show the spirit of the one described by Isaiah as never breaking a bruised reed or extinguishing a dimly burning wick (Isa. 42:3). . . . [We must learn that] love for them precedes the music they make, no matter how bad or good it is.[17]

We must accept them where they are. Only then can we learn from one another and take the next step together. This is Christian charity in action.

The Prohibition Prevented Intimacy

Peter is totally honest. He had thought of the Gentiles as tainted due to their dietary habits. The gospel was not for them. Observe, too, the astonishment of the six Jewish Christians present with Peter when the gift of the Holy Spirit is poured out "even" on the Gentiles (10:45). As for the Jewish Christians in Jerusalem, the revolutionary thought that forgiveness of sins might extend to the Gentiles is accepted only after Peter confirms that the same signs manifested in Acts 2 were manifested at the house of Cornelius (11:18). In his defense Peter says to them, "So if God gave them the same gift [the Holy Spirit] as he gave us . . . who was I to think that I could oppose God!" (Acts 11:17).

For Jews, eating with Gentiles was prohibited. It meant risking defilement. (Isn't that how some Christians look at some forms of contemporary and older music—as music that defiles!) Eating meant compromising the faith; it meant accepting Gentiles who, because of their unclean practices, were regarded as *inferior.* The prohibition on eating *prevented intimacy* between Jews and Gentiles. Think about that.

Moreover, to provide lodging for Cornelius's men, as Peter does (10:23), was contrary to Jewish practice. It could be construed as fraternizing, taking a first step toward accepting them—the "slippery slope theory." But for Peter to go further and actually stay at Cornelius's house for several more days and eat with them (10:48; 11:3)—an unambiguously clear infraction—*that* required some explaining to the Jewish Christians in Jerusalem even from the head apostle, because through that extended contact he must have become ceremonially unclean (11:2–3).

Two Applications

Two applications arise from this section of Peter's story. First, if you have problems communicating with someone, consider inviting that person to your home. When Peter stayed on at Cornelius's house, it undoubtedly deepened their friendship.

Second, when I have been involved in bringing about changes in the worship style in a church, I have often found it necessary to be a go-between like Peter. In one case, before we introduced a bass guitar into the morning service, I informed a few elderly members of our intention, anticipating they might have objections: "In a few weeks we plan to introduce a bass guitar sound during the singing of some worship choruses. I wanted you to know ahead of time. I'll get back to you. Tell me if it contributes to your worship."

When I saw the young man's guitar, I was worried. The guitar had a shapely, sensuous look and it was cherry red! I knew its appearance alone would cause a major distraction in this conservative church and we'd lose the day. So I had several of us play at low volume where we would not be readily seen—off to the side of the front row, not exposed on the platform.

The day we performed, the worship response improved. Previously the young people had not been singing, but the pastor (surprised) told me, "As soon as they heard the bass guitar they started singing." Interesting!

I went back to talk to my elderly friends. "Did the bass add to your worship?" I inquired. "Oh, did it happen today?" they responded. "We didn't notice. But thanks for asking."

I was greatly relieved. (Understand, I'm not intimating every church should use a bass guitar during worship.) I found out later how much they appreciated my taking the time to inform them personally beforehand. They became allies in subsequent changes.

Antioch at the Cutting Edge

The Christian Jews, however, were not quick to share their faith with Gentiles. Gentiles, other than those at Cornelius's house, first came to hear the gospel this way.

Some time after Acts 10, a wave of persecution hit Jerusalem. This persecution scattered Jewish Christians across the sea. These believers preached the gospel there to Jews *only* (11:19). Some Jews, however, came back from Cyprus and Libya (northern Africa), went to the Gentile city of Antioch, and began to tell the good news to *Gentiles* there. When the Jewish Christians in Jerusalem heard about this, they sent Barnabas to investigate this new ministry phenomenon. Fortunately, he not only put his blessing on it, but he also stayed to nurture it, seeking out Paul's assistance. Clearly, the cutting edge of ministry was now occurring abroad, not at the founding church in Jerusalem. But, happily, the home-based parent church (Jerusalem) and the outlying church (Antioch) were able to maintain cordial relations.

How does this apply to music? Changes in music style are not likely to occur as easily in the established churches as they are in younger suburban churches. Practices in outlying churches may raise eyebrows in parent churches.

Jerusalem Council Decision

We must remember that the voice commanded Peter to eat all the foods—*against his conscience*! Why? Peter is, in God's sovereignty, a model for us all, and his actions point to the normative, theoretical direction God wants us, the church, to go today. That's the basic teaching we need to instill first. The radical cultural shift that resulted is confirmed by Paul's teaching:

> Everything God created is good, and nothing is to be rejected if it is received with thanksgiving, because it is consecrated by the word of God and prayer.
> 1 Timothy 4:4–5

> To the pure, all things are pure, but to those who are corrupted and do not believe, nothing is pure.
> Titus 1:15

As the church set out to implement these principles of freedom to eat, impartiality to all peoples, and so forth, it encountered serious problems. Objections came from select Jews who attempted to impose circumcision on everyone (including Gentiles) as a condition for salvation:

> Some men came down from Judea to Antioch and were teaching the brothers: "Unless you are circumcised, according to the custom taught by Moses, you *cannot* be saved." This brought Paul and Barnabas into sharp dispute with them. So Paul and Barnabas were appointed, along with some other believers, to go up to Jerusalem to see the apostles and elders about this question.
>
> Acts 15:1–2, emphasis added

The Jerusalem Council convened and ruled *against* mandating circumcision for salvation: "We should not make it difficult for the Gentiles who are turning to God," they said (15:19, 28). The critical passage of a letter they sent back to the Antioch church reads:

> It seemed good to the Holy Spirit and to us *not to burden you* with anything beyond the following requirements: You are to abstain from food sacrificed to idols, from blood, from the meat of strangled animals and from sexual immorality.
>
> Acts 15:28–29, emphasis added

Consider the gracious responses by Peter, James, and Paul to the Gentiles:

- "we should not make it difficult" (15:19)
- "[we should] not . . . burden you" (15: 28)
- "[we should not put on your necks] a yoke" (15:10)

Peter, however, frames the question in theological terms, for he mentions "faith" (15:9) and "grace" (15:11), whereas James emphasizes the cultural dimension (15:19–21). Both are important aspects. There *was* a theological problem with circumcision as a condition for salvation because it undercut the free working of grace apart from works. And from a cultural standpoint, requiring the Gentiles to be circumcised would have caused them to undergo a nonessential, painful ritual that could have inhibited the unfettered dissemination of the good news, unnecessarily burdening the gospel.

Do we require non-Christians to go through "cultural circumcision" by the way we conduct our worship?

187

On nonessentials like music style (or circumcision), there should not be mandatory requirements. There is no *one*, established, "sacred" style. Just as King James English is not a requirement for a "good biblical" translation, so forcing a certain music style on people is not the New Testament pattern. Even the singing of hymns, for example, may be argued as a wise use of available cultural resources, but it cannot be mandated. In some cultures, Western hymns could be burdensome.

Summary of Concerns

This chapter has addressed a number of questions that deserve honest examination. Do we accept the idea of a Pentecost of musical styles? Do we denigrate local cultures, local styles? When we reject a person's style, do we also reject the person? Are we willing to undergo transformation and admit our shortcomings as Peter did? Have we imposed stylistic burdens (standards) that have impeded the reception of the gospel?[18] I leave this chapter to your conscience. There are, of course, other aspects. Let's take them up in the next chapter.

> If healthy change is to come to a culture, it must be guided by those who are identified with it, who love it and understand it. Actually, only they are really qualified to evaluate it.[19]

Questions for Reflection and Discussion

1. Explain and discuss the following statement: If a multilingual approach to propagating the gospel is accepted as normative, then a Pentecost of music styles should be accepted as normative.
2. Do you agree that when we reject a person's musical style, we may in effect reject the person?
3. Have you found it true that trained musicians and adults may undergo greater strain during change than young people?
4. Why is the issue of musical style so divisive?

Resolving Tensions over Musical Style: Paul

> Accept him whose faith is weak, without passing judgment on disputable matters. . . . Each one should be fully convinced in his own mind. . . . Why do you judge your brother? Or why do you look down on your brother?
>
> Romans 14:1, 5, 10

The rapid expansion of the faith presented Jewish and Gentile Christians with serious problems related to fellowship. Meat offered to idols was one of them, and it recurs repeatedly as an issue of conscience. The people were asking if it was proper for believers to eat meat that had been offered to idols. Just as Peter was the key figure God used to guide and effect change in the previous chapter, now Paul is, and he responds with this general principle: "Do not violate your conscience." Paul's principle of conscience is founded on the antecedent principle (in the previous chapter) that the eating of all foods, including meat, is permissible.

Paul Advises: "Don't Ask"

Dialoguing with Paul, some Christians expressed an additional question that troubled their conscience: "When we sit down to eat at someone's home, what if we are not sure the meat on our plates was offered to idols? Should we ask our hosts?" Paul advises them not to invite unnecessary feelings of guilt by asking if the meat has been offered to idols:

> Eat anything sold in the meat market *without raising questions* of conscience, for, "The earth is the Lord's, and everything in it" (1 Cor. 10:25–26, emphasis added).

> Someone who is not a believer may invite you to eat with him. . . . Eat anything that is put before you. *Do not ask questions* to see if it is something you think might be wrong to eat. But if anyone [any weak Christian or non-Christian?] says to you, "That food was offered to idols," then do not eat it . . . because it would be something that might be thought wrong. I don't mean that you think it is wrong. But the other person might think it is wrong (1 Cor. 10:27–29 ICB, emphasis added).

> But if anyone regards something as unclean, then for him it is unclean (Rom. 14:14).

> Until now, some people have had the habit of worshiping idols. So now when they eat meat, they still feel as if it belongs to an idol. They are not sure it is right to eat this meat. When they eat it, they feel guilty. But food will not make us closer to God. Refusing to eat does not make us less pleasing to God. And eating does not make us better in God's sight (1 Cor. 8:7–8 ICB).

How do these verses relate to the issue of musical style? If we substituted "musical style" for "meat" in the above passage, the following loose paraphrase could result: "Listen to any musical style in the marketplace without raising questions of conscience.[1] But if someone regards a music style as unclean, then for him it is unclean. When he listens to it, he feels guilty."

Another implication might be: If you like a certain melody, don't ask if a nonbeliever, a homosexual, or an adulterer composed it. If you love a certain rhythm, don't ask if it is a dance step. Don't share information with others that could cause problems of conscience.

I did a foolish thing that I sort of slipped into. I shared with a believer that a popular Christian song we sing at church was actually composed by a non-Christian, a Jewish musician who plied his gifts in a very intelligent manner.

This is how it happened. Several years ago the Jewish musician confided in a Hollywood studio-musician friend of mine that he was interested in writing Christian music. So my friend said, "Come to

190

my church!" He came and hung around the lobby listening to how evangelicals talked, and based on what he heard, he eventually wrote and published gospel songs and worship songs. He's made a good living.

When I told the believer this, he became troubled and later said the association of that song with the Jewish composer tainted its value for him. For him a good piece had been destroyed. On reflection, the root of the incident became crystal clear to me, and it was distressing. The piece was still a good one, but very simply, through engaging in a form of gossip, I had diminished its value.

Consider a compelling point along this line. Remember the story behind the hymn "It Is Well with My Soul" that I told in chapter 1? You'll recall that Horatio Spafford wrote the text close to the time that his four daughters died—when the *Lochearn* sank.

What I *didn't* tell you was that Spafford later had a mental disturbance "which prompted him to go to Jerusalem under the strange delusion that he was the second Messiah."[2] I wouldn't suggest you unthinkingly tell your congregation this part of the story! It could destroy a tremendous hymn. It turns out that Paul's ancient advice, "Don't ask," is radiant with contemporary wisdom.

Accept the Weak

Paul differentiates between the "weak" and the "strong." He advises us to treat the weak with sensitivity and he also asks the weak not to judge the strong:

> Accept him *whose faith is weak,* without passing judgment on disputable matters. . . . The man who eats everything must not look down on ["regard with contempt" NASB] him who does not, and the man who does not eat everything must not condemn the man who does, for God has accepted him.
> Romans 14:1, 3, emphasis added

The weak group described above is different from the Judaizers. The group here *does not wish to impose.* Rather, they want to continue on culturally as before, observing dietary restrictions and keeping the Sabbath and special days—doing the traditional things they have always done. These cultural, Christian Jews, says Paul, need acceptance too and should not be looked down on for *not* embracing or acting upon the freedom they have in Christ. Paul looks even-

191

handedly at both the "weak" and the "strong" in disputable matters, attempting to avoid attitudes of snobbery and exclusivity.

By way of application, what about the people in your church who by personality are conservative, resist change, and want to keep things as they have been? Shouldn't traditionalists also be treated with respect? How do you reconcile these two groups: the front-runners and traditionalists, which are present in every church to some degree?

All of us are strong in some areas and weak in others, aren't we? Take the practice of raising of hands in worship. I tend to be "weak" here—fearful. Isn't Paul saying by analogy that the strong (who feel free to raise their hands) should not look down on the weak (who don't)? Conversely, the weak should not condemn the strong by labeling them as fanatics. Each should respect the other.[3]

Some readers may even respond: "In my church it is the weak who raise their hands!" And that may be true. The raising of hands, by itself, doesn't indicate spiritual maturity.

Biblical teaching relative to cultural practices is not at all simplistic—it's sophisticated! Scripture tolerates inconsistencies in people: Something might be right for one person and wrong for another.

A central concern of Paul is for nurture. He's concerned about wounding a weak conscience (1 Cor. 8:12). Wounding could arise from even a seemingly infinitesimally small issue (as church leaders know). For musicians, music style often touches them deeply, for they have something major at stake—their job security and self-image. For others, music style can dredge up feelings of remorse and memories of past sins and unhealthy associations. When a musical style has the potential to inflict hurt, cause guilt, or threaten a person's spiritual progress, we can't excuse ourselves. We need to listen and try to work through the problem with them. Consider Paul's words:

> Be careful, however, that the exercise of your freedom does not become a stumbling block to the weak (1 Cor. 8:9).

> It is wrong for a man to eat anything that causes someone else to stumble (Rom. 14:20).

> Do not cause anyone to stumble. . . . I try to please everybody in every way. For I am not seeking my own good but the good of many (1 Cor. 10:32–33).

192

If Paul suspects his liberty may cause his brother to stumble, he will not eat. Nor will he flaunt his freedom verbally before his weaker brother: "Whatever you believe about these things keep between yourself and God" (Rom. 14:22). That is a demonstration of Christian sensitivity!

The Only Solution: Teach Everyone to Be Strong

Due to the large amount of space Paul devotes to "matters of conscience," he obviously believes that sound teaching on the subject is imperative. He identifies himself with the strong, explicitly stating "we who are strong" (Rom. 15:1). To be strong in the full sense of the word for Paul means to be able to eat all meats, yet be willing to set aside one's freedoms and preferences for the sake of one's brother or sister. Paul would like everyone to be "strong."

Several probing questions come inescapably to mind here. Do you desire to be one of the strong? Have you prayed to be one of the strong? Don't church musicians have a responsibility to teach people to be strong in the area of musical style? Something to think about.

Paul underscores the point of view of the strong because that is what all of us should work toward:

- "Eat anything sold in the meat market" (1 Cor. 10:25).
- "Eat whatever is put before you" (1 Cor. 10:27).
- "Everything God created is good, and nothing is to be rejected if it is received with thanksgiving" (1 Tim. 4:4).
- "I am fully convinced that no food is unclean in itself" (Rom. 14:14).

Teaching the entire church to be strong (as far as I can see) is the *only long-range answer* to reconciling the traditionalists and the front-runners. But the process cannot be forced. Paul maintains, "Each one should be fully convinced in his own mind" (Rom. 14:5). Again, musical style falls into the category of "disputable matters" (Rom. 14:1).

While the problem of meats brings out the issue of bad associations, the problem of "sacred days" brings out the issue of good associations: "One man considers one day more sacred than another; another man considers every day alike" (Rom. 14:5). This may refer to the Sabbath or to Jewish festival days or both. Individuals were apparently criticizing others for not properly observing religious days that upheld positive values. Paul again responds, "Let us stop passing judgment on one another" (Rom. 14:13).

People may consider certain music styles sacred and, like sacred days, demand that they receive special treatment. For example, Handel's *Messiah*, for some, *must* be performed at Easter. It's almost been sanctified. Young people, from an entirely different perspective, may insist that music that is suitable for youth meetings should be appropriate for Sunday worship services.

Paul does not seem to be advocating a "watery pluralism," however. People can choose a particular style for their worship. They can have strong convictions and should, in fact, be encouraged to produce the strongest possible reasons for their decisions. Another group may opt for a different style and be equally convinced. Both should not judge or condemn the other, but healthy sparring (if it can be done in a charitable manner) may improve both. Iron can sharpen iron (Prov. 27:17).

Biblical Arguments for Variety

I take the position that the Bible encourages Christians living today to be open to a variety of materials. Through biblical example and precedent, the case for variety (in music materials) can be argued at least six ways:

1. The created order displays immense variety.
2. The Psalm texts manifest enormous stylistic diversity (see chapter 2).
3. The early church employed a variety of materials—psalms, hymns, and spiritual songs (see chapter 2).
4. The descended sheet reveals all foods are clean.
5. The Pentecost of languages indicates all languages can propagate the gospel.
6. The eating of meat offered to idols teaches that idolatry doesn't spoil the goodness of the materials.

Let's enlarge on the last three points as they apply to music. My guess is that most readers will not have difficulty accepting the music-language analogy. For some, however, the music-meat analogy may seem "thin." True, it is a judgment call, and you have to decide if I've overstepped the bounds in drawing applications. Agreed, we are dealing with an analogy; neither Peter nor Paul makes specific reference to music. But when Peter reflects on the meaning of the descended sheet, he concludes the central issue is not meat but accepting people.

In the same way, Paul focuses on attitudes and principles when he deals with meat offered to idols. In fact, the way Paul argues his position and cites Christian principles guiding his response is probably more important to us today than the actual questions themselves. Our concern too must be for the underlying principles. Christian responsibility requires theologizing.

Here's my question: Don't we lose some authoritative insights and guidance when we see no connection—no applications—between meat and music or language and music?

At the same time, if we accept the meat-music analogy as having relevance, we must discern its limitations. Obviously, listening to and interpreting music is vastly more complex than eating meat.[4] For instance, meat sits on your plate; you decide whether or not to eat it. In a church setting, however, music is wafted in the air for all to hear. All *must* partake; we don't have earlids! That imposition makes it more difficult.

Are Music Materials Neutral?

Remember what Paul said: "I am fully convinced that no food is unclean in itself" (Rom. 14:14). This raises a similar question on which learned musicians disagree: "Are the materials of music style neutral?"[5] With this lead-in, consider the words of Jesus:

> Don't you see that nothing that enters a man from the outside can make him "unclean.". . . What comes out of a man is what makes him "unclean." For from *within*, out of men's *hearts*, come evil thoughts, sexual immorality, theft, murder, adultery, greed, malice. . . . All these evils come from inside and make a man "unclean."
>
> Mark 7:18, 20–23, emphasis added

Consider Christ's emphasis on the words *within* and *hearts*. To loosely paraphrase the paragraph relative to musical style: Jesus says, It's not the style itself that is so bad, that needs to be obliterated from the face of the earth. It's what's within our hearts that is so persistently sinful.

Let's draw an analogy to color. Is the color black inherently evil, and white holy? We could certainly draw that conclusion through the use of association. In the Book of Revelation there are white horsemen (symbolizing good) and black horsemen (symbolizing disaster). But wearing a black shirt or blouse doesn't make us wicked, nor does wearing white make us angelic. In the same way no instrumental color or rhythm is inherently satanic. The context and our experience are determinative factors.

Abuse Doesn't Invalidate Forms

The abuse of a form by one person should not invalidate its use by others.[6] When people do bad things with a form, it shouldn't prevent Christians from doing good things with it. Performers and listeners can derive different meanings from the same music. Meanings are created in our heads. Pass contends, "Whatever style of music communicates the gospel boldly and clearly according to convergences of person, group, culture, and historical moment is acceptable."[7] Paul shares his own reasoning, his modus operandi, for *kerygma* contexts: "that by all possible means" some might be saved. Culturally, Paul is conciliatory:

> To the Jews I became like a Jew. . . . To those not having the law I became like one not having the law. . . . To the weak I became weak. . . . I have become all things to all men so that by all possible means I might save some.
> 1 Corinthians 9:20–22

To translate this to music style, it means that if I had the ability, I might play some Mozartian riffs and ornaments to the classically oriented, some crushed thirds and open-string-violin-like fourths in the right hand to the country music fan, and raga pitch components (e.g., C-E-F$\sharp$-G-B) not found in Western scales to my East Indian or Turkish friends. I would play each style to the very best of my ability, appreciating the excellence that can be coaxed out of each one.

Now, this is not always possible. Very few of us are a Ken Medema capable of actually achieving this; but we can try to appreciate the diverse tastes within our cities and congregations and, more

196

broadly, nudge ourselves along the path toward becoming "world" Christian citizens. Moreover, hopefully we as a church will not be merely adapting to culture but transforming it.

A final thought along this vein. David Swanger, who has studied the process of making moral and aesthetic judgments, says there are parallels between judging moral issues and works of art. That's provocative, says Pass: "We tend to equate a certain music style with a certain morality and then pass off our aesthetic judgments as moral judgments."[8]

Is the Devil in the Music?

Where there are differences in background, exposure, and training, the potential for misunderstanding a musical style can be enormous. For this reason I am disturbed when people sound off that a certain beat is "of the devil" or a certain rhythm is "satanic." Graham Cray rightly asserts, "There is probably no musical form in existence which within its original cultural context does not send some messages which are in conflict with the Christian message."[9]

Is the devil in the music? It's not always that simple. A specific rhythm or beat can take on different meanings in different musical contexts. If a style hinders your walk with God, as much as possible, avoid it![10] Individuals troubled by certain associations should listen to their conscience.

In general, the basic counsel that Al Menconi gives parents seems sensible for everyone. Since the Bible does not outlaw specific music styles, he suggests that parents sit down with their children and *examine together (line by line) the philosophy behind the lyrics.* This way the issue is not so much the music style, but the *philosophy of life advocated.* Most of us (even musicians) do not have the expertise to talk about style precisely. We *are* better equipped to talk about words.

Moreover, we must state emphatically that music texts cannot be exempted from scrutiny. The profound can be made frivolous even by those with the best of intentions. The following lyric, which later develops several ideas seriously, takes (at one point) poetic license too far, in my opinion. The lyricist imputes to God casual, "groovy" expression in the phrase "praise looks good on you." God is speaking:

When you lift your hands up high
and you sing a song of praise to Me,
it brings Me great delight.
Such a lovely sight.
And yes it is true,
Praise looks good on you.[11]

Such language is too casual for my tastes. I feel it lacks the reverence due to God's person.

Did Israel Go to School with the Canaanites?

What about music style in Old Testament times? It may be shocking, but scholars believe Israel followed the uses and styles of her neighbors in her music. There is no style that is definitively biblical. "In the matter of her sacred song," von Rad writes, "Israel went to school with the Canaanites. . . . [There is] nothing unique about the Psalms as a literary form."[12] Sigmund Mowinckel concludes that temple singing "can be traced back to Canaanite patterns."[13] In fact, Hebrew musicians were such virtuosos that they acquired an international reputation. Foreign kings wanted them in their courts. The Israelites gave musicians as compensation for tribute money to the surrounding nations. Clearly, their performing ability was comprehensive enough to cross cultural boundaries.

Old Testament music style had no harmony as we know it, no scales comparable to ours, no music notation, no rhythmic meters akin to ours. Their rhythms followed the natural pattern in the Hebrew language of constantly *varying* accents; ours tend toward *regular* pulses in two or three beats.

Here's my point. If the Hebrew music differed so greatly from ours and was acceptable to God, must we not beware of imposing or elevating any one style as intrinsically sacred? There is no intrinsically sacred style. Any given style, however, may be a happy fit as determined by a particular people at a particular place and at a particular time.

Instruments and the New Testament

There is no record of instruments being used in worship in the Gospels or Epistles. Why is that? Why were instruments seemingly banned in synagogues and the early church? That question often arises, and it's difficult for us to understand. But there is an explanation.

Noted Jewish scholar Eric Werner answers that Greek music culture was exerting a powerful influence on Jewish culture in the time of Christ. Hellenism "had penetrated the daily life of Palestine." Jews employed Greek terms almost exclusively "for instruments, their parts, their tuning." The same instruments that Greeks used in their temple orgies, Jews used in their temple ceremonies. In revulsion, rabbis associated the instruments with immorality and banned them as unfit for the synagogues. Even instruments that had played a highly respected role in the psalter (aulos, kinnor, tympanon, and cymbals) were held in contempt. They were considered unclean because of their use in syncretistic religions. Rabbis pictured the aulos in pagan ceremonies as "full of frenzied tones." They recoiled at panpipe players "imitating" serpent songs. They imagined men called to war "in wild terms" when they saw a trumpet. Classic examples of guilt by association!

The same attitude of horror was reflected in Christian individuals like Clement of Alexandria up to the third century:

> One makes noise with cymbals and tympana, one rages and rants with instruments of frenzy . . . the flute belongs to those superstitious men who run to idolatry.

We don't regard flute playing today as linked to superstition. But Clement did! Recall again, these same instruments were *respected* in the Psalms. How could he forget that? From extrabiblical sources we know that the Sadducees used temple instruments in their synagogue services at the time of Christ, and in the Book of Revelation even elders carry harps!

A vital point on banning instruments in worship, therefore, needs addressing. Because of the powerful pressures of culture, the thinking of the rabbis and early Christians became distorted, just as our thinking may be today. By focusing too narrowly on *only* the Gospels and Epistles for the last authoritative word on worship style, we can draw misleading conclusions. The *whole* of the Bible as well as extrabiblical evidence should be consulted. We need to see the larger context. If instruments had not become associated with pagan worship and debauchery, their use in worship would never have been questioned.

Church Music: A Functional Art?

Is *every* style appropriate for church use? "Not so," says Donald P. Hustad, noted evangelical church musician. Church music should be "functional" (intelligible) and judged on whether it fulfils its "best function." "Free" or great art music may have to have restrictions within the local church:

> "Great art" in our culture . . . tends to be elitist. One of the requirements of the art music composer is that he must be free—free to communicate anything that is in his mind and heart, free even to fail to communicate (if that is his choice) so long as the work is his honest expression. Church music cannot be so "free." It must communicate the truth of God and express the response of the body of believers by whom it is used, and this means that it must have *the potential to be understood* by that particular community of faith. When it is so used and so understood, whether it be Palestrina or Felciano or Medema or Gaither, it is functional church music (italics added).[14]

Scriptural support for this principle of intelligibility comes from Paul, if we view music as a language:

> Now, brothers, if I come to you and speak in tongues, what good will I be to you, unless I bring you some revelation or knowledge or prophecy or word of instruction? . . . Unless you speak intelligible words with your tongue, how will anyone know what you are saying? . . . Undoubtedly there are all sorts of languages in the world, yet none of them is without meaning. If then I do not grasp the meaning of what someone is saying, I am a foreigner to the speaker, and he is a foreigner to me. . . . In the church I would rather speak five intelligible words to instruct others than ten thousand words in a tongue.
>
> 1 Corinthians 14:6, 9–11, 19

Hustad traces the emergence of functional church music to the sixteenth-century Protestant commitment to congregation participation. As the church moved away from "art music," serious composers shifted their loyalty from the church. By 1850 church music was more popular in appeal; it reflected the rising tides of humanism, democracy, "religion of the heart," mass revivals, choirs singing arranged hymns, and by the early twentieth century, gospel songs.

> Consequently, it [church music] moved to the level of the worshiper who rarely frequented the concert hall. . . . Church music was now expected to be functional in the evangelical sense that everybody should share it.

200

... What is performed in 99 percent of American churches today is functional church music that should not be confused with great art.[15]

The down side of the evangelical aesthetic is that many musicians feel a democratic leveling has occurred, such that the lowest common denominator *rules* in relation to music style. As a result, great, complex, and profound art cannot be performed or nurtured within the excessively "market driven" evangelical culture.[16] Isn't there something wrong here? But that is the subject of another book![17] Nevertheless, this realization underscores all the more J. S. Bach's amazing accomplishment in the early 1700s, for his music was practical, functional, and yet attained the highest standards of innovation and creativity.

Implementing Change

In Peter, Paul, James, and Barnabas, the early church experienced statesmanshiplike leadership. Through the power of the Holy Spirit, these men underwent remarkable transformations. Paul, formerly breathing threats on the church, became concerned about wounding believers! Peter, raised as a strict Jew, embraced all Gentiles. James, leader of the "establishment," steered the Jerusalem church away from entrenchment. Barnabas encouraged cross-cultural ministry. These were the people God used to be shapers of change. If we desire to exercise statesmanship in our time, we need to incarnate their attitudes.

Peter, particularly, was put on the spot. Music leaders, too, may feel that way when learning new styles. Ears strain to listen, tongues stumble over rhythms, and memories overload in striving to remember new phrases. Learning new styles means becoming vulnerable. No one wants to be humiliated. The more respected we are, the more "face" we have to lose!

For these reasons, every effort must go into providing conditions where *people can feel safe to try*. Don't expose people to ridicule. Hold weakness revealed in practice in strictest confidence. Guard self-respect. Don't mimic or poke fun. Remember Paul: He didn't want to wound anyone. Affirm individuals—"we know what you're going through ... we've been there ... let's break the learning down into manageable steps." Also, don't force public performance until the person feels ready. If possible, do a test run.

201

When I was a boy we had a magnificent evergreen tree in our front yard. One day Mom said to Dad, "The branches of the evergreen are hanging over the walkway. The tree needs trimming." Dad went out to do the job, and my brother and I went to see how he was coming along. We were aghast! My dad, normally a man bursting with creativity, had totally lost it—lost all sense of proportion. What we saw staggered us. The right side of the tree Dad left untouched, but the left side—there was nothing! Sheared off! It was like shaving off one side of your head; one side, a full head of hair, the other side, baldness. Stunned and bewildered, my brother Don and I exclaimed, "Dad! Dad! How could you do this!" We didn't know whether to laugh or cry.

And it remained an embarrassing eyesore for years and years. Today we get a bang out of affectionately telling this story about my dad, one of many, at family gatherings. But it was painful at the time.

All this to say that we need sensitivity in implementing change. Don't lop off, without careful forethought, your most prominent, cultivated branches. Don't dismantle an adult or children's choir program just because it's not the "in thing."

And this is especially important: *Don't undertake changes in worship unless there is a certain amount of calm in the church.* If your church is boiling because of some other issue, you're inviting more trouble.

If you are an established church, bring out sufficiently what is dissatisfying in order to generate motivation for change—for example, "the branches are hanging over the walkway." Or as Nehemiah proclaimed, "The walls are in ruins."

Arm yourself with some good anecdotes.[18] Humor is always helpful. And a sense of history can broaden one's perspective. These startling facts will cause your people to think:

- Harps were like guitars, small and portable, in the Old Testament.
- Asaph, David's chief musician, was a percussionist.
- Puritans in England took axes to organs, sang no hymns (only scriptural psalms), and prohibited instruments in worship (c. 1630).
- The Pope banned the piano as a secular instrument unfit for public worship (1903).

Consider the significant age groups in the congregation, the educational level, the size of the church, the local culture, and the unique abilities of members. For example, one reason I am personally interested in flowing praise is because I'm an improviser. The format suits my talents.

Give Your People Lead Time

Don't rush change. Give your people lead time to process.

A well-intentioned church elder missed this point completely. He experienced some worship under a "hot" worship leader, and without consulting the music leadership in the church, he invited him to lead worship for a couple of Sundays and give a few talks on worship. The worship leader's presence caused a big ruckus. The musicians were irked because they were not consulted. One key musician even withdrew from leadership. The incident was not unlike inviting an exceptional preacher into the pulpit for a few Sundays in order to demonstrate the correct way to preach—without the pastor's consent!

Obtain consensus. Consider the modeling of the New Testament church. A dual emphasis on listening to the Holy Spirit and applying the best of corporate judgment guided the crafting of the letter the Jerusalem Council sent to the church at Antioch: "It seemed good to the Holy Spirit and to us" (Acts 15:28).

Finally, pray about implementation long before you take action. Music directors have emphasized this point to me repeatedly.

Standards for Church Music

Consider carefully Hustad's standards for church music: they are weighty. According to Hustad, evangelicals should:

- express the gospel in a text and musical language richly understandable by the intended culture
- offer a worthy "sacrifice of praise" (our best performance) without arrogance or shame
- express the best Christian theology of each denomination or church subculture, supporting all tenets in proper balance
- support the best activities of the group's beliefs—worship, fellowship, outreach

- speak from the "whole person" to the "whole person," balancing the physical, intellectual, and emotional, while avoiding the sentimental
- be genuinely creative, shunning the hackneyed and trite as well as the elitist and abstruse

Hustad suggests that evangelicals, rather than narrowly focusing on *raising* music standards, be open to a *broader* musical experience; that is, be open to cultures other than their own, for in this way, he says, we may "get a new glimpse of God and his truth."[19]

Take Time to Process

I expect this chapter to raise questions. Readers may need time for processing. Some may echo a friend of mine who passionately responded: "Barry, I have a lot of trouble with this chapter. . . . I refuse to sing or affirm styles that trivialize the truths of the Word of God." I hope readers will not feel this way. I don't want truth trivialized either. I do take the position that music materials are neutral; any style is *theoretically permissible but not necessarily appropriate.* I cannot feel free to broadside any one style—jazz, rock, rap—as unfit, as unredeemable. Insightful artists have and will continue to "steal" elements from any music of interest and incorporate them into their style.

Music is like putty. The meaning of every chord, rhythm, timbre is in the hands of the context. Human "associations" greatly influence our perception of contexts. Shouldn't we logically expect tremendous diversity within Christian worship? Scripture says "*all* the families of the nations will worship before Thee" (Ps. 22:27 NASB, emphasis added). For sources that take a different position, I urge you to check this endnote.[20]

Harold Best tells a sad but true story that underscores the tremendous power of human associations.[21] A young man, heavily involved in a satanic cult that adamantly employed sophisticated music in its liturgies, was marvelously converted to Christ. He was serious about his newfound faith, had found a church home in a nurturing, well-respected body of believers, and was experiencing a great deal of inner healing. Then one Sunday the organist played a composition well-known and loved by the people. The man was traumatized. I'm told he literally bolted, ran from the church, terrified.

It turned out that the music was by none other than Johann Sebastian Bach, a composer of all that is considered noblest and best. But Bach was the cult's musical mainstay! And the piece flooded his mind with the most horrible memories. For him Bach epitomized all that was anti-Christian, devilish.

Should this church cut Bach from its music program? Definitely for the short term, but perhaps not for the long term. Clearly, the problem is not the music itself but the associations that it conjured up in the mind of the young man.

Talk to him! Lovingly work through the issues. Hopefully he will not have to seek another church home. Education and dependence on the Spirit of God to work in hearts is the only answer. This story further demonstrates that some problems of this sort are unpreventable—who could have predicted the young man's response? These problems will surely arise, so we need to be a praying people, patient, understanding, and open to the guidance of the Holy Spirit.

Summary of Principles

Musical style is a "disputable matter": let each be "convinced in his own mind" (Rom. 14:1, 5). Accept both the front-runners and the traditionalists (Rom. 14:1–8). Educate all the people to be strong (Rom. 15:1–2). Do not condemn those who do not embrace what you regard as "good style" or "good associations" (Rom. 14:5–6). If you like a certain melody or rhythm, don't ask (or don't tell) where it came from if that information could cause people to stumble (1 Cor. 10:25–29). Performers and listeners can derive different meanings from the same music: "For from within, out of men's hearts, come evil thoughts" (Mark 7:18, 20–23). Abuse of a form by one person does not disqualify its use by another. Be careful about equating aesthetic judgments with moral judgments. Lyrics are easier to evaluate than musical styles as being anti-Christian. Church music needs to be functional (intelligible): therefore, some styles may be permissible but not appropriate for a given local church.

The church has for centuries waged one brush war after another over . . . what it means to borrow styles, forms, processes, tunes, techniques, textures, shapes, gestures, and instruments from secular sources. . . . Despite

205

the numberless instances and their seeming diversity, one common thread runs throughout. At the time of the borrowing, the war rages, often quite bitterly and divisively. Then as time passes, the war dies down. The previously condemned becomes merely questionable, if not outrightly sacred.[22]

Questions for Reflection and Discussion

1. Is the choice of style as much a pastoral matter as a musical matter?
2. Is the analogy of meat to music appropriate, instructive?
3. Is every music style appropriate for church use?
4. Is there a "sacred" music style?
5. Does the criterion that evangelical music be understandable tend to reduce church music to the lowest common denominator? If so, is there a way out?

PART THREE

MINISTERING WITH OTHERS

Volunteer and Staff Relations

Be joyful always; pray continually; give thanks in all circumstances, for this is God's will for you in Christ Jesus.

1 Thessalonians 5:16–17

I saw him coming. Like a runaway locomotive with steam billowing in all directions, he broke through the line of departing parishioners and screeched to a halt in front of me.

"'What's the idea of changing the closing hymn this morning without telling me?' he demanded in a fortissimo voice. 'I worked so hard to plan the music and coordinate the service, then you had the nerve to throw in that . . . that *clinker*.'

"'Clinker?' I responded weakly, trying to appear calm before the startled people around me. I was a young pastor, he a talented musician. He was several years older than I, but we had never directly clashed before.

"'That hymn was a terrible selection. The congregation couldn't sing it. The organist couldn't play it. I didn't like it. It didn't fit in. Never, never do that again.'

"He turned abruptly and strode off, leaving me stunned as I mumbled something about the stress of ministry to the curious bystanders still in the hallway. Fumbling my way to the refuge of my office, I felt the blessing of the morning quickly fade. What began as bewilderment at the surprise attack turned rapidly to seething defensiveness.

"'Who does he think he is anyway?' I thought angrily. 'I have a right to do what's best for the service. After all, who's in charge here? I don't care if he has been at the church longer. Besides, that wasn't such a bad hymn. We used to sing it in seminary all the time. He should talk. The choir's been eating into my preaching time, yet he insists we need *two* anthems. No wonder we get out late. Makes you wonder if a music ministry is worth it.'"[1]

Sound familiar? Many pastors and chief musicians experience marvelous relationships. Others struggle. Yet the relationship between the music director and the pastor is of *crucial importance to the health of the entire church.*[2] In this chapter, I hope to shed light on what musicians are like and what is involved in their work. I also want to focus on some blind spots and common misperceptions where the pastor/musician relationship is liable to become strained, as well as highlight issues of leadership style, access, trust, teamwork, self-image, discipline, release time, and budget considerations, mostly taking the musician's point of view.

What Makes Musicians Tick?

Calvin M. Johansson, himself a church musician, describes the church musician the following way:

> Of necessity the church musician is a zealous, eager, and energetic worker who has little time for reflection, contemplation, and philosophic thought. What he most often craves is inspiration, new ideas, repertoire, methodological suggestions, problem solving, and technical review.[3]

Some musicians function comfortably with an authoritarian style of leadership, but most do not. Lyle E. Schaller, renowned church consultant, believes one-third to one-half of all professionally trained ministers of music resist the boss-subordinate leadership style.[4] This observation probably holds for volunteer and part-time musicians as well. Most desire a warm, egalitarian partnership with the senior pastor, perhaps more so than do other staff members.

Long- and mid-range planning is extremely helpful to musicians: "The more we strategize, the better we harmonize."[5] They also want regular, direct access to the pastor for the weekly planning of Sunday worship, preferably early in the week.

As Ray Lutke expressed to me, "It's important not to have to report to a committee to get to the pastor. It's better to answer directly to him; otherwise every part of the service can be changed by the committee or some other person. At first, the pastor kept the planning of the service tightly to himself. Now that he has come to trust me, I generally come to him with a plan and he looks at it and makes suggestions."

Trust and loyalty between pastors and musicians are essential if the pastor/worship director relationship is to be effective. The depth of loyalty and confidence each has for the other determines each leader's ability to lead. Those in

- level A will die for the leader.
- level B will fight, but not die, for the leader.
- level C will not fight for the leader, but neither will they oppose. This is the largest group of people. Their loyalty is more institutional than personal.
- level D doubt their leaders.
- level E are antagonists who . . . seek to erode . . . will fight against . . . may even be willing to sacrifice the institution to "get at" the leader.[6]

Staff members need to be in level A or B for an effective team relationship. If musicians behave in level E, the results can be devastating. Pastors may criticize the music program to get the musician, but they will generally protect the remaining church structure. Musicians, however, may assault wider dimensions of church structure to get the pastor. In this sense musicians may be more dangerous. Put differently, musicians may be concerned only with protecting the limited objectives of their music program, whereas pastors must protect the church's total welfare.

How do musicians feel about teamwork? Some musicians understand better than others what is involved in teamwork in order to function well as staff members. Doran C. McCarty observes that "a leader does not announce that a collection of people is a team."[7] A team *becomes* a team by wanting to be a team and by working together. A team forms over time through shared goals and mutuality. Team members turn to each other for information, help, and emotional support. What the team achieves corporately becomes more important than the personal agenda of each member.[8]

Schaller observes, however, that a large number of musicians are begrudging team members—as this vexed pastor relates:

I inherited a full-time minister of music. And I'm ready to see him move on. He's a great musician and an excellent choir director, but he also is the least cooperative member of our staff. In the three years I've been here I doubt if he has been on time more than twice. . . . It's almost impossible to get him to cooperate . . . it took me six months to get back the right to choose the hymns I wanted with my sermons. When I talk to him, I sometimes get the feeling that he is on another planet.[9]

To musicians, these may be painful, convicting words. Unless some mutual goals are found, a potentially "profitable partnership" could become a "wicked waste."[10]

Don't allow that to happen! The process of brainstorming—taking the sermon topics for the upcoming three months and considering the music and testimonies possible in the service—can really help in creating a feeling of mutual ownership. Brainstorming gets everyone talking and helps everyone "buy into" planning and preparation. Even if your normal format is liturgical or free-flowing praise, occasionally generate a tightly planned thematic service (seeker-sensitive or topical service). As a side benefit, it will draw your leadership together.[11] Again, "the more we strategize, the better we harmonize."

Understanding the World of the Artist

Creative musicians are also usually individualistic. As Schaller sees it, the problem is that there are two worlds: the creative-artistic world and the organizational-business world.

The first is a world inhabited by free-spirited individuals. The second is a culture that emphasizes groups, teams, and hierarchies. The best and most effective ministers of music come from the world of the creative artist . . . a relatively small number of ministers of music have mastered both worlds. Creative people tend to be individuals. . . . Some creative people are willing, as a price of their freedom, to visit that second world for a few hours every week for a staff meeting . . . but many cannot see the need or value of even those occasional visits. A few grew up in that second world, escaped from it many years ago, and simply cannot bear to return to it.

The wise pastor (1) understands the existence of these radically different worlds, (2) recognizes and affirms the native habitat of the creative artist, (3) sees the conflict in perspective and the values between the two worlds as a natural phenomenon, not as a product of personalities, (4) is reasonably comfortable with the fact this means trade-offs . . . , (5) does not require everyone to move and operate from that second world, (6) values the creative stimulation of artists, (7) does not project identical expectations on people regardless of the world they live in.[12]

Schaller's analysis is, I believe, accurate, and his response, more than fair—gracious. Pastors, when your musician seems to be in the "ozone layer," don't take it too personally. Remain emotionally secure and draw your musician out. Musicians, seek to become better listeners. Work at your faults.

There is a further complication. Generally speaking, popular musicians in our culture are not only free spirited but some also live promiscuous, drug-abusing lives. (Fortunately this image is changing for the better, at least publicly, even in Hollywood! Drugs are now considered bad for the business.) Moreover, too many musicians commit moral failure while in ministry.

Church musician Jim Barnett contends that evangelicals have bought into yet other bad ideas concerning artistic personality and, by thinking that they necessarily go with the turf, have unwisely (perhaps unintentionally so) perpetuated them:

> We excuse, exempt artists from discipline. We too readily apologize for their excesses, for their not leading a disciplined lifestyle. We accept the world's image of musicians.

Discipline is *required* of the church musician. We can't always major on what we like to do. Music has to be put away and properly filed; chairs need straightening. The choir room may need painting. The pain of valid criticism needs to be faced. We simply have to address our weaknesses, and at the same time continue to build on our strengths.[13]

Compliments That Count

We also need to emphasize positive models. If Christian leaders would hold high the positive image of musicians that the Old Testament projects, that would be helpful. The temple musicians are portrayed as responsible, conscientious, and intelligent. They were chosen as supervisors in the rebuilding of the walls of Jerusalem

(2 Chron. 34:12–13). Hezekiah complimented them for their intelligence and "good insight" in the temple service (2 Chron. 30:22). During the festival preparations, levitical musicians were found to be "more conscientious to consecrate themselves than the priests" (2 Chron. 29:34 NASB). One was chosen to distribute the tithe money because he was "reliable."

Positive affirmations! Share this information with your musicians!

Well-placed compliments can serve to point everyone in the proper direction. A music director shared with me the enormous impact her pastor had on the entire music program by the *nature* of the compliments he gave the choir and supporting musicians during their Sunday morning services: "Choir, you brought us into the very presence of God today," or "All of us thank you for projecting to us such an unusual sense of God's greatness this morning."

Instead of highlighting entertainment values—"That was fabulous, let's all give them a rousing hand!"—he focused everyone's attention on the heart of the worship experience. He used compliments to focus attention on the *proper* goal. This built integrity into their role of ministry and helped each member feel their faithful practicing was worthwhile. In dignifying the music ministry, go public with it, and let the whole congregation know how valuable it is and why. Musicians can also go public with their support of their pastor and the value of his ministry. Sharing, publicly and privately, how a sermon personally benefited you not only encourages but builds unity. Thank-you notes also go a long way in building team spirit. Don't underestimate their value!

Special Tips for Working with Volunteers

A pastor's relationship with a volunteer or part-timer will be different from that of a full-timer. Volunteers especially need training and equipping. McCarty advises, "Whatever the volunteer needs, the effective leader will contribute toward fulfilling it. That is the pay for the volunteer . . . The leader who overlooks the needs of volunteers is borrowing trouble."[14] The needs could be emotional or professional. Therefore, if a piano needs tuning or replacing, show support for tuning or replacing it. If keyboard lessons are advisable, share in the expense. If music materials are required, support their procurement. Obtain copyright permissions needed. *A good leader provides.* Tools and a sense of belonging are important! In general, volunteers leave when they lack fulfillment or anticipate greater fulfillment elsewhere.

The Part-Time Assignment

The part-time music position poses unique pressures for pastors. One pastor related:

> It hasn't worked for me. It is almost impossible to schedule staff meetings when everyone can be there, and a couple of part-timers have been so emotionally tied to their full-time jobs they're worn out when they show up at the church.[15]

For part-timers, fashion a precisely focused assignment, not a general job description. Determine the number of hours of work expected for preparation, rehearsal, and direct church performance. For every choir performance and service per week, at least two hours of preparation can be expected. The task of leading flowing praise each Sunday may be demanding enough in itself to take up the time left in a given week. Communicate early in the week by phone, or go out to lunch together if a scheduled staff meeting does not work. Having been a "moonlighter" myself, I know how hard it is to find time to talk about anything but the urgent.

Sundays come so fast and are so unrelenting that exhaustion is a common malady. But, somehow time *must* be found to discuss the deeper questions so that mutual growth can occur. Here's where previous chapters on letting Christ dwell richly, the dynamics of free-flowing worship, worship as performance, and the problem of style can be helpful as you privately work through the issues together. Intersperse some of this material (or thoughts of your own like it) into your sermons occasionally. Devote an entire sermon to worship at least once a year.

Schaller thinks there is a limit on what you should expect of part-timers: "The best part-time staff I've worked with has been more goal-oriented than relational. Their focus is on ministry and performance, not on staff relationships."[16] Nevertheless, a warm, personal relationship with the pastor is indispensable for longevity of ministry. Also, assist part-timers in taking seminars and workshops, or consider viewing a videocassette of another church's service together. From time to time, release your part-timers from the Sunday morning or evening service in order to let them rest, see the church service from the average church attender's perspective, or find what is going on at other churches. These measures will prevent staleness and promote self-development.

Are You Seeking a Full-Time "Miracle" Worker?

As for full-timers, Schaller reports there is a temptation for the church leadership to search for someone who can produce single-handedly a comprehensive music program. In other words, find a "miracle worker." A second, more realistic approach, he says, is to seek someone who can "cause" that to happen:

> This second approach is based on the assumption that it is unrealistic to expect one person to possess all the skills necessary to do everything or to relate effectively to all age groups. . . .
>
> The easiest way to distinguish between these two approaches is to listen in on the *budget* discussions. When the first approach is being discussed, the focus is on how much additional money will be required for the compensation package for a full-scale choir director. When the second approach is being considered, the discussion is on the total budget for a full-scale music program, including the salaries of several part-time directors, the purchase of additional sheet music, supplies, new instruments, organ maintenance, piano tuning, and a half dozen other items.[17]

The latter approach seems more appropriate. For example, consider Hustad's analysis of the full-time music position. The ideal music director must be (1) a musician, (2) an administrator, (3) an educator, and (4) a pastor.[18] That is, church musicians must be good conductors and have one strong performing area (composition/arranging could be included here).

Administratively, music has to be chosen, organized, and catalogued; recruitment is unceasing: people have to be called, programs planned, rehearsals scheduled and organized; the paper blizzard has to be attended to; and the machinery has to be kept oiled;[19] music budgets must be prepared and money raised for music, new technology, and instruments.

Educationally, in order to supervise or direct a graded choir program, musicians need to know something about child development processes and techniques on how to teach musicianship to different age groups.

Concerning their pastoral role, they should be able to teach Sunday school classes if necessary and do visitation work in caring for their choir members and worship team.

How many individuals are sufficiently gifted to fulfill each of these roles masterfully? Very few! (Again, the pastor faces the same tensions.) The wise senior pastor, though, will help assess the chief musician's primary gifts and help gather the correct support system so that the individual can major on what he or she does best. In particular, creative types (both part and full-time) will likely need some secretarial help with administration and in keeping themselves personally organized. Musicians are sometimes also expected to keep up with the responsibilities of other pastoral staff members in evangelistic calling, weddings, funerals, even preaching. The weight of too many of these tasks can make the job next to impossible.

The Hurting Musician

What about the inside, emotional life of the musician? Because of the nature of the "business," musicians reap strokes of adulation one moment and rejection the next. Sound familiar, pastors? Hear these words of testimony from a veteran musician whose pastor demonstrated remarkable sensitivity and compassion to him at a time of crisis, nursing him back to health:

> He was my spiritual father. He loved me, discipled me. He loved me for more than my gifts. He listened, prayed, stood by me—literally hugging me as I would cry out my emotional hurts, having no inkling I would later be his head musician.

These are the words of a worship director at one of the largest churches in America, burned out after serving four years at a previous church. He was telling me how grateful he was for his present pastor. "For several months," he told me, "I just sat in the services, doing nothing, recouping, replenishing." Now healed, he continued:

> I don't advocate a relationship like Johnny Carson and Doc Severinson had, who'd show up at a certain hour, do their thing, and depart; it's purely professional. They don't know each other. Ministry with that kind of professionalism backfires.

This story of burnout and hurt feelings, though, is not at all uncommon as I talk to church musicians serving in churches of all sizes. It has been said that "belonging is the foundation of all motivation."[20] Yet I hear of musicians who feel used—used for their gifts—but not appreciated as persons.

Like thoroughbred horses, they run hard *but feel unconnected emotionally.*

Or like underpaid hired hands leading maligned choirs, they take the brunt of criticism and ridicule, working on budgets allowing little creativity.

Or like organ grinders, they play the same tunes at the same location, at the same time, week after week.

Many feel thought of as *triflers,* as *appendages* or *distant cousins* to the really important ministry going on in the church, or worse yet, the bearers of low-level entertainment.[21]

Feeling used, not paid, underpaid, overworked, or thought of as a trifler—these are the wandering thoughts of musicians on bad days! Caring pastoral leadership can do much good in these circumstances. Unfortunately, some pastors appear insulated from and unaware of these feelings. They enter the sanctuary Sunday morning thinking, "I hope everything goes smoothly this morning. . . . Please! Please! Don't embarrass me!" Sometimes that's the extent of their awareness and concern:

> The minister is glad to have a conductor who will take the whole responsibility from his shoulders; and then, so that there be quiet in the choir and no disturbance in the congregation, he does not trouble himself any more about the matter.[22]

Where such attitudes exist, smoldering feelings can erupt. Hurting from a lack of respect and support, one such musician said to me, his voice choking with emotion, "I am a human being!!" What is interesting is that pastors experience the very same emotions.

What Can Be Done?

What can be done? First, realize that first impressions lay the foundation for deepening interactions. A musician warmly reminisced upon the sensitivity of his pastor:

> When we were candidating, pastor had flowers sent to my wife and me at the hotel. And the following day, he *personally* drove us around the town.

Just after we accepted the position and moved in, I came to a staff meeting one day and shared my wife's distress over the fleas infesting our new home. Pastor suggested I leave and go back home immediately. An hour later he was at the door: "What can I do?" I can't tell you how much his caring attitude impressed us.

One musician suggested a simple but often overlooked exercise:

Spend lunch together telling each other how you came to know the Lord. Walk through your spiritual odyssey. This is not a trite exercise! I've found that after exercises like that, the issue of authority isn't as much an issue. One's perception of position is different.

Another music director echoed a similar emphasis:

Team teach a Sunday school class. Claim a verse together. The way my pastor prayed for my family really touched me. It drew us together. He told me, "I want our relationship to be strong. If our relationship fragments, the entire church will know it."

This emphasis on intercessory prayer and pastoral care definitely needs underscoring. "Minister to, not just through, musicians."[23] Worship leaders need pastoral care and attention! People involved in true ministry feel the weight of the ministry. They carry the burdens of those under their care in addition to their own family cares. As pastor and musicians share and pray over these "weights," they can be refreshed. Together they can experience joy.

Is there an optimum time to offer feedback or correction? A TV play-by-play announcer watched amazed as an NBA basketball coach yelled instructions from the sidelines at his players, even though his team was way ahead late in the game. The announcer asked Bill Russell, the game commentator and former star center for the Boston Celtics, why the coach would want to criticize his team when they were running away with the game.

"That's the best time to do it," said Russell. "The guys are up now. They have their confidence. They can take a scolding and improve their skills even more."

Pastor Melvin Amundson eloquently shares his position on feedback: "My door is always open, and your suggestions are always welcome. I only ask that you use your ideas like seeds, not bullets. Plant them so they will grow, not wound."[24]

Do nothing out of selfish ambition or vain conceit, but in humility consider others better than yourselves. Each of you should look not only to your own interests, but also to the interests of others.

Philippians 2:3–4

Questions for Reflection and Discussion

1. Can you recall a time when you felt exceptionally loved and appreciated by the church community?
2. Can you remember feeling "used" by the church community?
3. Do pastors and musicians tend to live in "different worlds"? Which world do you inhabit? To what extent have you been able to master both worlds?
4. What joint activities could strengthen pastor/musician relationships?

Identifying and Attracting Church Musicians

> The days of the church musician as a silent partner in the religious enterprise are over. The tangled web of conflicting musical philosophy . . . makes it absolutely mandatory for the church musician to become an articulate spokesman and teacher.
>
> Calvin M. Johansson
> *Music and Ministry*

How can we identify and attract church musicians? Part of the answer is in the previous chapter. We have learned that the ideal music director is a musician, an administrator, an educator, and a pastor, and that the quality of the pastor/musician relationship is critical. But more specifically, what sorts of spiritual roles can the musician perform that *Scripture* indicates are important? Is music a distant cousin or a close brother to ministry? How important is the ability to improvise?

The Church Musician and the Spiritual Gifts

Donald P. Hustad received a letter from a former student serving as a church music director, who asked him the following question: "In Ephesians 4:11–12 Paul lists the ministries

God has given the church. Where does music fit in?" Here is the passage in question:

> It was he who gave some to be apostles, some to be prophets, some to be evangelists, and some to be pastors and teachers, to prepare God's people for works of service, so that the body of Christ may be built up until we all reach unity in the faith and in the knowledge of the Son of God and become mature, attaining to the whole measure of the fullness of Christ.

Hustad's answer indicates that, while music doesn't appear on Paul's list, it can relate to each of the five roles; and Hustad speaks (below) of the chief musician as a prophet, evangelist, pastor, teacher, and apostle, respectively. The principles enumerated are equally valid for volunteer, part-time, and full-time church musicians. Though not exhaustive, Hustad's exegesis also helps pastors consider what to look for in identifying a church musician.

1. [As music prophets or "forth-tellers," music directors] are as concerned with the words of hymns and anthems as they are with their music. . . . They must choose texts that bring the whole Word to the whole person, and they will equip themselves theologically to do this. . . . They "break the bread of life" in the anthem text, explaining it verbally in the choir rehearsal (sometimes even in the corporate worship service), or in writing in the church bulletin. . . .

   [If pastor's hymn selections] do not provide a healthy singing diet or their musical settings do not make the words more meaningful, they will help them find alternatives. . . .
2. [As evangelists, ministers of music should] be prepared to address another person with a simple, personal witness to "the old, old story." Furthermore, the solo or the invitation hymn may be the direct tool of the Holy Spirit in achieving . . . a decision that leads to Christian discipleship.

   The graded choir program, too, contributes to evangelism and church growth. Young children are attracted by musical activity, learn to sing the truth of God, and often come rather easily and naturally to personal faith. . . .
3. [As pastors, ministers of music] show love and special concern for the members of their musical groups, giving counsel when needed, visiting them in their homes or in the hos-

pital, and standing by them in the occasions of celebration as well as in the times of crisis and sorrow. . . .

4. [As teachers, ministers of music] teach worship and church-manship. In choosing music with strong scriptural texts, they teach theology and discipleship. They dramatize the Christian challenge to live and to worship creatively, and perhaps most importantly, they teach stewardship of life and of talent. . . .

5. [As apostles, some ministers of music] "follow in the train" of the *apostles,* the first missionaries! . . . They help churches around the world to develop their own indigenous expressions of musical worship.[1]

While we are thinking about gifts, here is another question to consider. Is the ability to improvise a gift? Can it be learned systematically like music notation, or do some people just "have it"? Does its importance vary from denomination to denomination? What are its key benefits? Let's address these questions.

The Value of a Reading and Improvising Church Musician

In gathering musicians around your ministry, seek those who are good at *both* reading music and improvising. These individuals are difficult to find. Again, the ability to do both is what I strongly want to emphasize—at least as an ideal to work toward. I do not wish to infer in any way, however, that a musician who does not improvise is not valuable, or one who does not read notation cannot be competent in ministry.

Regarding improvisation, graduates from conservatories and colleges possess good technique and read music well. Excellent accomplishments! But few improvise fluently; it is not emphasized in their curriculum. This needs addressing, for our whole culture is shifting from the written tradition toward the oral tradition (perhaps too much so). Self-taught musicians and youth involved in contemporary music, on the other hand, tend to improvise well but read poorly, and their technique is usually uneven. What we need is balance. Did you know Bach, Beethoven, and Mozart could *all* read *and* improvise expertly?

What about the use of improvisation across the various denominations today? We can see these "two systems" (reading and

223

improvising) operating in a continuum that extends over the whole spectrum of Protestant church culture, from the mainline churches to the Pentecostal churches. Mainline churches, such as the Episcopal (Anglican), Lutheran, and Presbyterian churches, in particular, emphasize the written tradition; while the charismatic and more Pentecostal-styled churches rely on improvisation.

Mainline churches have a worship book that lays out their Sunday morning structure of worship. It's indispensable to them. It contains a lectionary—systematic, predetermined Scripture readings laid out in advance for each Sunday of the year—creeds to recite, prayers to read, and hymn lyrics and short sung or spoken responses. Their spoken responses and music are generally written down. The people become expert in finding their way around their worship book/hymnal, as the following humorous story illustrates.

> Did you hear of the man visiting a liturgical church for the first time who kept punctuating the pastor's sermon spontaneously with "Praise the Lord"? A woman in the same pew hearing this held her feelings as long as she could but finally turned around, addressing the irritating offender, "Excuse me, sir, but *we don't 'praise the Lord' in the Lutheran church.*"
>
> A man down the row corrected her. "Oh yes we do; it's on page 19."[2]

Although the worship in liturgical churches has one basic structure, the current mood is "to reduce" the fixed features "to the bare essentials and to allow considerable mixing of homemade components with official ones. . . . The program has become wide open."[3] This flexibility is a notable change from the past. In regard to music, the new rites "allow for hymnody [and worship choruses] all over the place, and there are no controls at all."[4] This being the case, even in mainline churches today, the bastions of the written tradition, musicians are freer to exercise improvisatory skills.

In charismatic and Pentecostal-oriented churches a different culture prevails. They hold that structure must yield to the Spirit. The order of service may be laid out in the bulletin, but there's no assurance it will (or must) be followed. They require musicians who have grown up in their church environment, who know the tunes by memory, who have absorbed the style, who hear the sounds and rhythms in their heads, and who can improvise that style on the spur of the moment. Their musicians may read music, but more often than not their reading skills are elementary, whereas their improvisational ability is their most highly prized possession.

Toward the middle of this continuum fall the various Baptists, Brethren, the Christian and Missionary Alliance, Evangelical Free, Nazarene, Church of God, Independent Bible churches, and so on, most of which have a thematic rather than fixed order of service and frequently seek performers with both reading and improvisatory skills. What are the practical benefits of improvisation? They are more extensive than most people realize.

Practical Benefits of Improvisation

I can think of at least four practical benefits that improvisation provides.

1. *Improvising provides a bridge between musicians with different backgrounds.* This bridge is an important asset in our increasingly diversified culture. Let's use learning a foreign language as an analogy. It's marvelous to have good *reading* ability in a foreign language—this gives one access to books, newspapers, and the signs along the road. But it's also vital to be able to *talk* in real time when we meet people—that's improvisation. A musician who reads notation can tap into new and old styles through this reading skill. But improvisatory "jamming" can stimulate *direct* communication and fellowship even further. Plus, there's something special about the spontaneity of improvising that helps break down barriers and speaks to people.

Let's apply the analogy to pastors. When delivering a sermon, it's essential to be able to cut from one's notes and clarify a point in a personal way when the audience needs that.

Finney thought this way. He strenuously objected to preachers who bury their eyes in their written text and read their sermons without impromptu comments:

> The preacher preaches right along just as he has it written and cannot observe whether he is understood or not. . . . [But] if a minister has his eye on the people he is preaching to, he can commonly tell by their looks whether they understand him. And if he sees they do not understand any particular point, let him stop and illustrate it. If they do not understand one illustration, let him give another.[5]

That's what the music improviser can do too.

 2. *Music improvisers are valuable because they can listen and respond to what the people are feeling at any given*

225

*moment, and they can supply what is needed to assist the congrega-
tional song.* They can highlight certain words in the text musically.
They can drop the key when the congregational voice is rusty and
low in the opening minutes of the early morning service. They can
lower the key for adoration numbers emerging from times of prayer
and raise it for transcendent pieces. They can improvise smooth
transitions between numbers and modulate between stanzas.

They can play the "lay-back" rhythms characteristic of young
contemporary churches that are not easily captured in music notation. I hear whole congregations of young people "dropping" these
rhythms "right in the pocket" today. Rhythmic subtleties such as
these can't be learned immediately or effortlessly by older musicians—one needs experience in the style over time. It has to be
"felt." Improvisers are more adept at feeling and dealing with these
kinds of ongoing cultural adaptations. Clearly, the benefits of improvisation go deeper than mere "evangelistic playing."

3. *Improvisers are better equipped to take full advantage of the
potential of synthesizers and the latest music technology.* Electronic
technology is not going to go away! Digital keyboard sales are
increasing, whereas acoustic piano sales are decreasing. Young
people want to hear more than just piano and organ sounds with
their worship.[6] Many organs and acoustic pianos today have MIDI
capability, making more musical sounds a reality. Guitars have their
sound effects pedals. In churches where the platform area lacks
the space for a percussion set and other instrumentalists, space-
saving MIDI modules can provide percussion sounds.

The proper perspective is to see acoustic and electronic instruments as complementary, not competitive. As for sound quality,
while electronic strings can sound like a big string section, the presence of just one live violinist can add tremendously to the realism
of an electronic strings "patch."

Practically speaking, keyboardists need to know how to "work"
electronic instruments. If a synthesizer has string, guitar, and brass
presets, the synthesist needs to know the ranges of these instruments, how to improvise like a string section, be familiar with the
kinds of rhythms and voicings guitarists employ, know the kinds
of melodic lines and chord structures that make for brassy sounds.

Every patch (preset) needs to be played differently and serves
different functions. Electronic basses have a variety of timbres
including fretted and slap bass sounds. Some digital piano sounds

are bright, soloistic, and cut through music textures; while others are rich, dark, and blend with other instruments. The "Rhodes" piano sound, for example, is generally more effective with fewer notes (less active accompaniment) and thinner chord voicings (less doubling). Because of their "envelope" settings, some patches cannot respond to short note values—for example, spacy, sonic "pads" have slow-developing attacks. The sensitive improviser may have to revise what is on the written page to fit the patch. The skilled improviser acts as an orchestrator, bringing out the unique potentials of each sound to full advantage.

The emergence of interactive software programmed to produce music in any number of styles should also prove to be a boon to congregations. Improvisers can input the chords for given pieces and "play off" digitally generated accompaniments.

4. *Improvising avoids copyright infringement.* This is an enormous advantage. It's a way to avoid the moral quagmire of photocopying. Since the improvisation is not "fixed" in any form, improvisers can create spontaneous arrangements for any vocal or instrumental combination, any congregational hymn or chorus. Improvisers are free! Their only limitation is their imagination—what they can hear in their heads. So work up your own material! Jot down a few notes to remember what you have done. Tape record your work or make your own MIDI file. Choose to be free!

The average church keyboardist may not be able to realize all of these goals, yet each must be encouraged to "chip away" at them. Proceed at your own speed and ability level. *Learn at least one new thing each week.* Be adamant about details. Master each tiny task. Over time you'll get closer toward the tangible realization of your goals. One practical piece of advice. When purchasing an all-purpose electronic keyboard for congregational use, buy a "weighted" keyboard that allows octaves to be played cleanly. Unweighted keys, which provide no resistance, can be depressed unintentionally by even the slightest contact.

Isn't Improvisation a "Gift"?

Although improvisation is a goal to strive toward, some may *feel* as if they have no aptitude for it at all. And some people in fact may be better off not spending inordinate time with it. But I believe this holds true only for a small percentage of musicians. My first questions are these: "Have you worked at it? Do you know *how* to work at it?" The process is quite similar to learning a new language. Improvisation does *not* fall from the sky! It takes sustained, patient, and systematic practice, just as the skill of sight-reading does.

Memorize cliches and try to integrate them into your worship materials. (Studio musicians call them "licks.") Try them in different keys. In real life, children learn new words and try various ways of employing them. It takes time for children to integrate words into their vocabulary. They repeat cliches endlessly until they are fluent with them. Their sentences at first are short.

The same applies in music. You become aware of certain rhythmic patterns, certain chord spacings that fall easily for your hand, and certain chord progressions that are appealing. You try them out in different pieces and practice them in different keys. At first, your musical sentences will be short, and your music syntax rudimentary. Growth is gradual, but practically every musician can attain rudimentary proficiency. For example, if handed a lead sheet with the lyrics and "pop" chord symbols above the words, most musicians can learn to improvise a basic accompaniment. At the same time, every improviser should develop the ability to read notation, at least up to the level of hymnbook sight-reading.

"Deep Wounds Have Been Inflicted"

Do nothing out of selfish ambition or vain conceit, but in humility consider others better than yourselves.

Philippians 2:3

Again, I do not wish to belittle those who don't improvise or to make light of their hard-won accomplishments. Looking at the broader scene, we can see the effects of such behavior. Rather than affirming one another, we become threatened, competitive, and discount each other's gift or stylistic preference. What results? Wide chasms, resentments, and jealousies between those who improvise and those who don't, between those who champion the traditional music versus modern music, between the older and younger generations, or between art music and folk music. Robin Sheldon expresses the resulting devastation:

Deep wounds have been inflicted, sufficient indeed to cause total breakdown of communication.... Organists have no longer been able to continue where so-called inferior music is used because of their classically-oriented entrenched attitudes; conversely, music groups with their light instrumental accompaniments of guitars, synthesizers, percussion and the relevant electronic gadgetry have been insensitive to those who would naturally wish to use other styles.... Humanly speaking, reconciliation is merely a hope because the natural gulf is often so deep.[7]

If the apostle Paul were here, I think he would say, "Stop passing judgment on one another!" Especially when we are hurting. However, that's exactly what we do. *Hurting people hurt people.* Resentments from musicians are sometimes aimed at pastors:

Understandable though it may be that the clergy are for the most part musically uneducated, is it any wonder that through ignorance or disinterest they repeatedly come up with the wrong answers, or fail to clutch and build on the crucial relationship with their musicians which is so essential a factor. When clergy equate their authority with autocracy, is it surprising that disastrous consequences result?

Disbanding a traditional choir or organist doing a good job is one of the most unforgivable of actions, yet it frequently occurs. It causes untold hurt and can, as evidence shows, permanently alienate people from the Church. To what purpose is this waste, especially when as in many instances there is nothing, or nobody, available as a viable replacement?[8]

Are we hearing the pain in this paragraph? "Unforgivable actions," "untold hurt," "permanently alienated"—these words refer to the raw feelings of "establishment musicians" being replaced! Robert Hayburn observes, "Almost everyone is making music in the church, except trained musicians."[9] That should give us pause for consideration. In the Old Testament, an elaborate training system, the levitical "guild," was established for the very purpose of leading worship.[10] We, too, need to train and retrain rather than replace so we can grow together rather than sever members from Christ's body.

I received a call informing me of a crisis facing a church music director in Los Angeles. The people and pastor were calling for worship choruses to be incorporated into their service. This musician, although in his late twenties, did not identify at all with contemporary Christian music; his whole life history and training went against it. "I just can't bring myself to perform that contemporary stuff! I cannot get the feel of the beat," he told me. His voice began to break up with emotion, "I guess I'll have to take my family and go somewhere else one Sunday a month."

Your Favorite Style

Though church leaders may need to call for change, sensitivity needs to be demonstrated to musicians in this threatening predicament. To get to their present musical level has already been tremendously arduous and financially draining. The ability to acquire the feeling for new styles comes for most only with great difficulty.

A soloist at church once said to me while we were rehearsing, "Forget that Baptist stuff. Can you give it a jazzy feel?" I could not imagine, for the life of me, a jazzy feeling for that song. That comment, though, impelled me to begin to learn how to improvise various Latin rhythms as well as jazz and funk "feels." I know firsthand the tremendous effort it takes to internalize them. But consider this:

> Your favorite style of music is likely to be the one that was most part of your life in your *adolescence*. No matter how many years have passed, that music is your type of music, your music dialect, if you will.[11]

So, *when you hire someone, obtain at the very outset a clear idea of their stylistic comfort zone and church music philosophy*—you may have to live with that! It usually does not work to ask musicians to move into new styles. Ask your candidate, "What music did you like most in your adolescence? Describe the music culture of your youth."

How Do You Attract Good Musicians?

Premier church consultant Lyle E. Schaller contends: "The expansion of the ministry of music can be *the most effective single avenue* not only for enriching the peace and joy of the heart, but also for the expansion of the program, for reaching young children and enabling them to express their creativity, for the quick assimilation of new members, for expanding group life, for a ministry with the developmentally disabled, and for creating a distinctive community image. The larger the membership, the greater the priority that should be placed on a great ministry of music."[12]

But seasoned pastors have told me they believe it is harder to find quality music directors than quality pastors. Pastors frequently ask, "How can I attract good music leadership?" At times we feel the task is overwhelming and the supporters too few. Don't give up!

First, *do what you can, with what you have, where you are.* We all know people with shelves of unread books, unused recipes, and untasted spices. Use the resources you do have—people who can fashion banners, write reader's theater, who take the reading of Scripture seriously and yearn to see a spirit of prayer prevail. Create the proper environment, the right conditions in your heart and in your congregation now. Write down your goals; goals unwritten are seldom achieved.

Are you developing a philosophy of worship? Are your people hungry for authentic worship? Is there a willingness to accept change? Have you preached on worship lately? Have you attended a worship seminar?

Second, understand that *one good musician attracts another.*

Third, indicate your commitment to *minister pastoral care to musicians.* Remember your musicians are part of the church body. The church has nothing to lose when it ministers pastoral care and sensitivity to them.

Fourth, *adequately compensate those who are professionally equipped.*[13] Why should church musicians be paid when Sunday school teachers, for example, are not? The question deserves an answer. A musician is like an athlete. Trained musicians must commit precious time weekly to maintain and extend their skills—a necessity seldom sufficiently appreciated. And they have made an enormous financial investment in their instruments, their private lessons, and college tuition. No wonder musicians sometimes feel "used." They are! Sunday school teachers have not undertaken a comparative investment nor must they practice their skills each week.

Fifth, *search large churches for potential musicians.* Often large churches have an abundance of musicians ("One good musician attracts another!"), and some become frustrated when they are used infrequently.

Consider these additional ways of making positive preparation now:

231

- Look at your choir library
- Do an inventory of instruments in the church
- List all possible musicians
- Pay special attention to your accompanists[14]

If you do these things now, when the talented person comes along (professional or amateur) you can show a *demonstrated* interest in music and worship. You will have ideas to share. You will know the issues and show yourself able to defend your future music leadership. That will be highly attractive!

This is precisely what pastor David Niquette did. When he asked me to come to his church as a worship consultant for a specified period, I was more than sympathetic because of the work that had already gone on in his heart and people. There was a readiness that appealed to me. Dave had studied the theology of worship. We could talk intelligently about worship and present our ideas unitedly before the congregation. And he was an emotionally secure person.

Leaders of small and midsized churches, *be encouraged!* With the advent of MIDI and all the electronic technology available today, the enterprising musician has many tools to experiment with and keep busy. The poverty of music resources that afflicts small churches (lack of instrumentalists, etc.) can be compensated for electronically. Therefore, the gifted musician of today may well be more willing to devote energy to even a small church, *providing that church is philosophically and spiritually prepared* for the committed musician. Determine to be that church!

> Maturity is the ability to appreciate great musical diversity. . . . Musical narrowness is selfishness at its worst.[15]

Questions for Reflection and Discussion

1. "Your favorite style of music is likely to be the one that was most part of your life in your *adolescence*." Does this accord with your experience? Share what was your favorite style during your adolescence. Discuss the implications for hiring church musicians.

2. The benefits of music improvisation extend beyond mere evangelistic playing. Discuss.
3. Does improvisation occur in nonmusical parts of the worship service? Explain.
4. Did Jesus employ the improvisatory mode in his ministry style? Explain.

Why Seminaries Should Teach Music and Worship

It is not good to have zeal without knowledge.
Proverbs 19:2

Seminaries today are failing to exert leadership in reforming the worship practices presently occurring in local churches. Leadership in worship renewal has not come from the seminaries but from the grassroots—from a multitude of local pastors and musicians. Jack W. Hayford asserts this renewal's authenticity:

> I want to underscore the reformation in worship that is in progress. It's already begun, and its fruit has been tested and proven worthy in a sufficient number of situations to show we are not simply dealing with a fad.[1]

This leadership deficiency from seminaries continues to do incalculable harm to the effectiveness of pastors and musicians. It's not a peripheral factor; it is a central impediment to worship in local churches. If we are to move ahead in worship, then pastors, musicians, and seminaries must forge a strong partnership.

That worship for decades has received scarcely any attention in most North American seminaries or schools of theology is not mere statement. It can be documented. A study done in 1985 of 150 midwestern pastors indicated that only 3 percent rated their seminary worship experiences as most significant.[2] Of 103 seminaries surveyed in 1978, only *eight* offered degree programs in church music.[3] In theological institutions that do offer church music programs, Wohlgemuth reported in 1983 that a "cloudy picture emerges" of nonuniform standards, of "courses taught only in interim sessions that may be cycled every second or third year with no assurance that they will actually be taught."[4]

J. W. Schwarz found that seminary students are "aware of their need for training in church music and are desirous of having more of such training available to them."[5] Pastors in the field are also badly in need of worship training. J. F. White concluded that music and worship in seminaries are "where pastoral care was about twenty years ago. Today it is unthinkable not to teach pastoral care; someday it will be unthinkable not to teach worship."[6] In the few seminaries that teach music, the music and worship programs are often not combined. Prospective pastors and church musicians remain separated physically and academically.

The Great Divide

Not only have prospective ministers received scant training in worship, but musicians and pastors have also been divorced from each other. The great majority who become professional church musicians upon graduation receive a *different* education in a *different* location from seminarians.

Musicians receive their education at conservatories, colleges, or universities, whereas pastors and church educators receive theirs at seminaries and schools of theology. Musicians talk a *different* language from seminarians, and both languages can be highly technical and intimidating. Musicians experience no contact with seminarians, nor do they study theology or the pastoral dimension of ministry. The two groups share no common-core courses where they can dialogue with each other, nor do they have the privilege of rubbing shoulders together in practicums.

Moreover, since musicians and artists are not present at most seminaries, their practical skills and talents are not available to model worship. Consequently, seminarians tend to experience not

236

only an impoverished expression of worship in their chapels but also missed opportunities for spiritual formation. How lamentable! At the very least, seminaries could consider *utilizing adjunct church musicians drawn from the community* to assist in their chapel services and to co-lecture in their classrooms.

On the other side of the ledger, theologically naive musicians exhibit a woeful lack of theological grounding. Bruce Leafblad has observed that musicians have "a limited understanding of, and appreciation for, the true nature and work of the church."[7] No wonder then, when musicians and preachers are thrown together in a pastorate a lack of understanding and trust arises! The problem has become more acute because the new worship confers an enlarged role to music expression.

Robert Webber of Wheaton College attests to the state of affairs in seminaries:

> I speak from experience. I graduated from three theological seminaries without taking a course in worship. Even though I was planning to become a minister, no one ever sat down and said, "Look, worship is one of the most central aspects of your future ministry. Now is the time not only to learn all you can about the subject but also to become a worshiping person so you can offer mature leadership to your congregation." The simple fact is that my seminary professors knew little about the subject. . . .
>
> What is needed . . . is the recognition of worship as a legitimate discipline among the other disciplines . . . it is a field in its own right. Indeed it is an interdisciplinary study demanding expertise in biblical, historical, and systematic theology as well the arts, practical expertise, and personal formation.[8]

What can be done? If someone would endow a chair of worship at a seminary, that could have very positive results. Seminaries will not turn down money! Concerted pressure from pastors acting as concerned alumni to bring about corrective change is also needed. Seminary leaders will listen to pastors. Pastors, if the current state troubles your spirit, *write your letters and make your phone calls!* In the past this is how pastoral care, counseling, and Christian education emphases found a place in seminaries. Cracks of concern in seminaries are beginning to appear. They are most welcomed!

The present state of affairs, as observed by Martin E. Marty and Paul Westermeyer, engenders disharmony and strife:

> The potentials for conflict are clear. The clergy is trained to think. The musician is trained to perform. The pastor has had little or no training in worship. The musician has had little or no theological training. . . . The

pastor may see all of worship related to preaching, pastoral care, [or evangelism]. The musicians may see all of worship related to art, as the world views art, or to teaching higher standards of taste, or to performance. The schizoid condition of much American worship is the inevitable result. . . .

It will come as no surprise to many [pastors] that not all of them are popular with church musicians. . . . I have spoken at local and national meetings of the American Guild of Organists and at church music professionals' workshops. . . . I was surprised to hear as many expressions as I did of what has to be called anticlericalism, or at least deep resentment.[9]

What are some of these resentments and frustrations? Musicians resent seminaries and pastors who do not

- place value on worship
- preach on worship
- give time for it
- give the people an active role

Musicians are distressed when leaders

- break up the flow with long, intruding announcements
- do not inform them in advance of the main points in sermons so that an integration of music and message can occur

Musicians *need* lead time! Especially those leading thematic services. What musicians find even more disturbing is although pastors lack preparation and training in worship, they make the key decisions. This condition has led a growing number of musicians to undertake additional training to become pastors themselves!

Ten Reasons Seminaries Should Teach Worship and Music

1. Worship is central to every pastor's ministry.
2. Music is central to evangelical worship, and the new worship has intensified this centrality: music forms 50 percent of the service.
3. A peer relationship between pastors and musicians is demanded in contemporary worship.

4. Worship requires interdisciplinary study. Seminaries, as an institution, are most able to offer the variety of resources needed to provide a platform for teaching worship.
5. Worship aids spiritual formation.
6. Pastors need a theology of worship and music and a better understanding of the arts.
7. Musicians need theological grounding and a better understanding of ministry and the nature of the church.
8. Pastors and musicians should share classes, practicums, and become comfortable with each other prior to their partnership in ministry.
9. Pastors should experience numerous, varied, quality worship experiences in seminaries and have opportunities to design and execute them.
10. Some pastors and musicians have gifts in both preaching and music. Why should only one be developed?

Music and worship deserve formal recognition in the seminary curriculum. Ministers of music, be proactive! At the minimum, call for (1) a worship course and (2) the creation of choirs and/or worship teams composed of faculty and students. Make yourself available. Contact the seminary near you.

Properly understood, worship relates to all of life. Donald P. Hustad insists, "To experience full and authentic worship, 'in spirit and in truth,' is the greatest need of the church today."

> I am of the opinion that we should not be concerned about working for God until we have learned the meaning and the delight of worshiping Him. A worshiper can work with eternal quality in his work.[10]

Appendix 1

The Book in Brief

1 Hymns or Choruses? (19–31)

- Hymns and choruses are complementary—determine the appropriate blend.
- Hymns and choruses edify differently.
- Think of tradition as an ongoing, ever-renewing process.
- Roots down! Walls down!
- The words, rhythms, and tunes of established hymns have and will continue to undergo revision.
- Worship forms should not be confused with spirituality.

2 Psalms, Hymns, and Spiritual Songs (33–43)

- Let Christ dwell *richly* (Col. 3:16). Emphasis on rich.
- Dwelling in Christ is linked to a richness of expression and form.
- The phrase "psalms, hymns, and spiritual songs" may indicate collectively the total range of style or reflect three different styles.
- "Spiritual songs" probably involved improvisation.
- The Psalms demonstrate variety. The Hebrews preserved old songs, sang contemporary songs, called for new songs.

3 Free-Flowing Praise (45–60)

- The Five-Phase model: invitation, engagement, exaltation, adoration, intimacy.
- Faithfully image the character of God (both transcendence and intimacy).
- Sing not only "about" but "to" the Lord.
- Praise normally precedes adoration.
- Not repetition, but accumulation.
- Jerking about distracts. Use common words, common keys where possible. Employ smooth tempo changes: invitation/engagement (running), exaltation (jogging), adoration (walking), intimacy (stopping, gazing).

4 Journey into the Holy of Holies (61–70)

- Worship mirrors the "Journey into the Holy of Holies" at every point.
- Enter his gates with thanksgiving.
- Exuberant praise turns to solemn adoration.
- Silence is golden to worshipers. Just worship!
- The mind jumps faster than the spirit.
- The Five-Phase and "Journey into the Holy of Holies" models are similar.
- The Wimber, Cornwall, and Webber Syntheses include repentance.

5 Designing the Service (71–85)

- Scripture contains no prescribed order of service.
- There should be a full revelation and a full response.
- Keep congregational singing, praying, and Scripture reading central.
- Liturgical, thematic, and open worship forms predominate today.
- Innovation *between* and *within* the three forms is where the action is.
- The lectionary drives the liturgical service.
- The sermon drives the thematic service.
- Flowing praise resists a thematically conceived service.

- Thematic planners need the sermon outline.
- Historic liturgies allow for response after the sermon.
- Pauline worship reveals astonishing variety.

6 Creating Drama: Bulletins, Readings, Slides, Videos (87–98)

- Headings provide direction and orientation.
- Don't overwhelm guests with detail.
- Employ repetition of threes.
- Divide the congregation into sectors occasionally.
- When there is punctuation, take a breath.
- Boldface fonts enhance creative interaction.
- Nature backgrounds aesthetically enhance slides.

7 Inspiring the People's Song (99–117)

- Treat the congregation as your primary choir.
- Stand for praise, sit for adoration.
- Nest new hymns and choruses.
- Paraphrase abstruse hymn texts.
- Eliminate wordy hymn/chorus announcements.
- Pitch songs lower in early morning services.
- Introduce no more than one new song in a given service.
- Introduce new songs at the beginning of a set.
- Exert your personality during praise and relinquish it during adoration.
- Perfectionism characterizes both pastors and musicians.
- Pastors and musicians—protect each other!

8 Is Worship a Performance? The Concept (121–34)

- Yes! . . . but people distrust, musicians value, and pastors deny "performance." Let's reload the word.
- To perform is to minister is to serve.
- To perform is to do something complicated with skill in public with a view toward serving or ministering.
- Kierkegaard: God is the audience; pastors and musicians are prompters; the people are performers.
- Prompters must not distract from worship.

- Prompters serve two audiences (God and the people).
- Private worship should precede public performance.

9 Is Worship a Performance? The Implications (135–44)

- TV culture has imposed professional standards on worship.
- As your church grows, specialize.
- The larger the church, the higher the performance standards required.
- Practice! People appreciate quality. Offer costly worship.
- Exercise your technique but don't put your trust in it.
- Good technique means being "response-able."
- Restraining your technique may show wisdom.
- Pastors and musicians share a performance temperament.
- Find someone emotionally secure to work with.
- Pray that others around you will be more praised, more used by God than yourself.
- Service in small things helps discipline ego urges.

10 The Danger of Cosmetic Change (145–59)

- Danger of "worshiping worship."
- Church music should be determined by the nature of the church.
- Model: *kerygma* (to proclaim), *koinonia* (to fellowship), *leitourgia* (to worship).
- *Leitourgia* includes and subsumes *kerygma* and *koinonia*.
- No *kerygma—no koinonia—no leitourgia.*
- One definition of worship will never suffice.
- The Hebrew concept of worship is primarily gestural, not propositional.
- Invite a total response: let every knee bow and every tongue confess.

11 The Look of Music in Evangelism, Fellowship, and Worship (161–73)

- *Kerygma* confronts, *koinonia* comforts, *leitourgia* integrates.
- The church's mission: to incarnate all three modes.
- *Kerygma* music accentuates specialized performance.

- *Kerygma* provides the best context for choirs.
- *Koinonia* resembles a TV talk show.
- *Koinonia* music brings performers closer to the audience.
- New Orleans jazz exemplifies *koinonia* music.
- *Leitourgia* music is Godwardly directed, participant oriented.

12 Resolving Tensions over Musical Style: Peter (175–88)

- Music is relative: there is no one universal style.
- Music tracks language.
- Acts 2 ultimately leads to a Pentecost not only of languages but also of *music styles.*
- If language dialects are not despised, then music dialects (folk music) should not be despised.
- No melody, scale, chord, texture, rhythm, instrument, or timbre is theoretically off-limits. Peter was commanded to eat all the foods.
- The issue of style involves the broader issue of accepting people.

13 Resolving Tensions over Musical Style: Paul (189–206)

- Music style is a disputable matter: let each be "fully convinced in his own mind" (Rom. 14:5).
- Teach everyone to be "strong."
- Listen to any style without raising questions of conscience.
- If a style ministers, don't ask where it came from.
- Beware of elevating any one style as intrinsically "sacred."
- Some worship styles may be permissible but not appropriate.
- If someone regards a style as unclean, for him or her it is unclean.
- If a style causes spiritual harm, do not wound.
- Listeners derive different meanings from the same music.
- Abuse of a form does not disqualify its use by others.
- Lyrics are easier to evaluate than music style.
- Church music should be functional, richly intelligible.
- Those within the culture (who know it) are best suited to critique it.

14 Volunteer and Staff Relations (209–20)

- Dignify the music ministry.
- Minister not only "through" but "to" musicians.
- The more we strategize the better we harmonize.
- The ideal music director is a musician, administrator, educator, and pastor.
- The heart of "administration" is ministry. To administer is to minister.
- Musicians crave inspiration, repertoire, methodological suggestions, and technical review.
- Musicians often feel like organ grinders, underpaid and overworked, and feel thought of as triflers or distant cousins to the "real" ministry.
- The creative-artistic world differs from the business-organizational world.
- Musicians resist the boss-subordinate leadership style.

15 Identifying and Attracting Church Musicians (221–33)

- First, do what you can, with what you have, where you are.
- Be able to articulate your worship philosophy.
- Consider the spiritual gifts (Eph. 4) when determining qualifications for music directors.
- One good musician attracts another.
- Look in large churches for prospective candidates.
- Seek both a reading *and* an improvising musician.
- Compensate adequately those who are professionally equipped.
- Obtain a clear idea of your candidate's stylistic comfort zone—you may have to live with that.
- Your stylistic comfort zone was formed during adolescence. Ask your candidate, "What was your favorite music in your adolescence?"
- View electronic and acoustic instruments as complementary.
- Even one live violin combined with synthesizer strings greatly enhances the sound.
- Improvising musicians take better advantage of new technologies.

16 Why Seminaries Should Teach Music and Worship (235–39)

- Music and worship are central to the evangelical church.
- Contemporary worship demands a more equal peer relationship between pastors and worship leaders.
- Pastors are woefully inadequate in worship, whereas musicians are woefully inadequate in theology and ministry.
- Worship requires interdisciplinary study and spiritual formation.
- Prospective pastors and church musicians should have opportunity to dialogue during classes and practicums before entering ministry.

Appendix 2

Results of Poll on Church Music Styles

What is the state of music nationwide in our churches? The graph below presents the percentage of the Sunday morning worship music that is traditional in 286 randomly selected American churches (*Your Church,* April 1994). The poll found that Protestant churches fall into three groups: traditional churches (more than 75% of the worship music is traditional), moderately traditional churches (50 to 74% is traditional), and nontraditional churches (less than 50% is traditional). Which type represents your church?

Portion of Sunday Morning Music That Is Traditional

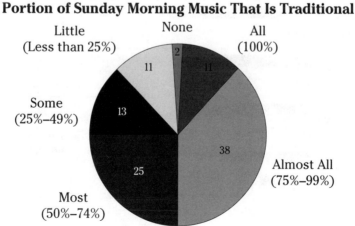

Little
(Less than 25%)

None

All
(100%)

Some
(25%–49%)

Almost All
(75%–99%)

Most
(50%–74%)

2
11
11
13
38
25

The poll shows that the majority of churches employ a blend of traditional and nontraditional music. In California the percentages for nontraditional worship are probably higher than the nationwide results. Within the next five years, I expect nontraditional music practice to increase dramatically.

The study also indicates the percentage of churches that use the following instruments weekly for worship: piano (69%), organ (67%), guitar (17%), drums (15%), synthesizer (11%), brass/woodwinds (7%), strings (4%). Pianos are more dominant than organs; and guitars, percussion, and synthesizer instruments (respectively) are used more than brass/woodwinds and strings. We should also expect the use of synthesizers and digital pianos to increase substantially. The results are accurate within plus or minus 6 percentage points 95% of the time.

How Often Instruments Are Used

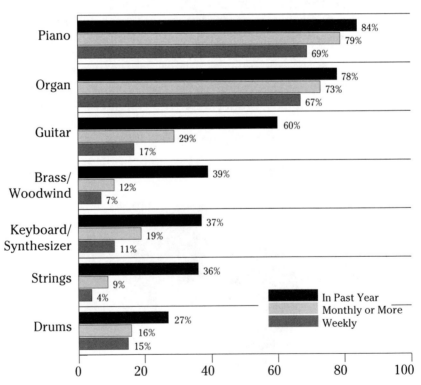

Appendix 3

The New Worship Musician Software

Have you ever wanted to sit down at the piano and lead a group of people in a time of free-flowing praise? That's precisely what this supplement helps you do.

The responsibility to segue from chorus to chorus and hymn to hymn falls to a knowledgeable musician. Yet many struggle, finding the performance of modulations baffling because little is taught or written about it.

This supplemental disk teaches you how to *create modulations yourself* and *develop a sense of flow*. Pastors or music directors may want to give the disk to their musicians. College music departments will also find it useful. This printable resource offers:

- a mini-course on modulation and improvisation
- 125 pages and 160 music examples
- coverage of classical and contemporary styles

An intermediate background in piano or organ will be beneficial to the user of the disk. It's primarily intended for musicians who have little or no experience in improvising, but even seasoned improvisers will find the information here will help clarify their thinking.

Ten chapters are divided into two sections. The first section focuses on modulations up a half step, a whole step, and the other modulations. The V7 I and ii7 V7 I progressions are employed initially, and then the Vsus9 is introduced to smooth chord connections and add color. Modulations of different lengths (2 beats to 4 measures long) are also treated.

Exercises develop your fluency and physical memory of strategic chords, and a variety of techniques are illustrated in actual hymns and choruses. A summary chapter puts a flowing praise service together and shows how to make modulations flow.

The second section focuses on a more difficult objective—improvisation. Alternatives to the V7 chord and added seconds and quartal chords are presented. Finally, an interview with a veteran Hollywood studio musician points the way to intelligent improvisation.

Contents

Modulation
1. Basic Stuff
2. Modulations Up a Half Step
3. Modulations Up a Whole Step
4. Modulations with Color and Resonance
5. Modulations in Flowing Praise: Demonstration

Improvisation
6. Ten Thoughts on Developing a Ministry
7. Fourteen Principles for Intelligent Improvisation
8. Reshape V7: Use "Four over Five"
9. Reshape Triads: Use Added 2/Quartal Chords
10. Shop Talk: Insights from Tom Keene

Whenever you see the disk logo in the margin of this book, it's your signal that follow-up material is available in the software. This shareware is available in Macintosh and Windows versions. The self-extracting, printable archive takes 2.2 Mb. Obtain your copy through Baker's World-Wide-Web page: http://www.bakerbooks.com. Or obtain a copy through the religion or music related areas of major on-line services or on the Internet. Look for the files named NWMUS.ZIP for Windows and NWMUS.SIT for Macintosh.

There is no charge for college students. After a 15-day trial period, all others are invited to send a check for $7 to the address below if the entire work is found personally valuable. A partial, three-chapter version of the work is available on-line at no cost.

If you want the disk mailed to you, specify the version and send a check for $10 to the address below. My goal is to glorify God and build up the church. Moneys collected will be used to finance disk give-aways at music camps and worship seminars and for software enhancements.

The New Worship Musician
P.O. Box 1461
La Mirada, CA 90637

Notes

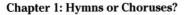

Chapter 1: Hymns or Choruses?

1. I'm not criticizing the use of slides; often congregations sing better when their heads are not buried in books. But hymnbooks also have advantages. They allow worshipers to peruse a vast hymn literature, meditate on their lyrics, become acquainted with music notation, and learn to sing parts. And it's edifying to have hymnbooks at home so families can gather around the piano and sing and play for one another. Shouldn't we seek to birth a musically literate generation of young people?

2. From Kenneth A. Myers, *All God's Children and Blue Suede Shoes: Christians and Popular Culture* (Westchester, Ill.: Crossway Books, 1989). Quoted by reviewer Douglas Groothuis in *Christian Scholar's Review,* June 1992, 422. Also see Milburn Price, "The Impact of Popular Culture on Congregational Song," *Hymn,* January 1993, 11–19; and Paul Westermeyer, "Beyond 'Alternative' and 'Traditional' Worship," *The Christian Century,* March 18–25, 1992, 300–302.

3. Some of the deficiencies cited were culled from a taped lecture by Jeremy Begsby at Regent College, Vancouver, B.C., Canada, June 1994, entitled "Where Is Church Music Going?" (tape RAV 24 9407).

4. Harold Best says something similar in his *Music Through the Eyes of Faith* (Harper San Francisco, 1993), 146, 183–84.

5. In my home church we have a rule: a minimum of two hymns for the Sunday morning worship service. Exceptions have been rare.

6. See Best, *Music Through the Eyes of Faith,* 71–73, 190.

7. Leonard Peyton comments, "This condition will have its bitterest fruit when young people reach age fifty—when their twenty-five-year-old children reject their worship and go off to form their own churches with whatever will be contemporary then. Balance at all times in history dictates that we honor our fathers and mothers, and their fathers and mothers. . . . and thus worship with their forms of worship, all the while following the biblical mandate to sing a new song to the Lord." Personal communication, June 27, 1992.

8. See Psalm 90.

9. The chart is adapted from Harry Eskew and Hugh T. McElrath, *Singing with Understanding: An Introduction to Christian Hymnody* (Nashville: Broadman Press, 1980), 47.

10. Roland H. Bainton, *A Life of Martin Luther: Here I Stand* (Toronto: New American Library of Canada, 1963), 267.

11. For an outstanding examination of the role of the electronic media in popular culture see Quentin J. Schultze, et al., *Dancing in the Dark* (Grand Rapids: Eerdmans, 1991).

12. These two stories are adapted from Kenneth W. Osbeck, *101 Hymn Stories* (Grand Rapids: Kregel Publications, 1982), 126, 172.

13. Transformation in long-established churches should be undertaken gradually over an extended time frame, without rushing it, and in tiny, measured steps. Matthew 9:16–17 seems applicable.

14. Bruce Thede, "How One Church Reached Out to Baby Busters," *Worship Leader*, July/August 1994, 12–14, 37.

15. See article by Tom Schwanda, entitled "The Personality of Worship: Using the Myers-Briggs Type Indicator to Understand Worship Preferences," *Reformed Worship*, March 1992, 25–28. A recent poll by *Your Church*, March/April 1994, shared in appendix 2 of this book, reports current worship styles.

16. Some churches that have multiple services tailor their worship to the tastes of different groups within their congregation.

17. *Songs of the Vineyard* (Anaheim: Mercy Records and Publishing, 1987), 103. I'm aware that the lyric comes dangerously close to affirming a "self-esteem" theology.

18. Saint Augustine, *The Confessions of Saint Augustine* (New York: Washington Square Press, 1960), 158.

19. See *The Worshiping Church: A Hymnal* (Carol Stream, Ill.: Hope Publishing Co., 1990).

20. The Worship Leader's Edition of *The Worshiping Church: A Hymnal* (1990) contains a copyright index that indicates which hymns are public domain and which are under copyright. The telephone numbers of publishers are indicated.

21. A recent change in copyright law does not require the copyright sign to be printed, but any well-researched hymnbook (like *The Worshiping Church*) will contain copyright information.

22. Purists have a place, but a limited one. For example, specialized choirs can limit themselves to the literature of certain historical periods, but church choirs in general must address themselves to the question of relevance to present-day culture.

23. See below a "blues" or "black" rendering of "Blessed Assurance."

Notice the right hand voicings (above) make much use of the pentatonic scale (C, D, E, G, A, C) for the basic chords in the key of C (C, F, G). Look at the D's and A's in the right hand; they tend to give the passage its black sound. To further clarify the style, below are two chord progressions (A1, B1). A1 is what you would expect to encounter in an ordinary hymnbook harmonization (I–IV–I or C–F–C), whereas B1 is its black counterpart (I–ii–I or C–Dm–C). Notice, again the C–D–C movement in B1.

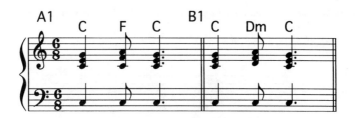

A2 and B2 (below) extend this idea a little further, giving a feeling of musical context, with (again) A2 representing a conventional hymnbook sound and B2 a black sound.

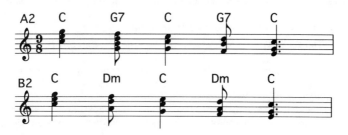

Below, find an exercise to assist you in improvising in black style. It's in C major, but practice it in other keys. Measure one centers on the C chord (I), measure two F (IV), and measure three G (V), the three chord areas you are most likely to encounter.

Feel free to also include some crushed notes like the A♯ below, which adds stylistic flavor to measure three:

24. I believe the word *harlots* also occurred. The word *prostitutes* is perhaps shocking, but the Wesley brothers were proclaiming the gospel to all segments of their society.

Chapter 2: Psalms, Hymns, and Spiritual Songs

1. Martin Hengel, "Hymns and Christology," in *Between Jesus and Paul* (London: SCM Press, 1983), 80.

2. The parallel passage in Ephesians 5:19 yields the same interpretation when the conjunction and comma are dropped, according to Peter O'Brien, *Word Biblical Commentary: Colossians, Philemon* (Waco: Word Books, 1982), 207–8.

3. Hengel, 79. Hengel concurs with O'Brien, Clement of Alexandria, Westcott and Hort, Lightfoot, and Lohmeyer on this point. They consider the Nestle text's preference to include the comma and the "and" to be incorrect.

4. Gerhard Delling, *Worship in the New Testament* (London: Darton, Longman and Todd, 1962), 86. Paul F. Bradshaw's well-researched book *The Search for the Origins of Christian Worship* (New York: Oxford University Press, 1992), reports that the connections between Judaism and Christian worship are not as clear as they were once thought to be.

5. Andrew T. Lincoln, *Word Biblical Commentary: Ephesians* (Dallas: Word Books, 1990), 346.

6. John S. Andrews, "Hymns," in *The International Dictionary of the Christian Church,* ed. J. D. Douglas (Grand Rapids: Zondervan, 1974), 494ff.

7. Andrews, "Music in the Early Christian Church," in *The New Grove Dictionary of Music and Musicians,* ed. Stanley Sadie, 1980, vol. 4, 363–64.

8. Ibid., 365.

9. Ibid., 364.

10. Egon Wellesz, "Early Christian Music," *The New Oxford History of Music,* vol. 2 (London: Oxford University Press, 1954), 2. This judgment has been disputed by Heinrich Schlier (p. 363).

11. Andrews, "Music in the Early Christian Church," 363.

12. Professor of New Testament at Talbot Theological School and author of *Ephesians, Power and Magic* (1989), personal communication, May 27, 1994.

13. Daniel W. Hardy and David F. Ford, *Praising and Knowing God* (Philadephia: Westminster Press, 1985), 59.

14. Donald P. Hustad, *Jubilate II: Church Music in Worship and Renewal* (Carol Stream, Ill.: Hope Publishing Co., 1993), 148.

15. Migne XXXVII, 1271; Nicene & Post-N, Ser. 1, VIII, 488. Quoted in Gustave Reese, *Music in the Middle Ages*, 64.

16. Eric Werner, *The Sacred Bridge* (New York: Schocken Books, 1970), 59. The term *melismatic* refers to the use of more than one pitch per syllable.

17. Edie Ensley, *Sounds of Wonder* (New York: Paulist 1977), 105. See also the chapter by George H. Williams "A History of Speaking in Tongues and Related Gifts" in the *Charismatic Movement*, ed. Michael P. Hamilton (Grand Rapids: Eerdmans, 1975).

18. Lincoln, *Word Biblical Commentary: Ephesians*, 246.

19. Peter O'Brien, *Word Biblical Commentary: Colossians, Philemon,* 210.

20. See the music journal *The Hymn,* January 1987, for informative articles on Pentecostal music and singing in the Spirit by Donald Hustad ("The Historical Roots of Music in the Pentecostal and Neo-Pentecostal Movements"), Larry T. Duncan ("Music Among Early Pentecostals"), Paul Wohlgemuth ("Praise Singing"), and Calvin M. Johansson ("Singing in the Spirit: The Music of Pentecostals"). I am indebted to this issue for this chapter.

21. For example, a fifth, D-A, in the key of D.

22. Here, D, F♯, A.

23. The Trinity Lutheran Church in San Pedro, California (Paul Anderson, pastor), performs "Give Thanks" this way.

24. The first line (below) is a representation of the drones over a pentatonic scale. Lines two and three are the improvisatory chord progressions.

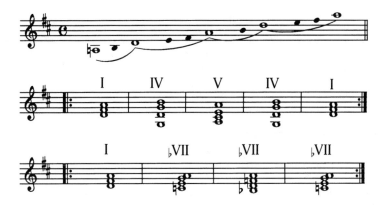

25. I debated the wisdom of including the paragraphs on "singing in the spirit," fearing some readers might find the emphasis objectionable and reject the book out of hand. However, as far as I can determine, the scholars cited on this issue are not charismatic (nor am I). They and I have no pet issue to grind. My sole purpose is to be fair and honest—to acquaint readers with the range of possibilities that seem worthy of consideration. Bob Sorge, who is charismatic, argues that the popular use in charismatic circles of the term "song of the Lord" is misleading. The "songs of the Lord" in the Old Testament were simple "songs of Zion." The term "prophetic songs" is more appropriate to today's situation.

26. *Your Church,* March/April 1994.

27. Paul Beckwith, Hughes Huffman, and Mark Hunt, eds., *Hymns II* (Downers Grove, Ill.: InterVarsity Press, 1978).

Chapter 3: Free-Flowing Praise

1. For a more scholarly analysis of the variety of Protestant worship traditions see James F. White, *Protestant Worship: Traditions in Transition* (Louisville: Westminster/Johns Hopkins Press, 1989), 23ff. He lists nine groups: Lutheran, Reformed, Anabaptist, Anglican, Separatist/Puritan, Quaker, Methodist, Frontier, and Pentecostal.

2. Robin A. Leaver and James H. Litton, eds., *Duty and Delight: Routley Remembered* (Carol Stream, Ill.: Hope Publishing Co., 1985), 89–91.

3. John Wimber is the founding pastor of the Vineyard at Anaheim Hills, California. This parent church has planted about three hundred Vineyard churches throughout the USA and Canada in about fifteen years. Their music and worship style has been central to their success.

4. Words and music by Bruce and Judi Borneman in *Maranatha! Music Praise Chorus Book* (distributed by Word, 1983), 173.

5. Paul Anderson, "Balancing Form and Freedom," in *Leadership,* spring 1986, 26.

6. Charismatics like Cornwall and Sorge make a distinction between "praise" and "worship." This distinction is confusing because praise is a part of worship. What they are attempting to say, I believe, is that in the dynamics of leading worship, praise and exaltation normally precede adoration and intimacy. Expressing it in this way clarifies the concept and helps avoid confusion.

7. An acronym for "Musical Instrument Digital Interface," which makes it possible for electronic instruments from different manufacturing companies to talk (relate) to each other. Thus, the organ keys can trigger a synthesizer, "fire" several synthesizers at one time, and even connect with a drum machine.

8. Try modulating up a P4 when repeating "Let there be glory and honor and praises" (D to G-major).

9. Also available are a book and two audiotapes on worship drumming: *Drums in Worship,* by Mike Kinard, Mike Kinard Productions, P.O. Box 476627, Garland, TX 75047 (214) 771–0205.

10. For an automated music accompaniment software program for use with IBM, Atari, or Macintosh computers, contact PG Music, Inc., Suite 111, 266 Elmwood Avenue, Buffalo, NY 14222.

11. For License Kit and licensing and copyright information, contact Christian Copyright Licensing, Inc., 6130 N.E. 78 Court, Suite C-11, Portland, OR 97218.

Chapter 4: Journey into the Holy of Holies

1. Graham Kendrick, *Learning to Worship as a Way of Life* (Minneapolis: Bethany House, 1984), 141–51; and Judson Cornwall, *Let Us Worship* (South Plainfield, N.J.: Bridge Publishing, 1983), 153–58. This chapter borrows from them.

2. Adapted from Hayyim Schauss, *The Jewish Festivals: History and Observance,* trans. Samuel Jaffe (New York: Schocken Books, 1962), 170–84.

3. Cornwall, *Let Us Worship,* 156.

4. Ibid., 109–10.

5. Ibid., 157.

6. Ibid., 157–58.

7. Ibid., 158.

8. James F. White claims the desire to begin the service with confession actually stems from the medieval emphasis on penance (*Protestant Worship: Traditions in Transition,* 66, 74).

9. I feel tentative in talking about the combination of worship and evangelism within a single morning service, for I have not recently had the privilege of serving for an extended time at a church where that was achieved continuously and effectively. I have *attended* churches, however, where the two purposes were powerfully comingled on Sunday mornings.

10. My appreciation to Daniel Bauman, pastor and former dean of Bethel Seminary, for these thoughts (March 3, 1994).

11. Saint Augustine, *The Confessions of Saint Augustine,* 3.

Chapter 5: Designing the Service

1. Hustad, *Jubilate II,* 317.

2. Some would add the weekly or frequent observance of the Lord's Supper to this list.

3. Robert E. Webber, *Worship Is a Verb* (Waco: Word Books, 1985), 50.

4. Hustad, *Jubilate!* 172. Appears here in an adapted form. See also *Jubilate II,* 330.

5. Hustad, *Jubilate!* 184–85. See also *Jubilate II,* 333, for an example of an extended prayer in contemporary language.

6. Hustad, *Jubilate II,* 322.

7. Adapted from A. W. Tozer, *The Knowledge of the Holy* (Harrisburg, Pa.: Christian Publication, 1961), 104.

8. Hustad, *Jubilate!* 170–71. See also *Jubilate II,* 319.

9. I'm assuming most readers are most accustomed to thematic services. For these readers, I hope the exposition of liturgical and open worship services may suggest new possibilities for use within the thematic framework. This kind of cross-fertilization seems to be precisely where interesting things are happening today.

10. Ronald Allen and Gordon Borror, *Worship: Rediscovering the Missing Jewel* (Portland, Oreg.: Multnomah, 1987), 74.

11. Allen and Borror, *Worship,* 71.

12. Kendrick, *Learning to Worship,* 141.

13. Ibid., 153.

14. Ibid., 157.

15. Ibid., 161.

16. Ibid., 164.

17. Ibid., 199–200.

18. Ibid., 169.

19. Ibid., 170–71.

20. Ibid., 165.

21. Ibid., 166.

22. Ibid., 209–10.

23. Hustad, *Jubilate II,* 234ff, 346, 391.

24. I understand many evangelicals believe the day of prophecies and tongues "has ceased." I am not trying to make a theological point. I think it does us good, however, to let scripture "fall out" just as written and try to understand, feel, and experience what the early Church experienced.

Chapter 6: Creating Drama

1. Daniel Bauman comments: "Planned spontaneity is best generally" (February 3, 1994).

2. From Vickie Fisher at Heights Evangelical Free Church, La Habra, California.

3. Barry Liesch, *People in the Presence of God* (Grand Rapids: Zondervan, 1988), especially chapter 17.

Chapter 7: Inspiring the People's Song

1. A 56-minute video, "Sing and Rejoice: Help for Hymn Singing with Alice Parker," is available from Worship Works, a National Worship Resource Network, 10619 Alameda Drive, Knoxville, TN 39932 (615) 966–0103; $39.95.

2. Kendrick, *Learning to Worship,* 206–7.

3. Provide additional options for individuals who want to exercise their music gifts regularly: senior citizen homes, small group Bible studies, monthly special music programs on Sunday evenings, church parties for outreach, etc.

4. Dale E. Ramsey, *Sing Praises: Management of Church Hymns* (Minneapolis: Bethany House, n.d.), 16.

5. Composed (c. 1987) by Dr. Jack Schwarz, head of the Music Department at Biola University, La Mirada, California.

6. John Wesley, *The Works of John Wesley* (Grand Rapids: Baker Book House, a 1978 reprint of the 1872 edition), 346.

7. All the tunes in this paragraph can be found in the *Maranatha! Music Praise Chorus Book* (distributed by Word, 1983).

8. The text is from Isaiah 6:3. Tune by Nolene Prince, choreography by Dorie Mattson, October 1985.

Holy Holy Holy Is the Lord of Hosts

Isaiah 6:3

Words/Music by
Nolene Prince
arr by Barry Liesch

whole earth is full of your glo - ry   Ho-ly is the Lord.

9. A few of these points were culled from Jay Martin, "That Congregational Singing," *Journal of Church Music* 25, no. 5 (May 1983).

10. See Harold P. Geerdes, *Music Facilities: Building, Equipment, and Renovating* (Reston, Va.: Music Educators National Conference, 1987); Harold P. Geerdes, *Worship Space Acoustics: A Guide to Better Sound in Your Parish* (Washington, D.C.: The Pastoral Press, 1989).

11. Pastor Ismael Gurrola responds, "I disagree. I know when people are with me and when I am not getting through. Body Language is everthing" (March 1994).

Chapter 8: Is Worship a Performance? The Concept

1. Personal communication, January 4, 1992. Tom has produced, performed, and arranged for more than three hundred Christian albums.

2. Daniel Bauman comments: "Bruce Leafblad talks of 'evangelistic music' for the outsider. Are we using outsider music for the insider?" (March 3, 1994).

3. John Cochran, Christian drama instructor. Personal communication, May 23, 1986.

4. Adapted from Edwin Lindquist, "The Dusty Demands of Worship Prompting," *Leadership,* spring 1986, 37.

5. *Webster's New Collegiate Dictionary* (Toronto: Thomas Allen, 1960), 625. "Perform is the general word, often applied to ordinary activity as a more formal expression than DO, but usually implying regular, methodical, and prolonged application or work" (*Random House Dictionary of the English Language: The Unabridged Edition* [1967], 1070). "Perform, often a mere formal equivalent for do, is usually used for a more or less involved process rather than a single act" (*Webster's New World Dictionary: Third College Edition* [N.Y.: Prentice Hall, 1994], 1003). "Perform implies action that follows established patterns or procedures or fulfills agreed-upon requirements and often connotes special skill" (*Merriam Webster's Collegiate Dictionary,* 10th ed.). "When you perform or play a piece of music or dance, etc., you do something to entertain an audience" (*Collins Cobuild English Language Dictionary* [London: Harper Collins Publication, 1988]). The word "rendition has become as popular as performance in the sense of providing musical, dramatic, or other forms of entertainment. Both

words mean the accomplishment or execution of acts, feats, or ceremonies" (*Dictionary of Problem Words and Expressions,* by Harvey Show [N.Y.: Washington Square Press, 1975]).

6. See also Numbers 8:22 NASB.

7. For further references on *ministering,* see the NASB 1 Kings 8:11; 1 Chron. 6:32; 2 Chron. 8:14; 23:6; Neh. 10:39; for *serving,* see Num. 8:11, 19, 22, 24; 1 Chron. 6:48; 25:1; Luke 1:8.

8. A number of translations use the word "to do" (e.g., KJV) in place of the word *perform.* This is the basic meaning of the Hebrew and Greek words. The word *perform* seems less general and more focused. The NASB version uses this word in the context of signs and wonders in the Old Testament more than ten times. In the New Testament the NASB version translates the New Testament Greek words *poyeo, ergazamai, ginomai, ioomai* as "perform," "performs," "performing," "performed" more frequently than the NIV. Moreover, in about thirty instances in the NASB, the Greek words refer to healing, signs, and miracles "performed," whereas only ten instances of the same occur in the NIV, for example. The ten occurrences in the NIV refer exclusively to signs and wonders. Obviously, the translators of both versions have been reserving the English word *performance* almost exclusively to the overtly spectacular in the New Testament. The NASB uses *perform* in relation to worship in Luke 1:8 and 1 Cor. 9:13.

9. Again, I am not suggesting that you must or should use the word *performance* in the pulpit. I am suggesting how to mute its negative connotations and keep everyone properly focused.

10. G. Johannes Botterweck and Helmer Ringgren, eds., *Theological Dictionary of the Old Testament* (Grand Rapids: Eerdmans, 1978), 4:249.

11. Jack R. Taylor, *The Hallelujah Factor* (Nashville: Broadman Press, 1983), 86.

12. Tasks that appear on the surface to be simple and short yet are absorbing emotionally and intellectually also qualify.

13. In relation to length, though, pastors and the people perceive things differently. Many pastors feel it is more difficult to preach a short sermon than a long one. For the people, however, it is more difficult to hear a long one than a short one, unless the pastor is unusually gifted. When a sermon or a song service is not going well, there is a tendency to extend it inordinately in order to "turn the corner." My experience is that this is seldom effective. We simply may be reaping the fruit of preparation that was inadequate or lacking in insight.

14. Ben Patterson, "Can Worship Leaders Worship?" *Leadership,* spring 1986, 36. Pastor Eugene Peterson says that his Sabbath (practically speaking) is Monday. Sunday he leads others in their Sabbath. Sunday is his "workday."

15. May I share with you something that offends me? Worship leaders are sometimes particularly insensitive immediately after the passing of the cup in the communion service. The people are at a point of repose, reflecting on the Lord, when suddenly the service veers off in another direction as if shot out of a cannon. It is as if the deep reverence felt in drinking from the cup has absolutely no continuing significance. Why can't we linger for a time in that reverence?

16. Harold M. Best, "Toward a Biblical Perspective on the Arts," 7.

Chapter 9: Is Worship a Performance? The Implications

1. 1 Sam. 16:18; 1 Chron. 15:22; 2 Chron. 34:12; Ps. 33:3; 47:7; Isa. 23:16.

2. I picked up the ideas of "response-able" and the definition of discipline from being around Richard Foster and Dallas Willard.

3. C. S. Lewis, *Christian Reflections* (Grand Rapids: Eerdmans, 1967), 10.

4. The introduction and notes of *The NIV Study Bible* (1985) give more than usual attention to the literary aspects of the Psalms. See page 783 and note on Psalm 6:6 on center line, for example.

5. Lewis, *Christian Reflections,* 1.

6. I don't mean to imply that human personality should be expunged or suppressed.

7. The scriptural reminder and thought is from Stelian Parvu, January 14, 1994.

8. Lyle E. Schaller, *The Senior Minister* (Nashville: Abingdon Press, 1988), 131.

9. Lyle E. Schaller, *The Middle-Sized Church: Problems & Prescriptions* (Nashville: Abingdon Press, 1985), 88.

10. I am not referring to the kind of divine compulsion Paul speaks of in 1 Corinthians 9:16. Rather, a more human, ordinary desire to perform is on my mind.

11. A pastor comments: "When art goes public, the public can say what they want. No one feels compelled to take a course in art before they criticize a painting, nor a course in homiletics before they critique a sermon" (March 3, 1994).

12. Richard J. Foster, *Celebration of Discipline* (San Francisco: Harper and Row, 1988), 130.

13. Dallas Willard, *The Spirit of the Disciplines: Understanding How God Changes Lives* (San Francisco: Harper and Row, 1988), 174.

14. The chart is adapted in part from Foster's *Celebration of Discipline*, 128–40.

Chapter 10: The Danger of Cosmetic Change

1. Harold Best, "Church Music Curriculum," *Proceedings of the Fifty-Seventh Annual Meeting*, National Association of Schools of Music (Dallas, Texas, 1982), 137–38. See Best's valuable contribution, *Music Through the Eyes of Faith*, which offers theological perspectives.

2. David B. Pass, *Music and the Church: A Theology of Church Music* (Nashville: Broadman Press, 1989). Particular phrases are drawn from his text without endnoting.

3. Pass, *Music and the Church*, 75–78. The international representation is: Bonhoeffer, Hoekendijk, Dulles, Kelsey, Trimp, Gelineau, Nxumalo, Bosch, Moody, and Deschner.

4. Some pastors believe social justice should be included in the church model.

5. Allen and Borror, *Worship: Rediscovering the Missing Jewel*, 55. *Leitourgia* also means "to serve."

6. John Stott suggests that good preaching is monological in practice but dialogical in function. The preacher engages his audience in a silent dialogue with him. The audience agrees or disagrees, rejects or affirms what it hears.

7. Karl Barth, *Church Dogmatics*, vol. 4, part 3, second half (Edinburgh: T. and T. Clark, 1962), 867, 870, 872, 874, 879, 895.

8. For example, recitative passages by J. S. Bach powerfully portray the image of prophetic utterance.

9. Pass, *Music and the Church*, 118.

10. *Leitourgia* is also used in reference to ministering to material needs (Rom. 15:27), as well as "helping" in the ministry in a general sense (Phil. 2:30)—emphases encountered in *koinonia*.

11. Theodore Jennings, *Life as Worship* (Grand Rapids: Eerdmans, 1982), 11.

12. Joseph Gelineau, *The Liturgy Today and Tomorrow* (London: Darton, Longman and Todd, 1978), 51. See also Acts 2:44–47.

13. Hans Urs von Balthasar, "The Grandeur of the Liturgy," *Communio*, winter 1978, 347.

14. Pastor Ismael Gurrola responds: "This leads me to think that the deeper and more profound the proclamation, the greater and more profound the worship if the proclamation is obeyed" (February 26, 1994).

15. Bruce Leafblad, *Music, Worship, and the Ministry of the Church* (Portland, Oreg.: Western Conservative Baptist Seminary, 1978), 21. Bruce, in using the word *first*, is addressing the issue of priority, not sequence.

16. Leafblad, *Music, Worship, and Ministry*, 21–39.

17. Jack W. Hayford, *Church on the Way* (Grand Rapids: Zondervan, Chosen Books, 1983), 53.

18. Ibid., 48–49.

19. Ibid., 78–80.

20. Ibid., 51.

21. Personal communication, February 22, 1987.

22. Allen and Borror, *Worship: Rediscovering the Missing Jewel*, 57.

23. Hustad, *Jubilate!* 64. See also *Jubilate II*, 100.

24. R. Daniel Reeves and Ronald Jenson, *Always Advancing: Modern Strategies for Church Growth* (San Bernardino, Calif.: Here's Life, 1984), 120–21.

25. Ibid., 64–65.

26. William Temple, *The Church and Its Teaching Today* (London: Macmillan, n.d.), 15.

27. Ralph P. Martin, *The Worship of God: Some Theological, Pastoral, and Practical Reflections* (Grand Rapids: Eerdmans, 1982), 210.

28. Botterweck and Ringgren, eds., *Theological Dictionary of the Old Testament,* 4:249.

29. Martin, *The Worship of God,* 11. Also, the word *bless* means "to kneel."

30. Botterweck and Ringgren, eds., *Theological Dictionary of the Old Testament,* 4: 249.

31. See Colin Brown, gen. ed., *The New International Dictionary of New Testament Theology* (Grand Rapids: Zondervan, 1978), 3:550–55.

32. Jack R. Taylor, *The Hallelujah Factor* (Nashville: Broadman Press, 1983), 86.

33. Only 90 of the 106 instances of the word relate to worship.

34. Paul Waitman Hoon, *The Integrity of Worship* (Nashville: Abingdon Press, 1971), 219.

35. See Best, *Music Through the Eyes of Faith,* 43–48, for an alternative position.

36. Sir John Bowring.

37. As quoted by Russell Chandler in *Racing Toward 2001* (Grand Rapids: Zondervan, 1992), 299.

38. "Worship evangelism" is the approach taken at the Christian Assembly in Eagle Rock, California.

39. Sally Morgenthaler, "Worship Evangelism: Bringing Down the Walls" in *Worship Leader,* December/January 1993, 23. See also *Starting a Seeker-Sensitive Service,* by Ed Dobson (Grand Rapids: Zondervan, 1993).

40. Best, *Music Through the Eyes of Faith,* 203.

Chapter 11: The Look of Music in Evangelism, Fellowship, and Worship

1. Pass, *Music and the Church,* 100. This chapter draws heavily on concepts from Pass.

2. Also read Stephen G. Meyer, "Neuropsychology and Worship," *Journal of Psychology and Theology,* fall 1975, 281–89.

3. I'm not suggesting we adopt their procedures uncritically.

4. Again, I'm not suggesting we employ techniques we see in TV talk shows wholesale. For example, the baring of private details of our lives can be more appropriately shared one-on-one, or in the intimate confidence of a small group of four to six believers who know each other well because they have met for nine or more months together.

5. Pass, *Music and the Church,* 113.

6. James I. Packer, personal communication, July 1978.

7. I would not press this distinction too hard. In the Book of Revelation, a leitourgical setting, the throngs also sing "about God."

8. Symbols are created when something interior and spiritual finds expression in something exterior and material. Some examples are the bread and wine, cross, candelabrum, Lord's Table, altar, open Bible, world missions map or globe, cornucopia, banners, icthus fish, dove, robes, vestments, incense, processionals, recessionals, laying on of hands, church building architecture, placement of choir(s) and pulpit(s), baptistry, artwork, and liturgical action.

9. The prepositions "to," "for," and "by" come from Robert Webber, *Discipleship Journal,* Issue 70, 47.

10. Joseph Gelineau, "Music and Singing in the Liturgy," in *The Study of Liturgy,* eds. C. Jones, G. Wainwright, and E. Yarnold (London: S.P.C.K., 1978), 443.

11. Nicholas Temperley, *The Music of the English Parish Church,* vol. 1 (Cambridge: Cambridge University Press, 1979), 453.

12. Paul Westermeyer, *The Church Musician* (San Francisco: Harper & Row, 1988), 16.

13. Pass, *Music and the Church*, 100.

14. Ibid., 128.

Chapter 12: Resolving Tensions over Musical Style: Peter

1. Elmer Towns, *Ten of Today's Most Innovative Churches* (Ventura, Calif.: Regal, 1991), 15. This source was found in Russell Chandler's *Racing Toward 2001*.

2. Doug Murren, *The Baby Boomerang: Catching Baby Boomers as They Return to Church* (Ventura, Calif: Regal, 1990), 189.

3. Bill Gaither is reported as having said the same thing at a seminar of the 1986 Gospel Music Convention (Nashville) by David B. Pass, *Music and the Church*, 18, footnote 3.

4. Thought from Daniel Bauman, March 3, 1994.

5. For a discussion of the tension between Paul and Peter in Galatians 2:1–14 see F. F. Bruce, *Commentary on the Book of Acts* (Grand Rapids: Eerdmans, 1954), 244ff., 298ff.

6. See chapter 10 for a definition of the Greek term.

7. Bruce, *Acts,* 55–56, believes the three thousand were assembled in the temple precincts.

8. Some may object to the assumption that fifteen geographical locations implies fifteen languages. But both the NIV and NASB seem to support this position, for they use the expressions "own language" or "native language." In fact, an alternative reading for "language" in the NASB is rendered "dialect" (2:6, 8). Moreover, if only Greek, Latin, and Aramaic were spoken, why were the expressions of amazement so intense? Also see Best's discussion on the musical implications of Acts 2 in *Music Through the Eyes of Faith,* 66-69.

9. Music innovation, though, is not exclusively tied to language. For a comparison between language and music, see Doris Stockmann, "Interdisciplinary Approaches to the Study of Musical Communication Structures," *Comparative Musicology and Anthropology of Music,* eds. Bruno Nettle and Philip V. Bohlman (Chicago: University of Chicago Press, 1991), 328ff. It can primarily involve rhythm, dance, and interlocking music textures (Christopher A. Waterman, "Uneven Development of Africanist Ethnomusicology," *Comparative Musicology and Anthropology of Music,* 178). Innovation involves a response to human personality, nature sounds, any sounds, the kinds of materials available (bamboo or metal or electronic), and other media. It involves a selective response to one's total culture (Stockmann, "Interdisciplinary Approaches to the Study of Musical Communication Structures," 75).

Reporting on tribal music in India, enthnomusicologists remark: "The music . . . of a tribe that has maintained a unique linguistic and cultural identity also tends to be unique, different from that of both its tribal and nontribal neighbors. Even linguistically related tribes living within the same geographical region appear to differ from each other more musically than they do linguistically." Bhattacharya 1990:66, 68; Parmar 1977a:47; Nag 1981:323 in *Comparative Musicology and Anthropology of Music,* 75.

10. Hustad, *Jubilate!* 242.

11. Others interpret "afar off" to indicate a later time period.

12. The phrase comes from F. H. Chase, *The Credibility of the Acts of the Apostles* (London: Macmillan, 1902), 79.

13. He has at this point ministered to the half-Jewish Samaritans, just as Jesus did.

14. Harold Dollar, "The Conversion of the Messenger," *Missiology* 21, no. 1 (January 1993),17.

15. Paul agrees with the assessment that the Cretans are "liars, evil brutes, lazy gluttons" (Titus 1:12), but he does not tell his workers to not associate with them.

16. I'm not saying they, in fact, would have reacted this way, but that is how I felt.

17. Best, *Music Through the Eyes of Faith,* 81–82.

18. J. Daniel Bauman: "I have argued that God has no particular favorite style—he looks at the heart" (March 3, 1994).

19. Hustad, *Jubilate II*, 44. See also Mellonee Burnim, "Culture Bearer and Tradition Bearer: an Ethnomusicologist's Research on Gospel Music," in *Ethnomusicology: A Century of Ethnomusicological Thought,* ed. Kay Kaufman Shelemay (New York: Garland Publishing, 1990), 359–71.

Chapter 13: Resolving Tensions over Musical Style: Paul

1. Harold Best takes the same position in *Music Through the Eyes of Faith*, 42, 54–60.

2. Osbeck, *101 Hymn Stories,* 127. The generic fallacy in logic also states that a statement can't be faulted simply because the source is uncredible. If Hitler stated the earth was round, the killing of six millions Jews wouldn't necessarily make the statement invalid (Garrett Brown, personal communication, August 13, 1994).

3. For a fuller treatment, see Liesch, *People in the Presence of God*, 174–79. Daniel Bauman says: "This must be taught. It doesn't happen by osmosis" (March 2, 1994).

4. This is not to undervalue the larger issues that ensue from an apparently simple act.

5. See Paul Hindemith, *A Composer's World* (Cambridge: Harvard University Press, 1952), 13ff for a contrasting view—that of Greek philosopher Boethius. His idea is that music has power over behavior. It has moral power.

6. Pass, *Music and the Church,* 44.

7. Ibid., 102.

8. Ibid., 45.

9. Graham Cray, "Justice, Rock, and the Renewal of Worship," *In Spirit and in Truth: Exploring Directions in Music in Worship Today,* ed. Robin Sheldon (London: Hodder and Stoughton, 1989), 22.

10. A survey by Hannelore Wass, "Adolescent Interest in and Views of Destructive Themes in Rock Music," *Omega: Journal of Death and Dying,* 1988–89, 177–86, indicates that adolescents themselves "expressed concern about destructive lyrics in rock music." Moreover, another study by Isadore Newman, "Drugs, Suicide, and Rock and Roll," a paper presented to the Annual Meeting of the Ohio Academy of Science (Dayton, Ohio, April 1990) reported that for those youths involved in clinical treatment, patient preference for heavy metal music "was related to suicide ideology and drug involvement." Adolescents not involved in clinical treatment were not as much affected.

11. Copyrighted 1990 by Integrity Hosanna! Music/ASCAP. I don't mean to slight other works by the author.

12. Gerhard von Rad, *Old Testament Theology,* 1:24.

13. Sigmund Mowinckel, *The Psalms in Israel's Worship,* vol. 3 (Oxford: Basil Blackwell, 1962), 81.

14. Hustad, *Jubilate II,* 56.

15. Ibid., 48–49.

16. I have especially in mind here the impulse to capture a "large" market without any attempt to transform culture.

17. The discerning reader will note that Pass's theology of church music (especially his emphasis on "*kerygma* music") begins to address this question.

18. See Liesch, *People in the Presence of God,* and the subheadings entitled "Percussion Instruments," "Harps Were Like Guitars," and "Discrimination in Reverse," 194–96.

19. This subsection adapted from Hustad, *Jubilate II,* 67–69.

20. For sources with a different viewpoint, see Calvin M. Johansson, *Music and Ministry: A Biblical Counterpoint,* especially chapter 5 (Peabody, Mass.: Hendrickson Publishing, 1984); "Aesthetics" and "Boethius" in *The New Grove Dictionary of Music and Musicians,* 1980, 1: 22 and 2:844, respectively; and the "Doctrine of Affections," in *The New Harvard Dictionary of Music* (Cambridge: Harvard University Press, 1986), 16.

21. Best, *Music Through the Eyes of Faith,* 39ff.

22. Ibid.,41.

Chapter 14: Volunteer and Staff Relations

1. Garth Bolinder, "Closer Harmony with Church Musicians," *Leadership,* spring 1986, 95.

2. See "Ethics and Staff Relations," by Brooks Faulkner, in *Review and Expositor*, 1989, 547–59. The whole issue is devoted to ethics.

3. Johansson, *Music and Ministry*, 1.

4. Schaller, *The Senior Minister,* 66.

5. Garth Bolinder, "Closer Harmony with Church Musicians," 99.

6. Doran C. McCarty, *Working with People* (Nashville: Broadman Press, 1986), 75.

7. McCarty, *Working with People,* 62.

8. Ibid., 61.

9. Schaller, *The Senior Minister,* 114.

10. Westermeyer, *The Church Musician,* 101.

11. My thanks to Laurey Berteig for bringing this emphasis to my attention (May 24, 1994).

12. Schaller, *The Senior Minister,* 117–18.

13. See the excellent article by Kent Hughes, "Going to Your Left," in *Leadership,* summer 1993, 110, on learning to work on our weaknesses.

14. McCarty, *Working with People,* 101.

15. Schaller, *The Senior Minister,* 173.

16. Ibid., 174.

17. Ibid., 107.

18. Hustad, *Jubilate!* 49–50.

19. Schaller, *The Senior Minister,* 99.

20. Bolinder, "Closer Harmony with Church Musicians," 97.

21. The racehorse, organ grinder, and trifler images come from Westermeyer, *The Church Musician,* 6, 90, 92.

22. H. W. Beecher, *Lectures on Preaching*, 2d series (1873; reprint, New York: n.p., 1973), 115.

23. Bolinder, "Closer Harmony with Church Musicians," 96.

24. Melvin Amundson, "Building Positive Staff Relationships," *Journal of Church Music,* March 1986, 13–14.

Chapter 15: Identifying and Attracting Church Musicians

1. Adapted from Hustad, *Jubilate!* 50–51.

2. Paul Anderson, "Balancing Form and Freedom," *Leadership,* spring 1986, 25.

3. Colin Buchanan, "Music in the Context of Anglican Liturgy," *In Spirit and in Truth,* 110–11. I would endorse biblical liturgies, however, and would decisively reject inclusive language that tampers with, changes, or repeals the male gender of God.

4. Buchanan, "Music in the Context of Anglican Liturgy," 105.

5. Quoted in an article by Nathan O. Hatch, "Evangelicalism as a Democratic Movement," in *Evangelicalism and Modern America,* ed. George Marsden (Grand Rapids: Eerdmans, 1984), 74.

6. Martin Luther encouraged a variety of instruments: "Christian musicians should let their singing and playing . . . sound forth with joy from their organs and whatever beloved music instruments there are (recently invented and given by God) of which neither David nor Solomon, neither Persia, Greece, nor Rome, knew anything." *What Luther Says: An Anthology,* comp. World M. Plass (Saint Louis: Concordia Publishing House, 1959), 2:982.

7. Sheldon, *In Spirit and in Truth*, viii.

8. Lionel Dakers, "The Establishment and the Need for Change," *In Spirit and in Truth: Exploring Directions in Music in Worship Today,* 86.

9. Robert Hayburn, *Papal Legislation on Sacred Music* (Collegeville, Minn.: The Liturgical Press, 1979), 408.

10. See Liesch, *People in the Presence of God*, 183–85, 188–91, 192–95, 227–28.

11. Pass, *Music and the Church*, 92. True, one's college education can also influence one's musical tastes.

12. Schaller, *The Senior Minister*, 131.

13. The following suggestive salary scale, devised by the Atlanta Chapter of the American Guild of Organists (1991), is given by N. Lee Orr, in *The Church Music Handbook: For Pastors and Musicians* (Nashville: Abingdon Press, 1991). No music degree or minimal experience, 10–19 hours: $9,000–15,000. Bachelor's degree in organ, choral conducting, or sacred music, 10–19 hours: $12,000–17,500, 20–34 hours: $18,000–26,000, 35 or more hours: $24,000–35,000. Master's degree in organ, choral conducting, or sacred music, 10–19 hours: $15,000–21,000, 20–34 hours: $18,000–26,500, 35 or more hours: $30,000–42,000, etc. See Orr for more detail, 73–74. Estimates may vary from one locale to another.

14. Garth Bolinder, Tom McKee, and John R. Ciona, *What Every Pastor Needs to Know about Music, Youth, and Education* (Waco: Word Books, 1986), 24.

15. J. Daniel Bauman, personal communication, February 1994.

Chapter 16: Why Seminaries Should Teach Music and Worship

1. Jack W. Hayford, *Worship His Majesty* (Waco: Word Books, 1987), 21.

2. Norman W. Regier, "Self-Evaluation of Pastor's Church Music Education and the Resultant Philosophy of Music in the Worship Service" (Ph.D. diss., University of Missouri-Kansas, 1985), 26.

3. Leaver and Litton, *Duty and Delight*, 93.

4. Ibid., 91–92.

5. J. W. Schwarz, "The State of Church Music Education for Ministerial Students in Protestant Seminaries in the United States," *Dissertations Abstracts International* 36, 1600 AD (University Microfilms no. 75–19043), 65.

6. J. F. White, "Liturgical Scholars: A New Outspokenness," *Christian Century,* April 11, 1981, 107.

7. Bruce Leafblad, "What Sound Church Music?" *Christianity Today,* May 19, 1978, 20.

8. Robert E. Webber, "An Evangelical and Catholic Methodology," in Robert K. Johnson, ed., *The Use of the Bible in Theology/Evangelical Options* (Atlanta: John Knox Press, 1985), 139–40.

9. Westermeyer, *The Church Musician*, 82, xi.

10. A. W. Tozer, *Whatever Happened to Worship?* Compiled and edited by Gerald B. Smith (Camp Hill, Pa.: Christian Publications, 1985), 12.

Index